DAILY IMPACT

365 DAILY DEVOTIONAL

Finding Inspiration and Purpose

DOUGLAS ASANTE

365 DAILY DEVOTIONAL: FINDING INSPIRATION AND PURPOSE

ISBN 978-1-916692-07-7

Email the author via **info@dasante.org.uk**
Visit website for more info **www.dasante.org.uk**

Unless otherwise indicated, quotations are taken from the New King James Version (NKJV) © 1982

Published in the United Kingdom by
Equip Publishing House

EQUIP PUBLISHING HOUSE

Asante

INTRODUCTION

Welcome to "Daily Impact," a 365-day devotional series to inspire, guide, and uplift you every day of the year.

Each day offers an insightful moment of reflection, a scripture to ponder, and the practical advice needed to apply God's wisdom to your life. Whether you are seeking a deeper connection with God, strengthening your relationships with others, or searching for personal growth, this devotional is your best companion.

It's a journey throughout the year, one day at a time, with God's Word as your guide. Enhance your relationships, find purpose in your actions, and grow closer to God with every page of this devotional.

Regardless of life's highs or lows, this devotional offers daily encouragement and perspective. Start your journey today and transform every day into an opportunity for growth and joy.

Key Features

Dear reader, this devotional book is truly designed for your daily spiritual enrichment. Here are its key features:

- **MONTH AND DAY:** Organized by month and day, providing a daily guide for spiritual exploration.
- **INSPIRING TITLES:** Each devotional is accompanied by a meaningful title, offering insight into its essence.
- **HEARTFELT DEVOTIONAL TEXTS:** Thoughtfully crafted passages to uplift and guide you on your spiritual journey.
- **REFLECTIVE QUESTIONS:** Thought-provoking questions for personal introspection and growth after each devotional.

May these features enhance your daily life and deepen your relationship with the Lord Almighty.

Wisdom for the New Beginning

The fear of the Lord is the beginning of wisdom,
And the knowledge of the Holy One
is understanding.

PROVERBS 9:10

IN THIS VERSE, KING Solomon emphasises the importance of reverencing God as the foundation of true wisdom and understanding.

Seeking wisdom is a lifelong endeavour. We live in a world filled with information and knowledge, but true wisdom comes from knowing and respecting our Creator. When we fear the Lord, we acknowledge His authority, wisdom, and sovereignty over our lives. This reverence cultivates a heart that is open and receptive to the wisdom and guidance that God graciously provides.

As we pursue a life of wisdom, let us remember that knowledge alone is not enough. It is through the knowledge of the Holy One, by seeking a personal relationship with God, that we gain true understanding. True wisdom and understanding are not found solely in books or academic pursuits but in knowing God intimately and aligning our lives with His principles and values.

Take a moment and consider taking practical steps, such as reading and studying God's Word, spending time in prayer and worship, seeking wise counsel from fellow believers, and being intentional about applying God's teachings to your daily life.

Remember, the fear of the Lord (which is the beginning of wisdom) and knowledge of the Holy One are not just intellectual pursuits but lived experiences that transform our hearts and minds.

REFLECTIVE QUESTION
How can you cultivate a greater fear of the Lord in your life and deepen your knowledge of the Holy One?

Charting the Path of Purpose

Trust in the Lord with all your heart, And lean not on your understanding; In all your ways acknowledge Him, And He shall direct your paths.

PROVERBS 3:5-6

THESE VERSES OFFER GUIDANCE on how to navigate life's uncertainties through a steadfast trust in God. Trusting in God requires surrendering our own understanding and relying on His divine wisdom. Our human understanding may be flawed and limited, but God's understanding is perfect and infinite.

Submission to God is crucial to experiencing the blessings of His guidance. It means seeking His will and aligning our plans and decisions with His purpose. It also means surrendering our desires, fears, and uncertainties to God.

When we trust and submit to God, we can be assured that He will lead and guide us and make our paths straight. This doesn't necessarily mean that our lives will be without obstacles or challenges, but it means that God will provide the wisdom, strength, and guidance we need to navigate through whatever lies ahead.

Take a moment to reflect on this: Identify areas in your life that you have not fully trusted God in and submitted to Him and make a conscious decision to surrender those areas to God today.

May we trust in the Lord with all our hearts, lean not on our own understanding, and submit to Him in all our ways as we experience the peace and guidance that come from walking in His path.

REFLECTIVE QUESTION

In what areas of your life do you struggle to trust and submit to God? How can you intentionally surrender those areas to Him today?

Joyful Worship

*Therefore with joy you will draw water
from the wells of salvation.*

ISAIAH 12:3

THESE WORDS REMIND US of the deep, abiding joy that comes from experiencing the salvation and restoration found in a relationship with God.

Drawing water from a well was a necessary physical task in ancient times. In this verse, it is used metaphorically to describe the spiritual sustenance and satisfaction that God provides because God's salvation satisfies the deepest longings of our souls.

As believers, we have access to the wells of salvation through Jesus Christ. Through His sacrificial death and resurrection, we have been redeemed and reconciled to God. Our response to this should be one of joy and gratitude, knowing that we have been saved from the power of sin and death.

Worship becomes a natural outpouring of the joy we experience in our relationship with God. It is through worship that we draw near to Him. Worship not only lifts our spirits but also strengthens our connection with God.

Take a moment to reflect on this: Consider incorporating intentional acts of worship , such as expressing gratitude, singing praises, reading and meditating on Scripture, and spending time in prayer in your daily routine.

May we joyfully draw water from the wells of salvation, worshiping God with gladness and continually seeking to deepen our relationship with Him.

REFLECTIVE QUESTION

How can you cultivate a spirit of joy and gratitude in your worship and daily life, drawing from the wells of God's salvation?

Embracing Seasons

To everything there is a season,
a time for every purpose under heaven.

ECCLESIASTES 3:1

THESE WORDS REMIND US of the ever-changing nature of life and the importance of embracing the different seasons we encounter.

Life is a series of seasons characterized by both joyful and challenging times. Each season has its unique purpose and lessons to teach us. In these seasons, it is essential to recognize that God is the orchestrator of time. He governs the rhythm and flow of our lives, and He works all things for our ultimate good.

Nature transitions from one season to another, and we, too, must learn to adapt and embrace the changes that come our way. Sometimes, holding onto a particular season can hinder our growth and prevent us from fully experiencing what God has to offer. By surrendering to God's timing and trusting in His wisdom, we find contentment and peace in every season.

Take a moment to consider the season you find yourself in at this moment. Are you in a season of waiting, healing, celebration, or perhaps transition? Reflect on the unique opportunities for growth that the season presents. Seek God's guidance to navigate it with grace and wisdom. Remember that every season is temporary, and each serves a purpose in shaping our character and faith.

May we trust in God's perfect timing and embrace each season with open hearts, allowing Him to guide us through the ever-changing journey of life.

REFLECTIVE QUESTION
Which season of life are you currently in, and how can you embrace it fully, seeking the lessons and opportunities it brings?

Persevering with God's Strength

Do not despise these small beginnings,
for the Lord rejoices to see the work begin.
ZECHARIAH 4:10 (NLT)

THESE POWERFUL WORDS ENCOURAGE us to have faith and persevere, even when our efforts may seem insignificant or challenging. In our journey with God, we often encounter seasons of starting something new or pursuing a dream or calling that seems small or insignificant in the eyes of the world. It is during these times that discouragement and doubt may arise, making us question the worth and impact of our endeavours.

However, God sees potential in our small beginnings. He delights in the steps we take, no matter how small they may seem. He rejoices when we step out in faith, trusting Him to fulfil His purposes through us.

We must remember that God's strength is made perfect in our weakness. It is not about our own abilities or the magnitude of our efforts; it is about relying on God's power and provision to accomplish His will. Our role is to be faithful and obedient, allowing Him to work through us.

Take a moment to consider any areas in your life where you may be feeling discouraged or facing challenges. In the face of these circumstances, acknowledge that God sees the potential in your small beginnings. Trust in His strength and timing, knowing that He is faithful to fulfil His purposes in and through you.

May we persevere with faith and trust, knowing that God rejoices in our small beginnings and will provide the strength and guidance we need to fulfil His plans for our lives.

REFLECTIVE QUESTION

Are there any areas of your life where you feel like your efforts are insignificant? How can you shift your perspective and trust in God's power and timing?

Embracing God's Grace

**And He said to me, My grace is sufficient for you,
for My strength is made perfect in weakness...**
2 CORINTHIANS 12:9

THESE WORDS FROM THE apostle Paul remind us of the incredible strength and sufficiency of God's grace in our lives. In our human frailty, we often encounter moments of weakness, struggles, and limitations. However, it is in these very moments that God's grace shines brightest. His grace is not only forgiving and compassionate but also empowering and transformative.

When we recognize our own inadequacies and surrender them to God, we open ourselves to His unlimited power and provision. In our weaknesses, God's strength is magnified. His grace sustains and empowers us, enabling us to persevere through challenges and accomplish things we could never do on our own.

Rather than hide or be ashamed of our weaknesses, we can embrace them, knowing that they are a platform for the display of God's power.

Take a moment to consider any weakness or limitations you may be facing in your life. Bring them before God, surrendering them to His grace. Trust that His power is made perfect in your weakness. Seek His guidance and strength to navigate through these areas, knowing that His grace is more than sufficient to sustain and empower you.

May we continually embrace and celebrate God's grace, allowing His power to shine through our weaknesses and thereby, experience the transformative work of His grace in our lives.

REFLECTIVE QUESTION
What weaknesses or limitations do you bring before God today? How can you trust in His grace to empower you and reveal His strength in your life?

Trusting in God's Guidance

**Trust in the Lord with all your heart,
and lean not on your own understanding.**

PROVERBS 3:5

THESE WORDS REMIND US of the importance of placing our complete trust in God surrendering our limited understanding to His infinite wisdom.

Trusting in the Lord calls for a deep reliance on His character and promises. It means acknowledging that His ways are higher than our ways and his thoughts are higher than our thoughts. When we fully trust in Him, our hearts are at peace, knowing that He is in control and working all things for our good.

Leaning on our own understanding can lead to a limited perspective and misguided decisions. Often, we try to rely on our own knowledge, experiences, or human wisdom to navigate through life's challenges. However, God's wisdom surpasses our own, and His guidance can lead us on the right path.

Take a moment to reflect on this question. Consider the areas of your life where you may be relying on your own understanding rather than fully trusting in God. It could be in relationships, career decisions, or personal plans. Surrender those areas to God, seeking His wisdom and guidance through prayer and a study of His Word.

Trusting in God's guidance requires humility, faith, and a willingness to surrender our own desires and plans to His. May we grow in our trust for the Lord, allowing His wisdom and guidance to lead us on the path of purpose and abundant life.

REFLECTIVE QUESTION

**In what areas of your life are you leaning on your own understanding instead of fully trusting in God?
How can you surrender those areas to Him today?**

Embracing Our God-Given Purpose

For we are His workmanship,
created in Christ Jesus for good works,
which God prepared beforehand
that we should walk in them.

EPHESIANS 2:10

AS BELIEVERS IN CHRIST, we can find great comfort and assurance in this verse. It reminds us that we are not accidents or random beings but rather intricately designed by our Heavenly Father. He has created each one of us with purpose and intentionality.

When we meditate on the fact that we are God's handiwork, it brings a sense of awe and wonder. Just like a skilled artist carefully crafts a masterpiece, God has carefully crafted us. We are His masterpieces, created uniquely and wonderfully. This truth should fill our hearts with gratitude and appreciation for the incredible privilege of being created by the Creator of the universe.

Furthermore, we are created in Christ Jesus to do good works. God has prepared specific tasks and assignments for each one of us. These works are not a burden but an opportunity to make a difference in the world and bring glory to His name. When we embrace our God-given purpose, we walk in fulfilment and experience the abundant life that Jesus promised.

Consider the talents, passions, and opportunities that God has provided. How can you use them to make a positive impact on those around you and bring glory to God? Take a moment to pray and seek guidance from the Holy Spirit, inviting Him to help you discover and fulfil your unique purpose. Trust that God will equip and empower you to walk in the good works He has prepared for you.

REFLECTIVE QUESTION
How can you embrace and live out your God-given purpose in your daily life?

The Peace of God

Peace I leave with you,
my peace I give to you;
not as the world gives
do I give to you.

JOHN 14:27

IN A WORLD FILLED with chaos, stress, and fear, the promise of peace from Jesus is a comforting and powerful reminder. The peace that Jesus offers is not dependent on external circumstances. It is an inner peace that can anchor our souls amidst the storms of life.

Jesus' peace is unique because it surpasses human understanding. It is not the temporary peace that the world offers but a deep and abiding peace that can only come from a relationship with Him. It is a peace that can calm our anxious hearts, soothe our troubled minds, and bring rest to our weary souls.

As followers of Christ, we have the privilege of accessing and experiencing this peace on a daily basis. We can find peace in knowing that we are loved unconditionally, forgiven completely, and accepted fully by our Savior. We can find peace in His promises, His presence, and His faithfulness.

Take a moment to reflect on any anxieties, worries, or fears that may be troubling your heart. Surrender them to Jesus and invite Him to fill you with His peace. Trust that He is able to calm the storms within you and grant you a peace that surpasses all understanding. Seek His guidance on how to cultivate a life of peace rooted in Him, even amidst the challenges of life.

REFLECTIVE QUESTION

In what areas of your life do you need the peace that only Jesus can provide?

The Eternal Word of God

Your faithfulness
endures to all generations;
You established the earth, and it abides.

PSALM 119:90

IN A RAPIDLY CHANGING world, we can find comfort in the fact that God's faithfulness remains constant throughout all generations. He is the same yesterday, today, and forever. Just as He established the earth with His unwavering power and wisdom, His Word stands firm and reliable, providing us with guidance, comfort, and truth.

The psalmist's words echo a deep truth: God's faithfulness is not limited to a specific time or place. It transcends generations, cultures, and circumstances. His promises are timeless and relevant for every stage of our lives.

As we delve into the rich depths of God's Word, we encounter His faithfulness revealed through stories of triumph, deliverance, and redemption. We witness the unchanging nature of His character and His steadfast love for His people.

Take a moment to reflect on the faithfulness of God throughout history and in your personal journey of faith. Consider the ways in which His Word has brought comfort, guidance, and transformation in your life. How can you prioritize the study and application of His Word to experience His faithfulness more fully? Seek His guidance and wisdom as you seek to deepen your understanding and connection with Him through His eternal Word.

REFLECTIVE QUESTION
How does the eternal nature of God's Word impact your life?

Harnessing the Power of Thoughtful Silence

Even a fool is counted wise when he holds his peace;
When he shuts his lips, he is considered perceptive.

PROVERBS 17:28

THIS VERSE EMPHASIZES THE value of thoughtful silence and the importance of choosing our words wisely. In a world where speaking our minds and sharing our opinions has become increasingly prevalent, it is crucial to recognize the significance of silence. The ability to listen, contemplate, and refrain from speaking impulsively is a mark of wisdom and discernment. Silence allows us to truly hear and understand others, fostering deeper connections and empathy. It gives us the space to reflect on our own thoughts and motivations, allowing for personal growth and self-awareness. It also prevents us from hastily responding in anger or frustration, avoiding unnecessary conflicts.

Moreover, silence shows respect for others and acknowledges the value of their perspectives. Thus, it allows us to honour the moments when words may not be required and presence may be more comforting. By choosing silence in certain situations, we demonstrate humility and a willingness to learn from others.

Take a moment to reflect on your communication patterns. Are there times when you could benefit from listening more and speaking less? Consider the impact that practising silence can have on your relationships, both with others and with God. How can you grow in wisdom and discernment by intentionally choosing when to remain silent? Seek guidance from the Holy Spirit to help you develop this valuable skill and to use your words in ways that bring life and understanding to those around you.

REFLECTIVE QUESTION

How can you cultivate a habit of thoughtful silence in your interactions with others?

The Beauty of God's Creation

The heavens declare the glory of God,
And the firmament shows
His handiwork.

PSALM 19:1

THIS VERSE REMINDS US of the awe-inspiring majesty of God's creation and His fingerprints that are evident all around us.

When we look up at the vast expanse of the heavens, whether it be during a clear day or a star-filled night, we catch a glimpse of God's glory. The intricacy and wonder of the cosmos, the beauty of a sunrise or sunset, and the delicate balance of nature all point to a Creator who is infinitely great and creative.

The psalmist invites us to join in the cosmic chorus of praise as we witness the skies proclaiming the work of God's hands. Every part of creation serves as a testament to His wisdom, power, and care. The rhythm of the seasons, the symphony of birdsong, and the diversity of life all declare His glory.

Take a moment to reflect on specific moments when you've felt a deep sense of awe and wonder while observing nature's beauty. Consider the ways in which God speaks to you through His creation. How can you cultivate a heart of gratitude and worship as you encounter His handiwork in your daily life? Seek opportunities to connect with nature intentionally, allowing it to remind you of the greatness and majesty of your Creator. Let His creation be a source of inspiration and refreshment for your soul.

REFLECTIVE QUESTION

How do you experience God's presence and glory through His creation?

Walking in Integrity

The integrity of the upright
will guide them,
But the perversity of the unfaithful
will destroy them.

PROVERBS 11:3

INTEGRITY IS THE QUALITY of being honest, upright, and consistent in our thoughts, words, and actions. It is a virtue that guides our choices and shapes our character. When we walk in integrity, we align ourselves with God's truth and His ways.

Living a life of integrity has numerous benefits. It brings clarity and peace to our hearts as our actions align with our beliefs and values. It strengthens our relationships, as others can trust and rely on us. It also honours God as we become reflections of His righteousness in a world often filled with deception.

On the contrary, duplicity and deceit lead to destruction. When we engage in dishonesty or manipulation, we not only harm others but damage ourselves as well. Our credibility and reputation suffer, and trust is eroded. Ultimately, the consequences of unfaithfulness catch up with us, leaving a trail of brokenness in its wake.

Take a moment to reflect on your thoughts, words, and actions. Are there areas where you've been tempted to compromise your integrity? How can you cultivate a lifestyle of honesty and consistency in your everyday life? Seek God's guidance and wisdom, asking for His help to walk with integrity even when faced with challenges or temptations. Remember that walking in integrity is a lifelong journey, and with God's grace, you can grow in this virtue day by day.

REFLECTIVE QUESTION
In what areas of your life do you need to strengthen your integrity?

The Joy of Giving

**It is more blessed
to give than to receive.**

ACTS 20:35

THIS VERSE REMINDS US of the joy and blessing that comes from a generous and selfless heart.

Jesus taught His disciples the importance of giving and serving others, exemplifying it in His own life. In a world that often promotes self-centeredness, the act of giving shifts our focus from ourselves to the needs of others. It is through giving that we reflect the character of Christ and participate in His redemptive work.

When we give, whether it be our time, resources, or kindness, we experience a deep sense of joy and fulfilment that surpasses any temporary satisfaction we may gain from receiving. Giving allows us to tangibly demonstrate our love and care for others, impacting lives and spreading the light of Christ.

Take a moment to reflect on the ways in which you can be a blessing to others. Is there someone in need whom you can reach out to and support? How can you use your time, talents, and resources to make a positive impact in your community? Ask God to reveal opportunities for you to give and serve, trusting that He will provide what you need to bless others. Remember, as you give, you are not only making a difference in someone else's life but also experiencing the abundant joy that comes from obeying the words of Jesus.

REFLECTIVE QUESTION

How can you cultivate a heart of generosity and giving in your own life?

The Beauty of God's Timing

He has made everything beautiful in its time.
Also He has put eternity in their hearts,
except that no one can find out
the work that God does from beginning to end.

ECCLESIASTES 3:11

THIS VERSE ENCOURAGES US to trust in God's perfect timing and recognize His sovereignty over all things.

In a world filled with constant change and uncertainty, it is reassuring to know that God works according to His divine timetable. He orchestrates the events of our lives, weaving together a beautiful tapestry even in the midst of our confusion or impatience.

Sometimes, we may question the delay of certain blessings or the presence of hardship in our lives. However, God's timing is perfect and purposeful. He sees the bigger picture, and His plans lead to a greater beauty beyond our understanding.

Moreover, God has instilled a longing for eternity within our hearts. This longing reminds us that there is more to life than the present and that our hope extends far beyond our current circumstances. As we trust in God's timing, we can find comfort in knowing that He is working all things together for our ultimate good and His glory.

Take a moment to reflect on times when you've grown impatient or anxious. How can you cultivate a heart of surrender and trust, even when you don't understand God's timing? Consider the ways in which past experiences have shown you that God's timing is always perfect. How can you embrace a perspective that aligns with His eternal perspective? Seek His guidance and peace as you surrender your desires and trust in His beautiful timing.

REFLECTIVE QUESTION
In what areas of your life do you struggle with trusting God's timing?

Be Still and Know

Be still, and know that I am God.
PSALM 46:10

THESE WORDS HOLD A powerful reminder for us in the midst of our busy lives, filled with noise, distractions, and incessant worries.

In this verse, the psalmist invites us to pause and reflect on the divine presence in our lives. It calls us to trust in God's sovereignty and to find peace in knowing that He is in control. "Be still" does not necessarily mean physical stillness but rather emphasizes the need for us to quiet our hearts and minds, let go of our anxieties, and surrender to the loving embrace of our Heavenly Father.

God doesn't want us to live in constant restlessness and fear. Instead, He invites us to abide in Him, finding peace beyond understanding. Through prayer and meditation, we connect with God, making space to recognize His power, faithfulness, and love for us.

Pause for a moment and consider the various ways you can prioritize stillness in your life. It may involve setting aside a specific time for quiet reflection, creating a peaceful environment for prayer, practising mindfulness, or engaging in activities that bring you closer to God, such as reading Scripture or journaling.

Remember, being still is not about doing nothing. It is about intentionally creating an atmosphere where you can tune out the noise of the world and tune into God's voice. It is in these still moments that we find clarity, strength, and a renewed sense of purpose.

So, let us heed the psalmist's call to "be still" and trust that as we cultivate a deeper awareness of God's presence in our daily lives, we will experience His peace, joy, and love in abundance.

REFLECTIVE QUESTION

How can you incorporate stillness into your daily routine and cultivate a deeper awareness of God's presence in your life?

Perseverance in Doing Good

And let us not grow weary while doing good,
for in due season we shall reap if we do not lose heart.
GALATIANS 6:9

LIFE CAN BE FILLED with challenges and setbacks that often make us feel weary and discouraged. But in this verse, the apostle Paul reminds us of the importance of perseverance and not losing heart.

As followers of Christ, we are called to live lives of love, kindness, and compassion. We are called to do good in the world and make a positive impact on those around us. However, there are times when our efforts may seem fruitless, and we may question if our actions truly make a difference.

In these moments of weariness, Paul's words serve as an encouragement to keep pressing on. The promise of reaping a harvest at the proper time reminds us that our acts of kindness and goodness are not in vain. God sees our efforts, and He will bring about the fruitfulness in His perfect timing.

Take some time to reflect on the areas of your life where you may have grown weary of doing good. It could be in your relationships, your work, or your service to others. Ask yourself what may be draining your energy and causing discouragement.

Next, seek God's guidance and strength to persevere. Ask Him to renew your passion, restore your energy, and help you see the impact of your actions even in the midst of weariness.

And then seek support from fellow believers . Remember, God calls us to be faithful in doing good, even when we can't see immediate results. Trust in His timing and His promise that our efforts will not be in vain.

REFLECTIVE QUESTION
In what areas of your life are you feeling weary in doing good, and how can you find renewed strength and perseverance?

Saved by Grace, Through Faith

**For by grace you have been saved through faith,
and that not of yourselves; it is the gift of God.**
EPHESIANS 2:8

THESE WORDS FROM THE apostle Paul highlight the beautiful truth that our redemption is not something we can earn or achieve on our own; rather, it is freely given by God.

In a world that often emphasizes self-reliance and achievement, it can be easy to fall into the trap of thinking that our salvation depends on our efforts or good works. However, this verse gently reminds us that our salvation is a result of God's grace and our faith in Him.

The truth is, we are all in need of God's grace. We have all fallen short of His perfect standard and are incapable of saving ourselves. But through His loving kindness and mercy, God extends the offer of salvation to each and every one of us. It is through faith, deep trust and reliance on Jesus Christ that we receive this incredible gift.

Take a moment to reflect on the profound truth of God's grace and the gift of salvation. Consider how this understanding can deepen your relationship with God and shape your interactions with others.

Knowing that your salvation does not rest on your own efforts but rather on God's unmerited favour should fill you with gratitude and humility. It reminds us of our complete dependence on God and His mercy. It also motivates us to extend grace and forgiveness to others, just as we have received. May this truth transform your relationship with God and inspire you to be an instrument of His grace in the lives of others.

REFLECTIVE QUESTION
How does understanding that salvation is a gift of grace through faith impact your relationship with God and others?

Persevering Through Trials

**But let patience have its perfect work,
that you may be perfect and complete, lacking nothing.**
JAMES 1:4

THIS VERSE REMINDS US that trials and challenges are a normal part of life, but they have the power to refine and strengthen our faith.

When we face challenges, our natural instinct may be to pray for an immediate resolution or to escape from the situation altogether. However, James encourages us to embrace perseverance and allow it to shape us into mature and complete individuals.

Trials have a way of revealing our true character and deepening our dependence on God. They teach us patience, humility, and the importance of relying on His strength. Just as a tree's roots grow deeper and stronger during times of drought, our faith can be fortified through perseverance in the face of trials.

Take a moment to reflect on the trials you have faced or are currently experiencing. Instead of wishing for a quick resolution, consider how these challenges can be opportunities for growth and transformation.

Ask God to grant you the strength and perseverance to endure these trials. Seek His wisdom and guidance by seeking support and encouragement from fellow believers, finding comfort in God's Word, and praying for the strength to press on.

Remember, the goal is not to avoid trials but to allow them to refine and strengthen your faith so you become mature in your relationship with God and man.

REFLECTIVE QUESTION
How can you embrace perseverance in the midst of trials and allow it to shape your character and faith?

Pursuing Peaceful Relationships

**If it is possible, as much as depends on you,
live peaceably with all men.**

ROMANS 12:18

THIS VERSE CHALLENGES US to be proactive in our pursuit of harmony and reconciliation with others.

Living in a broken and divided world, conflicts and misunderstandings are inevitable. However, as followers of Christ, we are called to be peacemakers. This verse instructs us to do everything within our power to maintain peaceable relationships with others.

Pursuing peace does not mean compromising our values or avoiding difficult conversations. It requires humility, patience, and a willingness to seek understanding. It means responding to conflict with grace and choosing to love and forgive, even when it's challenging.

Take a moment to reflect on your relationships, considering any areas where there may be tension or unresolved conflict. Ask God to reveal to you ways in which you can actively pursue peace with those around you.

Consider how you can cultivate a heart of forgiveness and extend grace to others, even when it may be difficult. Are there actions or words that you need to let go of to promote peace? Are there steps you can take to initiate dialogue and seek reconciliation?

Remember that pursuing peace requires intentional effort and a reliance on God's guidance and wisdom.

May your pursuit of peace be a reflection of God's love and grace, bringing healing and unity to your relationships and glorifying Him in the process.

REFLECTIVE QUESTION

How can you actively pursue peace in your relationships and contribute to a harmonious atmosphere?

The Freedom of Forgiveness

And whenever you stand praying, if you have anything
against anyone, forgive him, that your Father in heaven
may also forgive you your trespasses.

MARK 11:25

THESE WORDS FROM JESUS highlight the connection between
our willingness to forgive others and our own ability to receive
God's forgiveness.

Unforgiveness can be a heavy burden that weighs us down and
hinders our relationship with both God and others.

When we forgive, we free ourselves from the bondage of
anger and hurt and open ourselves to experience the healing
and restoration that comes from God's forgiveness. It is through
forgiveness that we create space for God to work in our hearts
and transform our relationships.

Take a moment to reflect on any unresolved conflicts or
feelings of unforgiveness in your heart. Ask God to guide you
in identifying those individuals who need your forgiveness and
to help you find the strength and willingness to let go of any
resentment or bitterness.

Consider the ways in which you can actively extend forgiveness
to others. It may involve having a conversation, writing a letter, or
simply letting go of negative emotions in prayer. Trust in God's
grace to empower you to forgive, even in difficult circumstances.

Remember, forgiveness is not condoning or forgetting the harm
done to you; it is an act of surrendering the pain to God and
choosing to release others from the debt they owe you.

REFLECTIVE QUESTION

Is there anyone in your life that you need to forgive?
How can you extend forgiveness and experience the
freedom that comes from letting go of grudges?

The Joy of Service

For even the Son of Man did not come to be served,
but to serve, and to give His life a ransom for many.
MARK 10:45

THIS VERSE CAPTURES THE essence of Jesus' mission on earth and provides a powerful example for us to follow.

In a world that often values power, status, and self-centeredness, Jesus calls us to a different way of living. He invites us to adopt a servant's heart, one that seeks to serve and bless others rather than seeking to be served.

Jesus demonstrated this servant attitude throughout His ministry. He humbly washed the feet of His disciples, healed the sick, and ultimately gave His life as a sacrifice for our salvation.

Take a moment to reflect on your own attitude and motives in your interactions with others. Consider the areas in your life where you can intentionally embrace a servant's heart.

Ask God to reveal to you opportunities to serve those around you – your family, friends, colleagues, and even strangers. Reflect on how you can be a source of love, support, and encouragement to others.

As you navigate your daily routines, challenge yourself to adopt the posture of a servant. Let your actions be fueled by a genuine desire to bless and uplift others.

Remember, true greatness lies in serving others selflessly, just as Jesus did.

REFLECTIVE QUESTION

How can you embody the spirit of service in your daily life, following the example of Jesus, who came not to be served but to serve?

Gentleness: Strength in Disguise

**Blessed are the meek,
for they shall inherit the earth.**
MATTHEW 5:5

THIS BEATITUDE HIGHLIGHTS THE importance of meekness and its unique role in the kingdom of God. Meekness is often misunderstood as weakness, but in reality, it is a virtue that demonstrates great strength under control.

To be meek means to have a humble and gentle spirit, submitting to God's will and relying on His strength rather than our own. It is an attitude that seeks to serve others and put their needs before our own. Meekness is not about being a pushover or being easily manipulated but rather about choosing to respond with kindness, patience, and love, even in challenging situations.

Jesus himself exemplified meekness throughout his life and ministry. He showed incredible patience and gentleness toward those who opposed him and willingly submitted to God's plan, even to the point of death on the cross.

As we reflect on this beatitude, we are invited to consider our own attitudes and actions. Are we willing to surrender our own desires and ambitions to follow God's will? Do we respond with love and kindness, even when it may be difficult? Are we willing to serve others, even if it means setting aside our own interests?

Take a moment to prayerfully consider how you can grow in meekness and seek God's guidance in this process.

Remember that meekness is not about being weak but about choosing to align our hearts with God's and relying on His strength.

REFLECTIVE QUESTION
In what areas of your life do you need to cultivate meekness?

The Power of Words

Death and life
are in the power of the tongue,
And those who love it
will eat its fruit.

PROVERBS 18:21

THIS PROFOUND VERSE REMINDS us of the immense power our words hold. Our words have the ability to bring both life and death, to build up or tear down, to encourage or discourage.

God created the world through His spoken Word, and as His image-bearers, we, too, possess the gift of language. However, with this gift comes great responsibility. Our words have the potential to shape our own lives and the lives of those around us.

It is crucial that we choose our words carefully and intentionally. Instead of using our words to gossip, criticize, or belittle, we should strive to speak life-giving words that bring encouragement, healing, and hope. When our words align with God's truth, we become instruments of His love and grace in the world.

Take a moment to reflect on the power of your words and consider how you can use them to bring life, healing, and encouragement to those you encounter.

Let us be mindful of the impact our words can have. May we seek wisdom from God in the words we choose to speak and ask for the Holy Spirit's guidance in using our words to build up, inspire, and bless others. Remember, our words have the power to bring life and create a positive ripple effect in the lives of those around us.

REFLECTIVE QUESTION
How do your words impact the lives of others?
Are there areas in your speech that need improvement?

Trusting God in the Storm

**God is our refuge and strength,
A very present help in trouble.**

PSALM 46:1

THESE WORDS PROVIDE IMMENSE comfort and assurance, reminding us that no matter what challenges we face, God is our safe haven and a source of unwavering strength.

Life can be filled with uncertainties, trials, and hardships. In such moments, we may feel overwhelmed, powerless, or alone. However, this verse encourages us to turn to God as our refuge – a place of shelter, protection, and solace. He is the one we can run to in times of distress, finding comfort and strength in His presence.

Furthermore, God is not distant or detached from our struggles. He is described as an ever-present help in trouble. His love and care are constant, and He is intimately aware of our circumstances. We can rely on Him to guide us, strengthen us, and provide the help we need.

Are you quick to turn to God as your refuge and source of strength, or do you tend to rely on your own abilities? Take a moment to reflect on your response to difficult situations and consider how you can deepen your trust in God as your refuge and strength.

May we be encouraged to seek God as our refuge and strength in times of trouble, knowing that He is always present and ready to help us. Let us lean on His guidance and find strength in His unfailing love, finding comfort and peace in the midst of life's storms.

REFLECTIVE QUESTION
How do you typically respond when faced with trouble or challenges?

Embracing Change with Faith

Behold, I will do a new thing,
Now it shall spring forth;
Shall you not know it?
I will even make a road in the wilderness
And rivers in the desert.

ISAIAH 43:19

THIS VERSE ENCAPSULATES GOD'S promise of renewal, transformation, and the restoration of hope. Even in times of desolation, God declares that He is at work, bringing forth something new and extraordinary.

In life, we may face seasons of dryness, despair, or feeling stuck in a wilderness. These moments can be disheartening and discouraging, making it challenging for us to see a way forward. However, God assures us that He is actively working amidst the barrenness, creating rivers of life where there seemed to be none. Just as God led the Israelites through the wilderness and provided streams of water, He continues to guide and sustain us today. He has the power to bring beauty out of ashes, to make a way where there seems to be no way. God's promise of doing a new thing should fill us with hope and anticipation, knowing that He can turn our deserts into flourishing landscapes.

Are there places that feel dry, desolate, or stagnant? Take a moment to reflect on God's promise of renewal and ask Him to reveal the new things He wants to bring forth in your life.

Remember that God's timing and plans are perfect. Trust in His faithfulness and rely on His guidance as He creates rivers of hope and restoration in the midst of seemingly impossible situations. Embrace the new things God is doing and walk in expectancy of His transformative power.

REFLECTIVE QUESTION
In what areas of your life do you need God to do a new thing?

Contentment in Simplicity

Better is a little
with the fear of the Lord,
Than great treasure with trouble.

PROVERBS 15:16

THIS VERSE EMPHASIZES THE importance of finding contentment in simplicity and the pursuit of godly values rather than being consumed by the pursuit of worldly wealth and possessions. In our modern society, the temptation to chase after material wealth, status, and excess can be overwhelming. We often associate happiness and success with the accumulation of material possessions or the pursuit of worldly ambitions. However, true satisfaction and peace come from having a reverent fear of the Lord and aligning our priorities with His wisdom.

The pursuit of wealth and material possessions can lead to trouble, anxiety, and discontentment. It can distract us from what truly matters and hinder our spiritual growth. In contrast, choosing to prioritize our relationship with God and seeking His wisdom brings about a peace and contentment that surpasses material wealth.

Are there areas where you have been chasing after worldly pursuits at the expense of your spiritual growth and inner peace? Take a moment to reflect on your priorities and ask God for help. Remember that true riches come from deepening our relationship with God and living in alignment with His values. Let us seek contentment in the fear of the Lord, valuing spiritual growth, integrity, and love above temporary wealth and worldly achievements.

REFLECTIVE QUESTION

How can you cultivate contentment in your life rather than pursuing worldly wealth?

The Power of Prayer

Be anxious for nothing,
but in everything by prayer
and supplication, with thanksgiving,
let your requests be made known to God.

PHILIPPIANS 4:6

THIS VERSE REMINDS US of the powerful invitation to find peace and freedom from anxiety through prayer and giving thanks to God. Anxiety and worry are common experiences in our lives. We often find ourselves fretting over the uncertainties of the future, our personal struggles, or the challenges we face. However, the apostle Paul urges us not to be consumed by anxiety but to bring all our concerns, fears, and needs to God in prayer.

Prayer is a transformative practice that allows us to surrender our worries to God and trust in His faithfulness. It is an opportunity to place our burdens before Him and seek His guidance and wisdom. Additionally, Paul instructs us to approach God with thanksgiving, acknowledging His goodness and provision even in the midst of our difficulties.

How can you incorporate prayer and thanksgiving into your daily routine to find peace and seek God's guidance? Take a moment to reflect on the power of prayer and thanksgiving in overcoming anxiety and strengthening your faith.

As we bring our concerns to God through prayer, expressing gratitude for His blessings, we open ourselves to receive His peace that surpasses all understanding (Philippians 4:7). May we cultivate a habit of turning to God in prayer, entrusting our worries to Him, and finding solace in His presence.

REFLECTIVE QUESTION
In what areas of your life do you struggle with anxiety and worry?

Embracing God's Grace in Weakness

**My grace is sufficient for you,
for My power is made perfect
in weakness.**

2 CORINTHIANS 12:9

GOD REMINDS US THAT His grace is more than enough to sustain us in our weaknesses and empower us to overcome any challenges we may face.

As human beings, we often try to hide our weaknesses and shortcomings, fearing that they make us inadequate or unworthy. However, God's message to us is that in our weaknesses, His power is displayed most vividly. It is through His grace that we find strength, comfort, and resilience.

God's grace is not dependent on our own abilities or achievements. It is His unmerited favour freely given to us, regardless of our shortcomings. When we surrender our weaknesses to Him, we allow God to work in and through us. In our moments of vulnerability, God's power shines brightly, bringing about transformation and growth.

Do you try to hide them or deny them, or do you surrender them to God and trust in His grace? Take a moment to reflect on your attitude towards your weaknesses and consider how you can embrace God's grace more fully in these areas.

May we learn to embrace our weaknesses, recognizing that they are opportunities for God's grace to be magnified in our lives. Through His power working in us, we can find strength and courage to face any challenge. So, let us humbly surrender ourselves to God, trusting in His sufficient grace to carry us through every season of weakness and empower us to live victoriously.

REFLECTIVE QUESTION
How do you typically view your weaknesses?

The Lamp for Our Path

**Your Word is a lamp to my feet
and a light to my path.**

PSALM 119:105

THIS BEAUTIFUL VERSE REMINDS us of the invaluable guidance and illumination that God's Word provides in our lives. Just as a lamp reveals the path in darkness, God's Word lights our way, showing us the direction we should take.

In a world filled with confusion, distractions, and moral ambiguity, we can find certainty and clarity through the Scriptures. God's Word serves as a source of wisdom, truth, and guidance, leading us to make choices that align with His will and purposes.

When we immerse ourselves in the Bible, studying and meditating upon its teachings, it illuminates our thoughts, decisions, and actions. It reveals God's character, His promises, and His plan for our lives. The more we engage with His Word, the more clearly we can discern the path He wants us to follow.

Are there areas where you can deepen your understanding and application of Scripture? Take a moment to reflect on the importance of allowing God's Word to guide and shape your thoughts and actions.

Just as a lamp is essential for navigating through darkness, God's Word is crucial for navigating the challenges and choices we encounter on our journey of faith. Let us commit ourselves to immerse in His Word, allowing it to illuminate our path and bring clarity to our lives. May we seek His guidance through Scripture and trust in its transformative power to lead us closer to Him.

REFLECTIVE QUESTION
How do you prioritize and engage with God's Word in your daily life?

Trusting in God's Plan

For I know the thoughts
that I think toward you, says the Lord,
thoughts of peace and not of evil,
to give you a future and a hope.

JEREMIAH 29:11

JEREMIAH 29:11 IS A powerful and reassuring verse that reminds us of God's faithfulness and His plans for our lives. In the midst of uncertain times or challenging circumstances, this verse serves as a profound reminder of God's promises and His commitment to our well-being.

Reflecting on this verse, we can draw comfort from the fact that God has our best interests at heart. He is not interested in causing us harm but rather desires to prosper us, both spiritually and in every area of our lives. This verse reveals God's compassionate nature, assuring us that He has a plan to guide us towards a future filled with hope and purpose.

When we face uncertainties or difficulties, it is natural to question God's plan. However, this verse reminds us to trust in His wisdom. It encourages us to surrender our doubts and fears, knowing that our Heavenly Father has a divine blueprint for our lives.

How does knowing that God has a plan for your life impact your perspective on challenging situations? How can you actively trust in His plan and find hope in the midst of uncertainty?

As you ponder on this verse and question, take a moment to pray and seek God's guidance. Ask Him to strengthen your faith and help you surrender any fears or doubts to Him. Trust in His plan, and embrace the hope and future He has promised.

REFLECTIVE QUESTION
How can you surrender to God's plans, trusting His intentions for your future are filled with hope and prosperity?

Love That Endures

Love suffers long and is kind;
love does not envy;
love does not parade itself,
is not puffed up.

1 CORINTHIANS 13:4

APOSTLE PAUL BEAUTIFULLY CAPTURES the essence of love when he writes, "Love is patient, love is kind." These simple words hold profound wisdom that continues to resonate through the ages.

To be patient means to bear with others, to endure with grace and understanding. It is a gentle reminder to approach relationships and situations with a calm and forgiving heart. Kindness, on the other hand, encourages us to act with compassion, empathy, and generosity towards others.

As we reflect on these qualities of love, let us consider how we can cultivate patience and kindness in our own lives. Are there areas in our relationships where we tend to be impatient or unkind? How can we practice more patience and kindness towards others, even in challenging circumstances?

Today, let us strive to embody the patience and kindness that Paul describes. Let us extend grace to those who may test our patience and choose kindness over harsh words or actions. In doing so, we can experience the transformative power of love and create a more harmonious and compassionate world around us.

REFLECTIVE QUESTION

How can you practice patience and kindness in your relationships today?

Unveiling the Power of Faith

Now faith is the substance
of things hoped for,
the evidence of things not seen.
HEBREWS 11:1

THE CONCEPT OF FAITH is central to the Christian journey. It is an unwavering belief in the promises and power of God, even when circumstances suggest otherwise.

Faith gives us the strength and perseverance to hold on to our hopes and dreams, knowing that God is faithful and able to bring them to fruition. It enables us to rise above doubt and fear, trusting in God's perfect timing and providence.

Consider the story of Abraham, who believed in God's promise of a son, even when it seemed impossible. Despite their old age, Abraham and Sarah held on to faith and eventually witnessed the birth of their son Isaac, fulfilling God's promise.

Similarly, faith empowers us to face life's challenges with courage and hope, knowing that God is in control. It reminds us that even in the midst of uncertainty, God is working behind the scenes, orchestrating the events of our lives for our ultimate good.

So, let us embrace faith as the bedrock of our existence, allowing it to inspire and guide us on our journey. By placing our trust in the unseen, we can experience a transformational perspective that brings hope, joy, and the fulfilment of our deepest desires.

REFLECTIVE QUESTION
How does having faith in the unseen impact your perspective on life and the fulfilment of your hopes and dreams?

Encouraging One Another

And let us consider one another in order to stir up
love and good works, not forsaking the assembling of
ourselves together, as is the manner of some,
but exhorting one another, and so much the more
as you see the Day approaching.

HEBREWS 10:24-25

As BELIEVERS, WE ARE called to inspire and encourage one another in our pursuit of love and good deeds.

In a world that often pulls us apart, the passage encourages us to consider how we can actively spur one another towards acts of love and kindness. It prompts us to think about the impact we can collectively make when we come together in unity, supporting and uplifting one another.

Furthermore, the verse stresses the significance of regular fellowship and gathering as believers. It urges us not to neglect this vital aspect of our faith journey, for it is within the community of believers that we find encouragement, accountability, and spiritual growth.

Consider the various ways you can engage with fellow believers and strengthen the bonds of love and unity in your community. This could include attending church services, joining small groups, participating in service projects, or engaging in meaningful conversations that edify and uplift.

As we eagerly anticipate the return of our Lord, let us prioritize love, good deeds, and regular fellowship with other believers. By actively spurring one another on and cultivating an environment of encouragement and unity, we can build a community that reflects the love and grace of Christ to a world in need.

REFLECTIVE QUESTION

In what ways can you actively spur others toward love and good deeds, and how can you prioritize regular fellowship with other believers?

The Power of Gratitude

In everything give thanks;
for this is the will of God
in Christ Jesus for you.

1 THESSALONIANS 5:18

THIS VERSE CHALLENGES US to cultivate a spirit of gratitude, not just when things are going well but even in the face of challenges and hardships. It's easy to be thankful when life is smooth sailing, but true gratitude shines brightest in the midst of adversity.

When we intentionally choose to be grateful, we shift our focus from what we lack to the blessings that surround us. Gratitude helps us recognize the goodness of God in every situation and appreciate the smallest joys in life.

Consider the apostle Paul, who wrote this verse from a prison cell. Despite his circumstances, he maintained an attitude of gratitude, rejoicing in the opportunity to share the Gospel and the transformative power of Christ.

Practicing gratitude can transform our perspective on life. It reminds us that even in the most difficult times, God is with us, working all things for our good. It enables us to find hope and strength, knowing that God's faithfulness endures.

So, let us cultivate a spirit of gratitude, expressing thankfulness to God for His love, provision, and guidance. As we embrace gratitude as a way of life, we will experience a profound shift in our perspective, finding joy and contentment in every circumstance.

REFLECTIVE QUESTION

In what ways can you cultivate a spirit of gratitude, even in the most challenging circumstances, and how can it transform your perspective on life?

Overcoming Fear With Faith

Have I not commanded you?
Be strong and of good courage;
do not be afraid, nor be dismayed,
for the Lord your God is
with you wherever you go.

JOSHUA 1:9

BEING STRONG AND COURAGEOUS does not mean we will never face fear or discouragement. Instead, it is a call to trust in God's unfailing support and guidance, even in the face of uncertainty.

Just as God promised Joshua His constant presence, He promises to be with us in every step of our journey. We can take courage knowing that God is our ever-present help, providing us with the strength and wisdom we need.

When we actively embrace this call to be strong and courageous, we begin to overcome obstacles that previously held us back. We find boldness to step out of our comfort zones, pursue our dreams, and face challenges with unwavering faith.

So, let us not be afraid or discouraged, for our God is mighty and faithful. As we trust in His presence and guidance, He equips us to navigate the unknown and walk confidently in His purpose for our lives. May we embrace the call to be strong and courageous, knowing that the Lord our God is with us wherever we go.

REFLECTIVE QUESTION

How can you actively embrace the call to be strong and courageous in your life, trusting in God's presence and guidance?

Walking in Love

Love suffers long and is kind; love does not envy;
love does not parade itself, is not puffed up;
does not behave rudely, does not seek its own,
is not provoked, thinks no evil;

1 CORINTHIANS 13:4-5

THIS PASSAGE BEAUTIFULLY DESCRIBES the qualities of love that should permeate our relationships. It reminds us that love is patient and kind, serving as the foundation for healthy and meaningful connections.

Patience allows us to extend grace and understanding, even when others fall short. It gives us the ability to walk alongside them as they grow and navigate life's challenges. Kindness, on the other hand, involves showing compassion, empathy, and genuine care towards others.

By actively practising patience and kindness, we create an atmosphere of acceptance and grace within our relationships. These qualities foster deeper connections, promote forgiveness, and enable us to build bridges of understanding.

Consider the example of Jesus, whose love for humanity was marked by immense patience and kindness. He demonstrated patience with His disciples' doubts and mistakes, and consistently showed kindness to those marginalized by society.

So, let us strive to exhibit patience and kindness in our daily interactions. As we do so, we demonstrate God's love to others and set a powerful example of what true and authentic relationships should be. May our relationships be marked by patience and kindness, reflecting the love of Christ to a world that desperately needs it.

REFLECTIVE QUESTION

In what ways can you actively demonstrate patience and kindness in your relationships, and how can it impact the depth and quality of your connections?

An Invitation to Ask

If any of you lacks wisdom,
let him ask of God,
who gives to all liberally
and without reproach,
and it will be given to him.

JAMES 1:5

WISDOM IS INVALUABLE IN our journey of faith. It enables us to make informed decisions, discern God's will, and navigate the complexities of life with clarity and discernment.

In the busy and chaotic world we live in, seeking wisdom from God becomes crucial. We need His guidance and insight to navigate relationships, make career choices, face challenges, and handle the difficulties life throws our way.

To actively seek God's wisdom, we can devote time to prayer, meditate on His Word, and seek counsel from wise and mature believers. God's wisdom is not limited to a select few but is available to all who earnestly seek it.

So, let us humbly approach God, acknowledging our need for His wisdom in all areas of our lives. May we seek His guidance daily, confident that He will generously provide wisdom for every situation. As we actively seek wisdom, we will grow spiritually and experience the abundant life that comes from aligning our choices with God's wisdom.

REFLECTIVE QUESTION

In what areas of your life do you need wisdom the most, and how can you actively seek God's guidance to navigate those situations?

The Joy of the Lord

The joy of the Lord
is your strength.
NEHEMIAH 8:10

TRUE JOY IS NOT dependent on our circumstances; it comes from knowing and experiencing the goodness and faithfulness of God. It is a lasting and unshakable joy that brings strength to our hearts, even in the midst of trials and challenges.

When we cultivate a sense of joy anchored in God's character and promises, we tap into a reservoir of strength that carries us through the storms of life. This joy doesn't ignore our pain or struggles, but it sustains us with hope and a sense of God's presence in every situation.

To cultivate this joy, we can spend time in God's presence, praising and worshipping Him, reminding ourselves of His faithfulness and goodness. We can seek gratitude for even the smallest blessings, shifting our focus from what is lacking to what we have been given.

So, let us choose to cultivate joy, regardless of our circumstances. As we anchor our joy in the Lord, we will find the strength to face whatever comes our way. May the joy of the Lord fill our hearts and become a constant source of strength and hope in our lives.

REFLECTIVE QUESTION

How can you cultivate a deep sense of joy in your life, anchored in the goodness and faithfulness of God, and how can this joy strengthen you in times of trials and challenges?

Delighting in the Desires of Your Heart

Delight yourself in the Lord,
and he will give you
the desires of your heart.

PSALM 37:4

"TAKE DELIGHT IN THE LORD, and he will give you the desires of your heart." This verse reminds us that when we prioritize our relationship with God and find joy in His presence, our desires will align with His will.

Sometimes, we may have desires that are not in line with what God wants for us. It's important to remember that God knows what is best for us, and His plans are far greater than our own. When we take delight in the Lord, our desires are transformed, and we begin to desire the things that please Him.

Instead of focusing solely on our personal ambitions, let us seek to understand God's purpose for our lives. This requires spending time with Him in prayer, studying His Word, and listening to His guidance. As we do so, we will find that the desires of our hearts align with His will.

In surrendering our desires to God, we open ourselves to His blessings and find true joy in His plans for us. So, let us take delight in the Lord and trust that He will fulfil the desires of our hearts in ways that surpass our imagination.

REFLECTIVE QUESTION

How can you align your desires with God's will and find joy in His plans?

Finding Rest in God

Come to Me,
all you who labour
and are heavy laden,
and I will give you rest.

MATTHEW 11:28

LIFE CAN OFTEN OVERWHELM us with its demands, worries, and challenges. Yet, Jesus offers us a profound promise: rest for our weary souls. He is the source of true rest, offering refreshment, peace, and comfort to those who seek Him.

To find this rest, we are called to come to Jesus—to approach Him with open hearts and lay our burdens down at His feet. It is in surrendering our worries, anxieties, and struggles to Him that we find relief and renewal.

Take a moment to reflect upon the burdens you are carrying today. Are you trying to handle everything on your own? Are there worries that consume your thoughts? Give these burdens to Jesus; let Him carry the weight for you.

In Him, we find rest from the weariness and burdens of life. He invites us to trust in Him, to release our worries, and to rely on His strength. So, come to Jesus and experience the rest that only He can provide.

REFLECTIVE QUESTION
How can you find true rest by surrendering your burdens to Jesus?

Walking in Faith

**For we walk by faith,
not by sight.**
2 CORINTHIANS 5:7

LIFE IS FILLED WITH uncertainties. We often face situations that challenge our understanding and test our faith. However, as believers, we are called to place our trust in God, knowing that He sees the bigger picture and has a perfect plan for our lives.

Walking by faith requires us to let go of our need for control and to surrender our desires, plans, and fears to God. It is a daily act of choosing to rely on His wisdom, strength, and provision, even when circumstances seem daunting.

Reflect on your current circumstances. Are there areas in your life where you are relying solely on what you can see and understand? How can you cultivate a deeper trust in God and lean on His guidance?

Remember that faith is not about having all the answers or seeing immediate results. It is about embracing the unknown with confidence in God's character and promises. By walking by faith, we open ourselves to the beauty of His plans and experience a deeper intimacy with Him.

So, let us choose to walk by faith, trusting in God's goodness, even when we cannot see the way before us.

REFLECTIVE QUESTION
**How can you cultivate a deeper trust in God and
navigate life with faith, even in the face of uncertainty?**

The Power of Humility

**God resists the proud,
but gives grace to the humble.**
JAMES 4:6

HUMILITY IS NOT ABOUT demeaning ourselves; it is about recognizing our need for God and acknowledging His sovereignty in our lives. When we approach God with humility, we open ourselves to the abundant grace He offers.

Cultivating a humble heart begins with surrendering our pride and selfish ambitions. It is about seeking God's will above our own and submitting ourselves to His plans. It involves recognizing our limitations and acknowledging that all our gifts and talents come from Him.

Reflect on your interactions with others. Are there areas where pride and self-centeredness might be hindering your relationships? How can you humble yourself and extend grace to those around you?

As we embrace humility, we experience the favour of God. He lavishes us with His grace, empowering us to live a life that reflects His love and mercy. It is through humility that we find true freedom and the ability to love and serve others selflessly.

So, let us embrace humility, recognizing that God's grace abounds for those who humbly seek Him. May we continuously surrender our pride and walk in the abundant grace He provides.

REFLECTIVE QUESTION
How can you cultivate a humble heart and experience the abundant grace that flows from God?

Contentment

Not that I speak in regard to need,
for I have learned in whatever state I am,
to be content.

PHILIPPIANS 4:11

IN A WORLD THAT constantly tells us that we need more to be happy, contentment seems elusive. However, true contentment is not dependent on external factors but rather on our perspective and relationship with God.

Contentment does not mean we become complacent, settling for less or neglecting growth. Rather, it is about finding peace and satisfaction in God's presence, trusting that He will provide for our needs and work all things for our good.

Reflect on your current season of life. Are there areas where you find it challenging to be content? How can you shift your focus to gratitude and trust in God's provision?

Cultivating contentment requires a shift in our mindset. It means learning to count our blessings, focusing on what we have rather than what we lack, and finding joy in the simple pleasures of life.

When we learn to be content, we free ourselves from the constant pursuit of worldly desires and find true fulfilment in our relationship with God. We can experience peace that surpasses understanding, even in the midst of difficult circumstances.

So, let us learn from Paul's example and strive to cultivate contentment in every season of life. Trust in God's provision, embrace gratitude and find joy in His presence.

REFLECTIVE QUESTION
How can you cultivate a heart of contentment and find joy in every season of life?

Love That Transforms

**A new commandment I give to you,
you love one another; as I have loved you,
that you also love one another.**

JOHN 13:34

LOVE IS NOT MERELY an emotion or feeling; it is an action. It is actively seeking the well-being and welfare of others, just as Christ demonstrated His love for us through His sacrificial death on the cross.

As followers of Jesus, we are called to love one another with the same depth and selflessness. This love goes beyond romantic or familial affection; it extends to all people, regardless of their background or beliefs.

Reflect on your interactions with others. Are there moments when you can extend kindness, compassion, and understanding? How can you actively demonstrate Christ-like love in your words and actions?

Loving one another means showing forgiveness, grace, and empathy. It involves putting aside our own interests and preferences for the sake of others. It requires humility and a willingness to serve.

When we love one another as Jesus loved us, we become a powerful witness of His love to the world. Our acts of love can touch hearts, heal wounds, and bring transformation to the lives of others.

So, let us embrace the command to love one another, making intentional efforts to extend Christ's love to those we encounter. May our love reflect His character and bring glory to His name.

REFLECTIVE QUESTION
How can you demonstrate Christ-like love to others in your daily interactions?

The Strength of Self-Control

A man without self-control
is like a city broken into
and left without walls.

PROVERBS 25:28 (ESV)

SELF-CONTROL IS A VALUABLE virtue that allows us to govern our thoughts, emotions, and actions. It empowers us to resist temptations, make wise decisions, and maintain healthy relationships.

Reflect on moments when anger or lack of self-control has caused harm or regret in your life. How can you cultivate self-control and guard against the destructive consequences of anger in the future?

Cultivating self-control requires self-awareness and intentional effort. It involves pausing before reacting, seeking to understand others' perspectives, and practising forgiveness. Developing habits like prayer, meditation, and seeking guidance from God's Word can strengthen our self-control.

When we exercise self-control, we build stronger relationships, avoid unnecessary conflicts, and prevent harm to ourselves and others. It enables us to respond with wisdom, grace, and compassion in challenging situations.

May we strive to be like a well-fortified city with strong walls of self-control. Let us surrender our desires for immediate gratification, seeking instead God's guidance and strength to overcome our weaknesses. Through His power, we can grow in self-control and experience the transformative impact it has on our lives.

REFLECTIVE QUESTION
How can you cultivate self-control and guard against the destructive consequences of anger?

The Gift of Encouragement

Therefore
encourage one another
and build each other up,
just as in fact you are doing.
1 Thessalonians 5:11 (niv)

ENCOURAGEMENT IS NOT SIMPLY a kind word or a fleeting act; it is a deliberate choice to speak life, hope, and affirmation into the lives of others. It is a means to uplift, inspire, and support those around us.

Reflect on the impact of encouragement in your own life. Are there people who have spoken words of encouragement that have made a lasting difference? How can you actively bring encouragement and upliftment to others?

We all face various challenges, doubts, and setbacks. Through intentional acts of encouragement, we can help others find strength, motivation, and resilience. A kind word, a listening ear, or a gesture of support can have a significant impact on someone's day or even their life.

As followers of Christ, we have the opportunity and responsibility to be agents of encouragement. By building each other up, we create a community that is marked by love, compassion, and unity.

So, let us heed the call to encourage one another and actively look for ways to uplift those around us. May our words and actions be a source of hope, joy, and strength, bringing God's light into the lives of others.

REFLECTIVE QUESTION
How can you actively encourage and uplift others in your daily interactions?

Nurturing a Spirit of Generosity

Give, and it will be given to you:
good measure, pressed down,
shaken together, and running over
will be put into your bosom.
For with the same measure that you use,
it will be measured back to you.

LUKE 6:38

GENEROSITY IS NOT LIMITED to material possessions; it encompasses our time, talents, and acts of kindness. When we give selflessly, without expecting anything in return, we cultivate a heart that mirrors the character of God.

Reflect on your current attitudes towards giving. Are there areas where you can be more generous with your resources, time, or talents? How can you cultivate a heart of generosity in your daily life?

God's economy works in a way that defies logic. When we give freely, not only do we bless others, but we also experience the overflow of God's blessings in our own lives. We are enriched by the joy of giving and witness the transformative impact our generosity can have on others.

As we pour out love, kindness, and resources to those in need, we become channels of God's grace. He multiplies our gifts and pours blessings into our lives, often in ways we could never anticipate.

So, let us cultivate a heart of generosity, knowing that when we give generously, we open ourselves up to experience the abundance of God's blessings. May our lives be marked by selfless giving and a willingness to share God's love with others.

REFLECTIVE QUESTION
How can you cultivate a heart of generosity and experience the blessings that come from giving?

Staying Faithful in Trials

Blessed is the man
who endures temptation;
for when he has been approved,
he will receive the crown of life
which the Lord has promised
to those who love Him.

JAMES 1:12

JAMES 1:12 REMINDS US of the incredible reward in store for those who endure trials with steadfast faith. This verse encourages us to view trials as opportunities for growth and to persevere with hope, knowing that a crown of life awaits us.

When faced with trials, it can be easy to lose sight of the bigger picture. However, James reminds us that our trials are not in vain. The promise of the crown of life gives us a greater perspective, reminding us that our faithfulness in the face of trials has an eternal reward. So, take a moment to reflect on how this promise impacts your perspective on trials and difficulties. How does knowing that a crown of life awaits you empower you to press on and remain faithful?

May you find strength and endurance in the assurance of the crown of life as you navigate the trials of life, knowing that your faithfulness will be richly rewarded by the Lord.

REFLECTIVE QUESTION
How does the promise of the crown of life impact your perspective on trials and difficulties?

Cultivating Joy in Everyday Life

Rejoice in the Lord always.
Again I will say, rejoice!
PHILIPPIANS 4:4

IN THE MIDST OF our busy and often chaotic lives, finding joy can sometimes feel elusive. Yet, the Apostle Paul reminds us in Philippians 4:4 to rejoice always in the Lord. This goes beyond temporary happiness based on circumstances; it is an enduring and deep-seated joy found in our relationship with God.

Rejoicing does not mean ignoring or dismissing life's challenges, but rather, it is a choice to focus on God's goodness and faithfulness despite the circumstances. When we cultivate a spirit of rejoicing, it transforms our perspective, brings peace to our hearts, and strengthens our faith.

Imagine a life where, even in the face of difficulties, we can confidently say, "I choose to rejoice!" This requires a genuine trust in God, knowing that He is in control and working all things together for our good.

REFLECTIVE QUESTION
How can you cultivate a spirit of rejoicing in your life today, regardless of the circumstances?

The Role of Discipline in Spiritual Growth

But also for this very reason, giving all diligence,
add to your faith virtue, to virtue knowledge,
to knowledge self-control, to self-control perseverance,
to perseverance godliness.

2 PETER 1:5-6

APOSTLE PETER ENCOURAGES US to diligently nurture our faith by adding various virtues into our lives. Each virtue builds upon the previous one, resulting in a life that reflects the character of Christ.

First, Peter calls us to add goodness, which encompasses acts of kindness, compassion, and integrity. As we grow in goodness, it naturally leads to acquiring knowledge and understanding of God's Word. This knowledge then empowers us to exercise self-control, enabling us to resist temptation and make wise choices.

But the journey doesn't stop there. We are also called to develop perseverance, the steadfastness to endure trials and challenges that come our way. And ultimately, the pinnacle of our spiritual growth is godliness, embodying the characteristics of God and reflecting His love in all that we do.

As we intentionally cultivate these virtues in our lives, we align ourselves with God's promises and experience a transformed and purposeful existence.

REFLECTIVE QUESTION

Which of these virtues (goodness, knowledge, self-control, perseverance, godliness) do you feel called to focus on and develop further in your life? How can you actively pursue growth in that area?

Seize Every Opportunity, Live with Purpose

Whatever your hand finds to do,
do it with your might; for there is no work
or device or knowledge or wisdom
in the grave where you are going.

ECCLESIASTES 9:10

IN ECCLESIASTES 9:10, WE are reminded to approach life with a sense of urgency and purpose. The author encourages us to seize every opportunity that comes our way, giving our utmost effort and wholehearted dedication to the tasks at hand.

Life is fleeting, and the certainty of death reminds us that time is limited. Therefore, instead of succumbing to complacency or indifference, we are called to engage in the present moment with diligence, determination, and enthusiasm.

Whether it's our work, relationships, or personal pursuits, we are reminded to do everything as if it matters because, in God's eyes, it does. Our actions and attitudes have an impact not only on ourselves but also on those around us.

By embracing this wisdom, we can live a life that is marked by purpose, fulfilment, and a deep appreciation for the opportunities that come our way.

REFLECTIVE QUESTION

How can you apply the wisdom of Ecclesiastes 9:10 in your daily life? What practical steps can you take to approach every task and opportunity with all your might?

Maintaining Hope in Challenging Times

I would have lost heart,
unless I had believed That
I would see the goodness of the Lord
In the land of the living.

PSALM 27:13

IN PSALM 27:13, THE psalmist expresses unwavering confidence in God's goodness and faithfulness. Despite facing challenges and uncertainties, the psalmist reaffirms their hope that they will witness the goodness of the Lord in their present circumstances.

This verse reminds us that as believers, we can cling to the assurance that God's goodness is not confined to some distant future but it is something we can experience here and now. Even in the midst of trials, we can choose to remain hopeful, knowing that God is with us and working for our ultimate good.

Rather than being consumed by fear or despair, we can place our trust in the One who is faithful and steadfast. Our confidence in God's goodness provides the strength to endure hardships and the perspective to see the beauty and blessings that surround us.

REFLECTIVE QUESTION

How can you cultivate a confident hope in God's goodness in the midst of your current challenges? What specific ways can you seek and acknowledge His goodness in your life today?

The Practice of Daily Prayer

Continue earnestly in prayer,
being vigilant in it
with thanksgiving.
COLOSSIANS 4:2

IN COLOSSIANS 4:2, THE apostle Paul urges believers to make prayer an integral part of their lives. Prayer is not merely a casual interaction with God; it is a devoted and intentional act of communication with our Heavenly Father.

To devote ourselves to prayer means to prioritize it, creating regular and intentional moments to connect with God. Prayer enables us to seek His guidance, express our gratitude, and present our needs and concerns before Him. It is through prayer that we align our hearts with God's will and experience His presence and peace.

Paul also encourages us to be watchful and thankful. Prayer should not be done absentmindedly but with alertness and attentiveness. We should be watchful for God's guidance, open to His promptings, and sensitive to His voice. And in every circumstance, we are to maintain an attitude of thankfulness, recognizing and appreciating God's faithfulness and blessings.

REFLECTIVE QUESTION

How can you enhance your devotion to prayer and cultivate a mindset of watchfulness and thankfulness in your prayer life? In what ways can you deepen your connection with God through intentional and heartfelt prayer?

Enduring Love, Unfailing Faithfulness

The Lord has appeared of old to me,
saying: 'Yes, I have loved you with
an everlasting love;
Therefore with lovingkindness
I have drawn you.

JEREMIAH 31:3

IN THIS VERSE, WE are assured that God's love for us is not based on our merits or accomplishments; it is an everlasting love that remains constant and unwavering.

God's love is not fleeting or temporary, but it endures throughout all circumstances and seasons of life. It is a love that surpasses human understanding and is rooted in His very nature.

Not only does God love us, but He also extends His unfailing kindness towards us. His kindness is not limited or conditional but extends to all who turn to Him. His love and kindness draw us closer to Him, inviting us into a personal relationship with the Creator of the universe.

In a world that often offers conditional love and fleeting affections, we can find comfort and security in the everlasting love of God.

REFLECTIVE QUESTION

How does the knowledge of God's everlasting love and unfailing kindness impact your view of yourself and your relationship with Him? How can you respond to His love and kindness in your daily life?

Good Words and Good Deeds

Pleasant words
are like a honeycomb,
Sweetness to the soul
and health to the bones.

PROVERBS 16:24

IN PROVERBS 16:24, WE are reminded of the profound impact our words can have on others. Gracious words, filled with kindness, encouragement, and positivity, have the power to bring healing and refreshment to the soul.

Our words have the ability to build up or tear down, to inspire or discourage. When we choose to speak graciously, we become agents of healing, spreading goodness and love to those around us.

Just as honey is sweet and soothing to the taste, gracious words have a similar effect on the soul. They uplift spirits, instil hope, and provide comfort in times of need. They have the power to mend brokenness and wounded hearts.

As followers of Christ, we are called to imitate His example and use our words to show grace and love to others. Let us be intentional in choosing words that bring life and healing, for they have the power to transform lives and leave a lasting impact.

REFLECTIVE QUESTION

How can you cultivate a habit of speaking gracious words that bring healing and refreshment to those around you? In what specific areas of your life can you focus on sharing kindness and encouragement through your words?

Examine Your Faith, Embrace Transformation

Examine yourselves
as to whether you are in the faith.
Test yourselves.
Do you not know yourselves,
that Jesus Christ is in you?
—unless indeed you are disqualified.

2 CORINTHIANS 13:5

IN 2 CORINTHIANS 13:5, the apostle Paul encourages believers to examine their faith and test themselves to ensure they are walking in the truth. It is essential for us to periodically evaluate our relationship with God, taking a sincere and introspective look at our beliefs and actions.

Self-examination allows us to identify areas of spiritual growth and areas where we may need to renew our commitment to Christ. It helps us discern whether we are truly living according to God's Word and aligning our lives with His will.

As we examine ourselves, we are reminded that Christ Jesus dwells within us through the Holy Spirit. This truth should motivate us to pursue a genuine and transforming relationship with Him.

Let us embrace the opportunity to reflect on our faith, inviting God to reveal His truth to us. May we humbly seek His guidance and willingly submit to the transformative work He desires to accomplish in our lives.

REFLECTIVE QUESTION

How can you actively engage in self-examination and testing to ensure you are walking in alignment with God's truth? What steps can you take to embrace transformation and grow deeper in your relationship with Christ?

Using Your Gifts to Make Room for Greatness

A gift opens the way and ushers
the giver into the presence of the great.
PROVERBS 18:16

PROVERBS 18:16 REMINDS US of the power and influence of our God-given gifts and talents. Our unique abilities, when used wisely and purposefully, have the potential to open doors of opportunity and bring us into the presence of those who can recognize and appreciate our abilities.

Each one of us possesses gifts and talents that have been entrusted to us by God. These gifts are not to be hidden or squandered but rather nurtured and utilized for His glory. They provide a means for us to make a positive impact in the world around us, whether big or small.

When we faithfully steward our gifts, we position ourselves for greatness. Our abilities become a doorway through which we can enter into meaningful connections, influential relationships, and impactful endeavours.

Let us be intentional in recognizing and developing our gifts, using them to serve others and bring honour to God. As we do so, we will find ourselves being led into greater opportunities and experiencing the fulfilment that comes from living out our unique purpose.

REFLECTIVE QUESTION

What gifts and talents has God entrusted to you?
How can you actively utilize and develop these gifts in a way that brings glory to God and opens doors for you to make a positive impact in the lives of others?

Finding Joy in a Cheerful Heart

**A cheerful heart is good medicine,
but a crushed spirit dries up the bones.**
PROVERBS 17:22

IN THIS FAST-PACED AND often stressful world, maintaining a cheerful heart can be challenging. Yet, the wisdom of Proverbs reminds us of the tremendous benefits a cheerful heart brings. A cheerful heart acts as a healing balm, bringing comfort, joy, and strength to both ourselves and those around us.

Imagine encountering someone with a cheerful heart. Their infectious laughter and positive energy are like a breath of fresh air. They have the ability to uplift others, lighten burdens, and create an atmosphere of joy. A cheerful heart is not dependent on external circumstances but is a genuine attitude of gratitude and contentment.

In contrast, a crushed spirit can drain us of vitality and rob us of our joy. It can make even the smallest tasks seem overwhelming and leave us feeling weary and discouraged. It is crucial to guard our hearts against negativity and cultivate a spirit of cheerfulness.

May you find joy in cultivating a cheerful heart, remembering that it is not only good medicine for your soul but also a blessing to others who cross your path.

REFLECTIVE QUESTION
How can you cultivate a cheerful heart today, and what impact might that have on your life and the lives of those around you?

Embracing Change as a Path to Growth

And we know that all things work together for good to those who love God, to those who are the called according to His purpose.

ROMANS 8:28

IN OUR JOURNEY OF faith, we often encounter challenging circumstances that leave us feeling perplexed and discouraged. In these moments, Romans 8:28 serves as a powerful reminder that God is at work in our lives, orchestrating everything for our ultimate good. It is a comforting assurance that even in the midst of trials, there is a divine purpose unfolding.

Consider the story of Joseph in the book of Genesis. Betrayed by his brothers, sold into slavery, and unjustly imprisoned, Joseph could have easily lost hope. Yet, he chose to trust in God's plan. In the end, Joseph's hardships led to his position of power in Egypt, which not only saved his family from famine but also fulfilled God's purpose.

Similarly, when we face adversity, we must remember that God can bring beauty out of ashes. Though we may not always see the immediate good, we can have faith that our loving Creator is working behind the scenes. By aligning our lives with His purpose, we can find solace and strength in knowing that everything has the potential to lead us closer to Him.

So, let us trust in God's providence, surrendering our fears and doubts to Him. As we do, we open ourselves to the transformative power of His love, allowing Him to guide our steps and shape our lives according to His perfect plan.

REFLECTIVE QUESTION
How can we trust and surrender to God's plan, even when life seems uncertain or difficult?

The Enduring Love of the Lord in Lamentations

The steadfast love of the Lord never ceases;
His mercies never come to an end;
they are new every morning; great is Your faithfulness.

LAMENTATIONS 3:22-23 (ESV)

IN THE BOOK OF Lamentations, amidst the backdrop of deep sorrow and mourning, we discover a powerful promise that echoes throughout the ages.

Life is filled with challenges and uncertainties that can easily leave us feeling overwhelmed and consumed. But the steadfast love of the Lord is our anchor, preventing us from being engulfed by the storms of life. His compassion is a constant source of comfort, assurance, and renewal.

Each morning, as we awaken to a new day, we are greeted with fresh mercies from God. It is an invitation to experience His faithfulness in tangible ways. We can rest in the knowledge that His compassion is not limited or depleted; it is continually renewed to meet our needs.

In times of adversity, let us fix our gaze upon the unchanging character of God. By anchoring our hope in His compassion and faithfulness, we can find strength to endure, courage to persevere, and peace that surpasses all understanding. May we hold fast to the truth of Lamentations 3:22-23 and allow it to guide us through every season of life.

REFLECTIVE QUESTION

How can we anchor our hope in the unchanging compassion and faithfulness of God, even when facing adversity?

Finding Strength in Community Support

**Two are better than one,
because they have a good reward for their labour.**
ECCLESIASTES 4:9

FRIENDSHIP IS A PRECIOUS gift from God that brings joy, encouragement and shared experiences. True friends provide support, comfort, and accountability in both the highs and lows of life's journey. They celebrate our victories and provide solace in our struggles.

To cultivate meaningful friendships, we must invest time and effort into building strong connections. It requires vulnerability, empathy, and a willingness to listen and understand. A genuine friendship thrives on trust, honesty, and mutual respect.

In our pursuit of friendship, let us seek those who share our values, dreams, and passions. Together, we can navigate the challenges of life, inspire one another, and make a positive impact on the world around us.

Consider the incredible impact of great friendships throughout history. From David and Jonathan in the Bible to influential partnerships in various fields, their collaborations have left lasting legacies. Similarly, our friendships have the potential to change lives and leave a meaningful imprint.

As we reflect on Ecclesiastes 4:9, let us cherish the friendships that enrich our lives. May we be intentional in fostering deep connections that bring mutual support, growth, and joy. Remember, the journey is brighter and more fulfilling when we walk hand in hand with trusted companions.

REFLECTIVE QUESTION
How can we cultivate meaningful friendships that bring mutual support and blessings?

Living in Faith, Not Fear

For God has not given us a spirit of fear,
but of power and of love and of a sound mind.

2 TIMOTHY 1:7

FEAR CAN BE A paralyzing force in our lives. It can hinder us from pursuing our dreams, stepping out in faith, and living the abundant life God has planned for us. However, as believers, we have been given the Holy Spirit, who empowers us to live fearlessly.

When we feel afraid, we can lean on God's strength and tap into the power that resides within us. We can trust in His perfect love that casts out fear and enables us to face any challenge with courage. Additionally, the Holy Spirit helps us develop self-discipline, which allows us to control our thoughts and actions, even in the face of fear and uncertainty.

So, let us embrace the spirit of fearlessness that God has bestowed upon us. Let us surrender our fears and worries to Him and allow His power, love, and self-discipline to guide us in every aspect of our lives.

REFLECTIVE QUESTION

How can you tap into the power, love, and self-discipline that God has given you to overcome fear and walk in confidence?

The Blessing of Obedience

**If you are willing and obedient,
you shall eat the good of the land;**
ISAIAH 1:19

THIS VERSE REMINDS US that obedience to God leads to abundant blessings and a fruitful life. When we choose to align our will with His and follow His commands, He promises to provide for us and bless us with His goodness.

Obedience is often a challenging concept to fully embrace, as our human nature often leans toward self-will and independence. But God's Word urges us to willingly submit to His ways, knowing that His plans for us are far greater than anything we could ever imagine.

When we choose obedience, we position ourselves to receive the abundant blessings God has in store for us. This doesn't mean life will be free from challenges or difficulties, but it means that even in the midst of trials, we can trust that God is working all things together for our good.

Let us strive to cultivate a willing and obedient heart, consistently seeking God's guidance and following His commands. As we do so, we will experience the richness of His provision, the beauty of His plans, and the fulfilment of His promises in our lives. Trust and obey, for there's no greater way to live.

REFLECTIVE QUESTION

How can you cultivate a willing and obedient heart, surrendering your desires and submitting to God's will in every area of your life?

Finding Strength in Weakness

And He said to me, "My grace is sufficient for you,
for My strength is made perfect in weakness."
Therefore most gladly I will rather boast in my
infirmities, that the power of Christ may rest upon me.

2 CORINTHIANS 12:9

WHEN WE LEAN ON His grace, we discover a source of power that far surpasses our own abilities.

In a world that often values strength and self-sufficiency, Paul's words serve as a humbling reminder that our weakness can be an opportunity for God to display His strength. When we recognize our limitations and surrender to His grace, we open ourselves to His divine power working in and through us.

God's grace is not only sufficient to meet our needs; it is abundant and overflowing. It sustains us when we feel inadequate, empowers us when we face challenges, and uplifts us when we are weary. We can find solace and strength in knowing that God's power is not dependent on our abilities but on His infinite love and grace.

So, let us embrace our weaknesses as opportunities for God to display His power. May we lean on His grace, trusting that His strength will carry us through every trial. In our surrender, we find true strength and experience the transformative power of God's love.

REFLECTIVE QUESTION

How can you learn to embrace and rely on God's grace in your moments of weakness, trusting that His power will sustain you?

Pursuing God's Abundant Blessings

The blessing of the LORD makes rich,
and he adds no sorrow with it.

PROVERBS 10:22

IN A WORLD THAT often equates blessings with material possessions, Proverbs 10:22 offers a different perspective. While God can certainly bless us with material abundance, true blessings go deeper than that. They encompass the joy, peace, and spiritual richness that come from a relationship with Him.

God's blessings are immeasurable, and they extend to every aspect of our lives. They bring contentment, guidance, and a sense of purpose in all circumstances. When we seek God's blessings with a heart that is aligned with His will, we experience a deep and lasting fulfilment that cannot be attained through worldly possessions alone.

Let us shift our focus from an obsession with material wealth to a pursuit of God's blessings that encompass spiritual and emotional prosperity. As we align our understanding of His blessings with His greater purpose for our lives, we discover a life of true abundance and satisfaction that surpasses anything the world can offer.

REFLECTIVE QUESTION
How can you align your understanding of God's blessings with His greater purpose for your life, seeking His joy and fulfilment rather than solely focusing on material wealth?

Walking in Love

And walk in love, as Christ also has loved us
and given Himself for us, an offering and a sacrifice
to God for a sweet-smelling aroma.
EPHESIANS 5:2

THIS VERSE REMINDS US to imitate Christ's sacrificial love in our daily lives. Just as Christ gave Himself up for us, we are called to align our actions and attitudes with the selfless love demonstrated on the cross.

In a world often characterized by self-centeredness, Ephesians 5:2 challenges us to embrace a different way of living. We are called to "walk in love," demonstrating Christ's sacrificial love to those around us. This means putting the needs of others before our own showing kindness, compassion, and forgiveness.

Walking in love requires intentional effort. It may involve forgiving someone who has hurt us, going the extra mile to help a friend in need, or extending grace and understanding in challenging relationships. When we choose to love sacrificially, our actions become a fragrant offering to God, reflecting His character and drawing others closer to Him.

Let us be mindful of the example set by Christ, who laid down His life for us out of love. As we daily seek to walk in love, may our lives become a living testament to His grace, compassion, and selflessness.

REFLECTIVE QUESTION
How can you actively walk in love, following Christ's example of sacrificial love in your interactions with others?

Growing in the Spirit

**But the fruit of the Spirit is love, joy, peace,
patience, kindness, goodness, faithfulness.**
GALATIANS 5:22

THE FRUIT OF THE Spirit represents the outward manifestation of the Holy Spirit living within us. As followers of Christ, we are called to cultivate these qualities in our lives, allowing them to shape our interactions and relationships.

Love, joy, peace, patience, kindness, goodness, faithfulness, gentleness, and self-control are not merely characteristics to possess but attitudes and behaviours to embody. They reflect Christlikeness and become a witness to the transformative work of the Holy Spirit in our lives.

Nurturing the fruit of the Spirit requires surrendering our will to God and being receptive to His guidance. It involves seeking His strength to love sacrificially, finding joy in all circumstances, and extending grace and kindness to others.

May we continually examine our hearts and allow the Holy Spirit to prune, refine, and grow the fruit within us. As we yield daily to His transformative work, the fruit we bear will draw others to the love and grace of Christ.

REFLECTIVE QUESTION
How can you actively nurture and cultivate the fruit of the Spirit in your daily life, allowing it to shape your attitudes and actions?

Finding Peace in Trust

You will keep him in perfect peace,
whose mind is stayed on You,
because he trusts in You.

ISAIAH 26:3

THIS VERSE REMINDS US that when we trust in God and fix our minds on Him, He grants us a profound and unwavering peace that surpasses all understanding.

In a world filled with chaos and uncertainty, Isaiah 26:3 offers a powerful promise: perfect peace in the presence of our steadfast and trustworthy God. This peace is not dependent on favourable circumstances but on our unwavering trust in Him.

To experience this perfect peace, we must intentionally fix our minds on God. We do this by immersing ourselves in His Word, spending time in prayer, and seeking His guidance and wisdom. As we cultivate a deep trust in Him, we invite His peace to guard our hearts and minds.

While life may bring trials and tribulations, we can rest assured that our God is faithful and sovereign. He sees our struggles and promises to be our refuge and strength. In Him, we find solace, security, and an unshakeable peace that transcends any situation we may face.

REFLECTIVE QUESTION

How can you cultivate a steadfast trust in God and keep your mind focused on Him, even in the midst of life's challenges and uncertainties?

The Call to Worship

O come, let us worship and bow down;
let us kneel before the Lord our Maker.

PSALM 95:6

PSALM 95:6 URGES US to come before the Lord with a heart of worship, acknowledging Him as our Maker and King. Worship is not confined to a specific time or place; it is a posture of the heart, an expression of our love and awe for God.

Cultivating a heart of worship involves intentionally setting aside time to praise and honour Him, both individually and in the community. It can include singing songs of worship, praying with gratitude, meditating on His Word, and reflecting on His goodness and faithfulness.

As we engage in genuine worship, we draw closer to God, experiencing His presence and receiving His peace and guidance. It is in these moments of adoration that we align ourselves with His purposes and find renewed strength and joy in our relationship with Him.

REFLECTIVE QUESTION

How can you cultivate a heart of worship and incorporate meaningful moments of praise and reverence into your daily life?

The Joy of Serving

For you, brethren, have been called to liberty;
only do not use liberty as an opportunity for the flesh,
but through love serve one another.

GALATIANS 5:13

THIS VERSE SPEAKS TO the balance between the freedom we have in Christ and our responsibility to serve others.

As Christians, we are called to embrace the freedom that comes from a relationship with Jesus. This freedom is not a license to indulge in selfish desires or destructive behaviours. Rather, it is an invitation to live in accordance with God's love and to serve others selflessly.

As we consider this question, let us remember that service can take many forms. It could be offering a helping hand to a neighbour in need, volunteering at a local charity, or simply taking the time to listen and support a friend or family member. By using our freedom in Christ to serve others, we not only demonstrate God's love, but we also experience the joy and fulfilment that comes from living out our faith in practical ways.

May our lives be a reflection of the freedom we have in Christ as we selflessly serve others in love.

REFLECTIVE QUESTION

How can you use your freedom in Christ to serve others today?

The Gift of God's Word

**Your word is a lamp to my feet
And a light to my path.**
PSALM 119:105

THIS VERSE BEAUTIFULLY CAPTURES the significance of God's Word in our lives. Just as a lamp guides our steps in a dark room, God's Word illuminates our path and provides direction and guidance.

In a world filled with uncertainty and confusion, God's Word serves as a dependable and unwavering source of truth. It reveals God's character, teaches us His ways, and offers wisdom to navigate life's challenges. It brings clarity to our thoughts, comfort to our hearts, and strength to our spirits.

Answering this question requires intentional effort and a genuine desire to seek God through His Word. It may involve setting aside dedicated time for reading and studying the Bible, meditating on specific verses throughout the day, or joining a community of believers for regular Bible study and discussion. By prioritizing the study of Scripture, we open ourselves to the transformative power of God's Word and allow it to shape our thoughts, actions, and decisions.

Embrace the light that God's Word provides and allow it to be a constant guide as you journey through life.

REFLECTIVE QUESTION
How can you make God's Word an integral part of your daily life and allow it to guide your steps?

Living Out Your Faith

**So also faith by itself,
if it does not have works, is dead.**

JAMES 2:17

THIS VERSE CHALLENGES US to examine the relationship between our faith and our actions. True faith is not passive or stagnant; it is meant to be active and transformative.

As followers of Christ, our faith should compel us to live out the teachings of Jesus through acts of love, kindness, and service. It is not enough to simply believe in God; our beliefs should be evident in our words and actions. Our faith should lead us to make a positive impact in the lives of others and in the world around us.

Consider the opportunities that present themselves throughout your day. It could be as simple as offering a word of encouragement to someone in need, extending a helping hand to a stranger, or advocating for justice and equality in your community. When we actively live out our faith, we become a reflection of Christ's love and bring hope to those we encounter.

Let your faith be alive and fruitful as you engage in acts of love and service, making a difference in the lives of others and bringing glory to God.

REFLECTIVE QUESTION

**How can you demonstrate faith in action today,
and how might it impact those around you?**

The Grace of God

For by grace you have been saved through faith, and that not of yourselves; it is the gift of God.
EPHESIANS 2:8

THIS VERSE EMPHASIZES THE foundational truth of our salvation: it is not based on our own efforts or works but on God's grace and our faith in Him.

God's grace is His unmerited favour extended to us. We cannot earn or deserve it, but it is freely given to us through the sacrifice of Jesus Christ. Our salvation is a gift, and it is through our faith in Him that we receive this gift.

Understanding that our salvation is solely a result of God's grace should humble us and fill us with gratitude. It reminds us that we are completely dependent on Him and that we can never earn our way into His kingdom. It also frees us from the burden of striving to prove ourselves worthy. Instead, we can rest in the assurance of His love and embrace a relationship with Him based on faith, trust, and obedience.

Embrace the gift of God's grace and allow it to transform your perspective and relationship with Him. Let it inspire you to live a life that reflects His love and grace to others.

REFLECTIVE QUESTION
How does understanding that our salvation is a gift of God's grace impact your perspective on your relationship with Him?

The Call to Be Light

You are the light of the world.
A city set on a hill cannot be hidden.
MATTHEW 5:14

IN THIS VERSE, JESUS challenges His followers to recognize their role as lights in a dark world. Just as a city on a hill is visible from afar, our lives should stand out as beacons of hope and truth.

As believers, we are called to reflect the character of Christ and shine His light in every aspect of our lives. This means living with integrity, demonstrating love and compassion, speaking words of encouragement and truth, and making a positive impact on those around us.

Consider the opportunities God has placed before you. It can be as simple as showing kindness to a stranger, offering a listening ear to a friend in need, or standing up for justice and righteousness in your surroundings. By living out your faith authentically and intentionally, you have the power to inspire and influence others for the better.

Embrace the calling to be a light in the world and let your life illuminate the darkness around you. Through your actions and words, may others see the love and truth of Christ shining through you.

REFLECTIVE QUESTION

How can you actively shine your light in the spheres of influence you find yourself in, whether at work, school or in your community?

The Power of Forgiveness

Then Peter came to Him and said, "Lord, how often
shall my brother sin against me, and I forgive him?
Up to seven times?" Jesus said to him, "I do not say to
you, up to seven times, but up to seventy times seven.
MATTHEW 18:21-22

FORGIVENESS IS NOT ALWAYS easy, but it is a necessary component
of our journey with Jesus. Just as God forgives us repeatedly
and abundantly, we are called to extend that same forgiveness
to others. It is through forgiveness that we experience healing,
freedom, and reconciliation in our relationships.

Consider any harboured resentment, bitterness, or anger that
you may be holding onto. Reflect on the freedom and peace that
come from choosing to forgive. Forgiveness does not negate the
hurt caused, but it allows us to release the burden and make
room for healing. It opens the door for restoration and growth
in relationships.

Choosing forgiveness may require courage and vulnerability,
but the rewards are immeasurable. As we walk in the footsteps of
Jesus, let us be willing to forgive others as we have been forgiven.
May our hearts be filled with grace, compassion, and a willingness
to extend forgiveness, reflecting the character of Christ.

Embrace the transformative power of forgiveness and experience
the freedom it brings to your life and relationships.

REFLECTIVE QUESTION
**Is there someone in your life whom you need to forgive,
and how might choosing forgiveness impact your
well-being and the relationship?**

The Joy of Giving

So let each one give as he purposes in his heart,
not grudgingly or of necessity;
for God loves a cheerful giver.

2 CORINTHIANS 9:7

THIS VERSE REMINDS US that giving is not just about the act itself but the attitude of our hearts.

God calls us to give from a place of joy and generosity, not out of obligation or pressure. He values the cheerful giver - someone who gives willingly and with a glad heart. When we give cheerfully, we reflect God's character and demonstrate our trust in His provision.

Consider your motivations for giving. Are there any areas where you may feel reluctant or compelled to give? Reflect on the blessings you have received and the joy of being a channel of God's goodness to others. Ask God to transform your heart and enable you to give with a cheerful spirit.

As you embrace the joy of giving, you will experience the delight that comes from being a blessing to others. Trust that God will multiply your generosity and use it to impact lives and further His kingdom. May your giving always be marked by a cheerful and willing heart.

REFLECTIVE QUESTION
How can you cultivate a cheerful and generous heart in your giving, whether it is with your time, resources, or talents?

Casting Your Cares on God

Casting all your care upon Him,
for He cares for you.
1 PETER 5:7

1 PETER 5:7 ENCOURAGES and reminds us that God is not indifferent to our worries and concerns. He invites us to entrust our burdens to Him, knowing that He deeply cares for us and desires to bring us comfort and peace.

As human beings, we often carry the weight of our worries and anxieties on our own shoulders. However, God lovingly reminds us that we don't have to bear the burden alone. He is ready to shoulder our cares and provide a refuge of rest and restoration.

Take a moment to identify the concerns that weigh heavy on your heart. Surrender them to God in prayer, acknowledging His love and care for you. Trust that He is able to handle every burden and find solace in knowing that you are not alone in the midst of your struggles.

As you cast your cares on God, you will experience His peace that surpasses all understanding. Allow His love and care to permeate every area of your life, knowing that He is faithful to provide for your needs and carry you through every trial and challenge.

REFLECTIVE QUESTION
What anxieties or worries do you need to release to God today, and how might surrendering them to Him bring you comfort and peace?

Seeking Wisdom from God

For the Lord gives wisdom; From His mouth
come knowledge and understanding; He stores up
sound wisdom for the upright; He is a shield
to those who walk uprightly.

PROVERBS 2:6-7

THESE VERSES HIGHLIGHT THE importance of seeking wisdom
from God recognizing that true understanding and success come
from Him.

In a world filled with information and opinions, true wisdom
is found in God alone. He is the source of all knowledge and
insight. As we seek Him and His Word, He imparts wisdom
and understanding to us, guiding us on the path of righteousness
and blessing.

Consider incorporating daily habits such as reading and
meditating on Scripture, praying for discernment, and seeking
wise counsel from trusted mentors. By prioritizing the pursuit
of God's wisdom, our decisions become aligned with His will,
and we experience the fruits of His guidance and direction.

Embrace the wisdom that comes from God and let it shape
your thoughts, actions, and choices. Trust in His promises and
allow His wisdom to guide you on the path of righteousness
and success.

REFLECTIVE QUESTION

**How can you intentionally seek wisdom from God today,
and how might it impact your decisions and direction
in life?**

The Peace of God

And let the peace of God rule in your hearts,
to which also you were called in one body;
and be thankful.

COLOSSIANS 3:15

THE PEACE OF CHRIST extends beyond the mere absence of conflict. It is a deep sense of tranquillity and contentment that transcends our circumstances. When we allow His peace to rule in our hearts, it governs our thoughts, emotions, and actions, enabling us to navigate challenges with grace and gratitude.

Consider the areas of your life where you may be experiencing unrest or anxiety. Surrender them to Christ and invite His peace to permeate those places. Additionally, take time to reflect on the blessings in your life and express gratitude to God for His goodness.

As you allow the peace of Christ to rule in your heart and cultivate a heart of gratitude, you will experience a profound transformation in your perspective and outlook on life. May His peace be your guiding force, bringing harmony and gratitude to every aspect of your journey.

REFLECTIVE QUESTION

How can you allow the peace of Christ to rule in your heart today, and what are you grateful for in your life right now?

The Call to Perseverance

**And let us not grow weary while doing good,
for in due season we shall reap
if we do not lose heart.**
GALATIANS 6:9

LIFE CAN BE FILLED with challenges and obstacles that can easily discourage us from doing good. It is tempting to give up when we don't see immediate results or when we face rejection or opposition. However, Paul reminds us to keep pressing on, for our efforts are not in vain.

Just as a farmer must patiently sow and tend to his fields before seeing the fruits of his labour, we, too, must endure and continue doing good, even when it seems difficult or unrewarding. Our faith calls us to sow seeds of love, kindness, forgiveness, and generosity in the lives of others.

We find the strength to persevere in the knowledge that our labour in the Lord is not in vain. Even if we do not see the harvest immediately, we can trust that God is at work in and through our acts of goodness. Our faithfulness in sowing seeds will eventually yield a bountiful harvest of blessings.

Let us not grow weary or disheartened but continue to sow seeds of goodness in our daily lives. The harvest may not come in our timing, but it will come at the appointed time. So, let us persevere, knowing that our labour is valuable and will be rewarded.

REFLECTIVE QUESTION
How can we find the strength to keep sowing seeds of goodness, even when we face discouragement or setbacks?

Walking in the Light

> But if we walk in the light, as He is in the light,
> we have fellowship with one another,
> and the blood of Jesus Christ His Son
> cleanses us from all sin.
>
> 1 JOHN 1:7

WALKING IN THE LIGHT means living our lives in alignment with God's Word and following His commands. It requires us to be honest with ourselves, with others, and most importantly, with God. When we choose to live in the light, we enter into a deep fellowship with God and our fellow believers.

Living in the light also means allowing the truth of God's Word to expose and cleanse our sins. Jesus' blood purifies us from all sin when we confess and repent, restoring our fellowship with God. This freedom from sin enables us to live in the fullness of God's grace and love.

To continually live in the light, we can cultivate daily habits such as spending time in prayer and studying the Bible. Regularly examining our hearts and confessing our sins to God helps us maintain a close relationship with Him. Additionally, surrounding ourselves with fellow believers who also desire to walk in the light can provide accountability and encouragement on our spiritual journey.

REFLECTIVE QUESTION

How can we continually live in the light of God's truth and experience the freedom it brings?

The Prayer of Faith

And whatever you ask in prayer,
believing, you will receive.
MATTHEW 21:22

PRAYER IS A DIRECT line of communication with our Heavenly Father. It is through prayer that we can pour out our hearts, express our needs, and seek God's guidance and intervention in our lives. However, Jesus reminds us that faith is essential in approaching God with our requests.

Having faith in prayer means trusting that God hears us, knowing that He is able to answer according to His perfect will. It involves aligning our desires with God's purposes and submitting ourselves to His wisdom and timing. Faith understands that even if the answer may not come in the way or at the time we expect, we can rest assured that God is working all things for our good.

To cultivate a faith-filled prayer life, we can begin by studying God's Word and growing in our understanding of His character and promises. As we deepen our relationship with God, our faith will naturally grow. We can also seek the guidance of the Holy Spirit, who helps us pray according to God's will and grants us the faith to believe for His best.

REFLECTIVE QUESTION
How can we cultivate a faith-filled prayer life that aligns with God's will?

Refining Through Trials

The crucible is for silver, and the furnace is for gold,
and the Lord tests hearts.

PROVERBS 17:3

PROVERBS 17:3 PAINTS A vivid picture of the refining process
for precious metals, comparing it to the way the Lord examines
and tests the hearts of His people.

Just as silver and gold are purified through intense heat, our
character and faith are often refined through trials and challenges.
Difficult circumstances have the potential to shape us, mould us,
and strengthen our faith if we allow them to.

When we face hardships, it is natural to seek relief and comfort.
However, viewing these challenging seasons as opportunities
for growth can transform our perspective. We can choose to see
trials as refining moments where God is purifying our hearts,
teaching us valuable lessons, and moulding us into the people
He desires us to be.

Rather than becoming resentful or bitter in the face of adversity,
we can humble ourselves and seek God's guidance and wisdom.
We can ask Him to reveal the lessons He wants us to learn and
the areas of our hearts that need refining. Through prayer and
surrender, we can grow in character, perseverance, and faith.

Moreover, we can find solace in the truth that God is with us in
the midst of our trials, providing comfort, strength, and hope. He
promises to walk alongside us, using even our most challenging
circumstances for our ultimate good (Romans 8:28).

REFLECTIVE QUESTION
**How can we view difficult circumstances as
opportunities for growth and character development?**

Guarding the Heart

Above all else, guard your heart,
for everything you do flows from it.
PROVERBS 4:23

OUR HEART ENCOMPASSES OUR thoughts, desires, emotions, and beliefs. It is the centre of our being, the wellspring from which our actions and words flow. Therefore, we must be intentional in guarding our hearts to ensure that they are aligned with God's truth and filled with love, faith, and goodness.

To actively guard our hearts, we must prioritize our relationship with God. Spending time in prayer, reading His Word, and seeking His guidance are essential practices that help shape and guard our hearts. By immersing ourselves in God's truth and seeking His presence, we allow His Spirit to mould and transform our hearts.

We also need to be discerning about the influences we allow into our lives. Negative influences, such as harmful relationships, unhealthy media consumption, or toxic thoughts, can corrupt our hearts and lead us astray. By intentionally surrounding ourselves with positive influences, godly community, and uplifting content, we can protect our hearts and stay aligned with God's purposes.

Additionally, forgiveness and gratitude play a vital role in guarding our hearts. Forgiving others and ourselves frees our hearts from bitterness and resentment. Gratitude shifts our focus from negativity to recognizing God's blessings, generating a heart filled with joy and contentment.

REFLECTIVE QUESTION
How can we actively guard our hearts and cultivate a healthy spiritual life?

Renewed Hope

**Then He who sat on the throne said,
"Behold, I make all things new." And He said to me,
"Write, for these words are true and faithful.**

REVELATION 21:5

As followers of Christ, we are invited to participate in this ongoing process of renewal. We are called to surrender our old ways, our brokenness, and our sinful patterns to God, allowing Him to make us new. It is through His transformative power that we can experience the beauty of new beginnings.

To embrace this newness, we need to acknowledge areas of our lives that require God's touch. It may be our thought patterns, relationships, habits, or attitudes that need to be surrendered to God's loving and refining work. Only when we let go of the old can we fully grasp the newness that God wants to bring forth.

This process of transformation is not always easy. It requires humility, surrender, and a willingness to let go of our own plans and desires. However, when we entrust our lives to God, He promises to bring about a new creation in us, one that reflects His love, joy, peace, and righteousness.

Let us reflect on our lives and invite God to examine and transform every area that needs His touch. Through His power, the broken can be made whole, the wounded can be healed, and the old can be replaced by the new. May we embrace the promise of Revelation 21:5 and experience the beauty of God's transformative work in our lives.

REFLECTIVE QUESTION

In what areas of your life do you need to surrender to God's transformative power to experience the beauty of new beginnings?

The Path Less Travelled

But small is the gate and narrow the road
that leads to life, and only a few find it.
MATTHEW 7:14

JESUS USES THE METAPHOR of a narrow road to emphasize that the path to eternal life is not easy. It requires us to make intentional decisions and prioritize our relationship with Him above all else. The broad road, on the other hand, represents the easier path of following worldly desires.

By walking the narrow path, we choose to live in accordance with God's will. It means seeking His guidance, obeying His commandments, and surrendering our lives to Him. It may involve sacrificing our own desires and comforts, but the reward of eternal life far outweighs any temporary hardships.

So, let us take a moment to reflect on our own journey. Are we willing to stay committed to Jesus, even when faced with obstacles and temptations? Will we choose the narrow path that leads to life, or will we be swayed by the allure of the broad road?

Remember, God's grace and strength are always available to equip us for the journey ahead. Let us walk in faith, trusting that the narrow path leads to the abundant and everlasting life that Jesus promised.

REFLECTIVE QUESTION
Are you willing to walk the narrow path, even when it is challenging?

Thy Kingdom Come

Your kingdom come.
Your will be done on earth as it is in heaven.
MATTHEW 6:10

WHEN WE PRAY FOR God's kingdom to come, we are acknowledging His sovereignty and inviting His will to prevail in every aspect of our lives. It is a prayer that aligns our desires with His and invites Him to work and rule in our lives, just as He does in heaven.

But it is not only about praying; it is about actively participating in bringing His kingdom on earth. It involves living in obedience to His Word, showing love and compassion to others, seeking justice, and being agents of peace and reconciliation.

Reflect on how you can actively participate in manifesting God's kingdom. Are there areas in your life where you can surrender more fully to His will? Are there opportunities to extend acts of kindness, forgiveness, or generosity? Are you using your gifts and talents to bring glory to God and serve others?

Let us strive to be vessels through which God's kingdom shines forth. As we align ourselves with His will, His kingdom will become evident in our lives and have a transformative impact on the world around us.

REFLECTIVE QUESTION
How can you actively participate in bringing God's kingdom on earth?

Victory through Christ

**But thanks be to God, who gives us the victory
through our Lord Jesus Christ.**
1 CORINTHIANS 15:57

IN THIS VERSE, THE Apostle Paul reminds us to give thanks to God, for it is through the Lord Jesus Christ that we have victory. Victory is not dependent on our own strength or abilities, but it is a gift freely given by God.

Life is filled with challenges and battles, both big and small. Whether it be overcoming a personal struggle, dealing with difficult circumstances, or facing spiritual warfare, we can find encouragement and hope in the assurance of victory through Christ.

Knowing that we have already been given the victory changes our perspective on these challenges. It gives us strength and confidence to face them head-on, knowing that the ultimate outcome is already secured through Christ's triumph over sin and death.

When we face difficulties, we can approach them with the assurance that we are not alone. Christ is with us, empowering and guiding us through every trial. He has already overcome the world, and when we abide in Him, we too can experience the victory that He has won.

So, as you reflect on 1 Corinthians 15:57, consider how knowing that victory comes through Christ impacts your outlook on life's challenges. How does it inspire you to face them with courage and hope?

REFLECTIVE QUESTION
How does knowing that victory comes through Christ change your perspective on life's challenges?

Faithful Stewardship

A faithful man will abound with blessings,
but he who hastens to be rich will not go unpunished.
PROVERBS 28:20

FAITHFULNESS IS AN ESSENTIAL quality that honours God and affects every aspect of our lives, including our finances. It involves being responsible and trustworthy with what God has entrusted to us - our time, talents, and treasures.

To cultivate a heart of faithfulness in stewardship, we can start by recognizing that everything we have ultimately belongs to God. He is the source of our provision, and we are called to be good stewards of the resources He has given us.

This requires practising wise financial management, such as budgeting, saving, and giving generously. It also involves using our resources in ways that align with God's values and purposes, seeking to bless and help others rather than seeking personal gain at any cost.

Take time to reflect on your current approach to stewardship. Are you faithfully managing your resources and seeking to honour God in your financial decisions? How can you grow in faithfulness and align your actions with His principles?

Remember, as you embrace faithfulness in stewardship, you open yourself up to the rich blessings that God desires to pour into your life, both spiritually and materially. Trust in His provision and be faithful, knowing that He is faithful to bless those who honour Him with their resources.

REFLECTIVE QUESTION
How can you cultivate a heart of faithfulness in your stewardship of resources?

Seeking God's Presence

**Seek the Lord while he may be found;
call on him while he is near.**

ISAIAH 55:6

SEEKING GOD'S PRESENCE INVOLVES setting aside time to pray, meditate on Scripture, and engage in worship. It means intentionally seeking moments of solitude and silence to listen to His voice and draw near to Him. It also entails continually seeking His guidance and direction in decision-making and seeking His wisdom and peace in times of trouble or uncertainty.

One practical way to seek God's presence is by carving out a dedicated time each day for prayer and Bible study. This intentional habit enables us to deepen our relationship with Him and opens our hearts to hear His voice.

We can also seek God's presence throughout the day by practising mindfulness and being aware of His presence in every moment. We can offer prayers of gratitude, seek His guidance, and invite Him to be part of our daily activities.

So, as you reflect on Isaiah 55:6, consider how you can actively seek the presence of God in your daily life. Are there any habits or practices you can incorporate to cultivate a greater awareness of His presence? Remember, seeking God is not a one-time event but a lifelong journey of drawing near to Him and experiencing His love, grace, and guidance.

REFLECTIVE QUESTION

How can you actively seek the presence of God in your daily life?

The Call to Compassion

Therefore, as the elect of God, holy and beloved,
put on tender mercies, kindness,
humility, meekness, longsuffering;

COLOSSIANS 3:12

IN TODAY'S READING, APOSTLE Paul encourages the believers to clothe themselves with compassion, kindness, humility, gentleness, and patience. These virtues are the attire we must wear daily, reflecting the character of Christ in our interactions with others.

Compassion is the tenderhearted response to the suffering and difficulties of others. It prompts us to show empathy, lend a helping hand, and offer words of encouragement. In a world where self-centeredness and indifference often prevail, choosing compassion is counter-cultural yet impactful.

Imagine a coworker struggling with a heavy workload. Instead of adding to their stress, we can extend compassion by offering assistance, words of affirmation, or simply listening attentively. In doing so, we become a source of comfort and support, reflecting God's love to them.

Compassion is not confined to grand gestures; it can be expressed through small acts of kindness. It could be offering a smile to a stranger, being patient with a loved one's shortcomings, or showing understanding towards someone going through a challenging season.

Today, let us intentionally embody compassion, allowing it to shape our thoughts, words, and actions. By doing so, we become vessels of God's love, making a positive impact on those around us.

REFLECTIVE QUESTION

How can you intentionally demonstrate compassion today?

Resilience in Trials

**Consider it pure joy, my brothers and sisters,
whenever you face trials of many kinds.**
JAMES 1:2 (NIV)

WE ARE ENCOURAGED TO consider it pure joy when we face trials of many kinds. This may seem counterintuitive, but it challenges us to change our perspective on difficulties.

Trials are a part of life, and they come in various forms, such as health issues, relationship challenges, financial struggles, or personal disappointments. Instead of allowing these trials to overwhelm us, James encourages us to approach them with a joyful attitude.

Choosing joy in the face of trials does not mean denying or minimizing our pain. Rather, it involves trusting in God's sovereignty and His ability to work all things for our good. It means finding strength and hope in the midst of adversity, knowing that God will never leave us.

Cultivating joy in trials requires a shift in our perspective. It involves focusing on the lessons we can learn, the character growth that can occur, and the opportunity to deepen our faith. It means seeking God's wisdom and guidance through prayer, studying His Word, and relying on His promises.

Today, let us choose joy in the midst of trials, knowing that God can bring beauty out of ashes. As we embrace a joyful attitude, we become a testament to the transformative power of God's grace.

REFLECTIVE QUESTION
How can you cultivate joy in the midst of trials today?

Walking in Integrity

The integrity of the upright will guide them,
but the perversity of the unfaithful will destroy them.

PROVERBS 11:3

THE INTEGRITY OF THE upright guides them, while the unfaithful are destroyed by their duplicity. This verse highlights the importance of living a life of honesty, transparency, and moral uprightness.

Integrity is the quality of being honest and having strong moral principles. It involves consistently aligning our thoughts, words, and actions with truth and righteousness. In a world where dishonesty and deceit are prevalent, choosing integrity sets us apart and allows us to reflect the character of God.

Practising integrity in our interactions can take many forms. It starts with being truthful and trustworthy in our words and commitments. It means honouring our responsibilities and treating others with fairness and respect. It involves being transparent and accountable for our actions, even when no one is watching.

In our professional lives, integrity may manifest through refusing to compromise on ethical standards, being diligent in our work, and treating colleagues and clients with integrity. In our personal lives, integrity can be seen in how we handle relationships, manage our finances, and make decisions that honour God and others.

Today, let us strive to walk in integrity, allowing it to guide our thoughts, words, and deeds. By doing so, we become a testimony of God's faithfulness and a blessing to those around us.

REFLECTIVE QUESTION
How can you practice integrity in your interactions today?

Embracing God's Sovereignty

But our God is in the heavens;
He does whatever He pleases.

PSALM 115:3

SURRENDERING TO GOD'S SOVEREIGN plan requires trust and faith in His wisdom and goodness. It means acknowledging that He is in control and that His ways are higher than ours. Though we may not always understand His ways, we can be confident that He is working all things for our ultimate good.

To surrender to God's plan, we must let go of our own desires and submit our will to His. It involves seeking His guidance through prayer and studying His Word, allowing Him to direct our paths and shape our decisions. It means trusting that He knows what is best for us, even when the circumstances may be challenging or unclear.

Surrendering to God's sovereign plan also requires patience and perseverance. It means trusting in His timing and being willing to wait for His purposes to unfold. It means embracing the journey, knowing that God is with us every step of the way.

Today, let us surrender to God's sovereign plan, trusting that He is working all things according to His purposes. As we yield to His guidance and walk in faith, we will experience His peace and see His faithfulness displayed in our lives.

REFLECTIVE QUESTION
How can you surrender to God's sovereign plan in your life today?

The Courage to Stand Firm

Watch, stand fast in the faith,
be brave, be strong.

1 CORINTHIANS 16:13

LIVING OUT COURAGE AND strength in our faith involves stepping out of our comfort zones, trusting in God's guidance, and boldly proclaiming His truth. It means speaking up for justice and righteousness, even when it's unpopular or goes against societal norms. It means facing adversity with resilience and relying on God's strength to overcome it.

Courage is not the absence of fear but rather the willingness to act in spite of it. It means taking risks for the sake of God's kingdom and walking in obedience, knowing that He is with us every step of the way. It means standing up for our beliefs, even if it means facing opposition or criticism.

Strength in our faith comes from relying on God's power rather than our own. It involves seeking His strength through prayer, studying His Word, and leaning on the support of fellow believers. It means persevering through trials and trusting that God's grace is sufficient to sustain us.

Today, let us embrace the challenge to stand firm, be courageous, and be strong in our faith. As we do so, we become agents of change and vessels for God's glory, making a difference in the world around us.

REFLECTIVE QUESTION

How can you demonstrate courage and strength in your faith today?

Growing in Grace

But grow in the grace and knowledge of our Lord
and Savior Jesus Christ. To Him be glory
both now and forever! Amen.

2 PETER 3:18

GROWING IN GRACE INVOLVES cultivating a deeper understanding and experience of God's unmerited favour and love. It means recognizing our need for His forgiveness and extending that same grace to others. It involves regularly seeking His presence, embracing His mercy, and allowing His transformative power to work in our lives.

Growing in knowledge refers to increasing our understanding of God's Word, His teachings, and His plans for our lives. It means dedicating time to study and meditate on Scripture, seeking wisdom and discernment through prayer, and actively pursuing opportunities for spiritual growth, such as attending Bible studies or listening to sermons.

Pursuing growth in grace and knowledge requires intentionality and a desire for a deeper relationship with God. It means being open to His instruction, humbly admitting areas where we need to change, and actively applying His principles in our daily lives.

Today, let us embark on a journey of continuous growth in grace and knowledge. As we do so, we will experience a deeper closeness with our Savior, a greater understanding of His ways, and a transformation that reflects His love and character to the world around us.

REFLECTIVE QUESTION
How can you actively pursue growth in grace and knowledge today?

Empowered Through Christ

**I can do all things through Christ
who strengthens me.**
PHILIPPIANS 4:13

IN MOMENTS OF DIFFICULTY or when facing seemingly insurmountable challenges, it is essential to remember that our strength does not come from our own abilities but from our union with Christ. We can tap into His strength by seeking His guidance, surrendering our fears and doubts to Him, and relying on His promises.

Prayer is a vital conduit through which we can access Christ's strength. By praying fervently and honestly, we invite Him to work in and through us, providing the supernatural strength required to face our challenges. Additionally, meditating on God's Word and filling our minds with His truths equips us with the mindset of victory and helps us overcome negative thinking patterns.

By acknowledging our dependence on Christ, we can embrace a posture of humility and trust. In times of weakness, we can seek encouragement and support from our Christian community, knowing that they can remind us of God's faithfulness and the strength available to us through Him.

Today, let us lean on the empowering strength of Christ to face our challenges. As we rely on Him, we will experience His grace, overcome obstacles, and be amazed at what He can accomplish through us.

REFLECTIVE QUESTION

How can you tap into Christ's strength to face your current challenges today?

Choosing Kindness and Forgiveness

**Be kind to one another, tenderhearted,
forgiving one another,
even as God in Christ forgave you.**

EPHESIANS 4:32

THIS VERSE REMINDS US of the importance of extending grace, kindness, and forgiveness in our relationships with others.

Practising kindness involves intentionally showing love, empathy, and compassion to those around us. It means speaking words of encouragement, extending acts of service, and treating others with respect and dignity. Kindness can bring comfort and healing to someone who is hurting or in need.

Forgiveness is an essential aspect of our Christian walk. It involves releasing grudges, letting go of resentment, and choosing to forgive as Christ forgave us. Forgiveness does not mean condoning harmful actions but rather freeing ourselves from the burden of bitterness and allowing God's healing to take place. It may also involve seeking reconciliation when appropriate.

In our interactions, we can pause before responding in anger or frustration, choosing instead to respond with kindness and understanding. We can offer forgiveness even when it feels difficult, trusting God's example of forgiveness and the transformative power it brings.

Today, let us strive to practice kindness and forgiveness, reflecting the love and grace of our Heavenly Father. As we do so, we become agents of reconciliation, peace, and healing in our relationships and communities.

REFLECTIVE QUESTION
How can you practice kindness and forgiveness in your interactions today?

Guarding Your Mind with Truth

Finally, brethren, whatever things are true,
whatever things are noble, whatever things are just,
whatever things are pure, whatever things are lovely,
whatever things are of good report,
if there is any virtue and if there is anything
praiseworthy—meditate on these things.

PHILIPPIANS 4:8

CULTIVATING A MIND FOCUSED on positive and praiseworthy things requires intentionality and discipline. It involves being mindful of the influences we allow into our lives—the books we read, the movies we watch, the music we listen to, and the people we surround ourselves with.

Reading and studying the Word of God is a powerful way to align our minds with truth. It provides wisdom, guidance, and inspiration for our daily lives. Regularly meditating on Scripture and memorizing verses can help us combat negative thoughts and replace them with God's truth.

Surrounding ourselves with positive influences also uplifts our mindset. Spending time with encouraging and like-minded believers nourishes our souls. Engaging in uplifting conversations, sharing testimonies of God's faithfulness, and joining in worship and praise deepen our connection with God and foster a positive attitude.

Today, let us be mindful of the inputs we allow into our minds. Let us intentionally fill our thoughts with things that are true, noble, right, pure, lovely, admirable, excellent, and praiseworthy so that we can experience a greater sense of peace, joy, and contentment.

REFLECTIVE QUESTION

How can you cultivate a mind focused on positive and praiseworthy things today?

Heart of Service Through Volunteerism

As each one has received a gift,
minister it to one another, as good stewards
of the manifold grace of God.

1 PETER 4:10

WE ALL HAVE UNIQUE talents and abilities, bestowed upon us by God. These gifts are not meant to be hidden or used solely for our own benefit but rather to bless others and bring glory to God.

A talented musician may devote their time and skill to leading worship in church, bringing the congregation into a powerful, worshipful experience. They use their gift to create an atmosphere where others can enjoy the presence of God.

Similarly, someone with a gift for teaching may dedicate themselves to mentoring others, helping them grow in knowledge and wisdom. Their gift empower others to develop their own gifts and reach their full potential.

Reflecting on Peter's words, it is important to ask how we can actively use our gifts to make a positive impact in the lives of others. Whether it is through acts of kindness, or lending a listening ear, we have the opportunity to be faithful stewards of God's grace in various forms.

As you go about your day, be intentional in recognizing the unique talents and abilities you possess. Remember, your gifts are not just for your own benefit but are meant to used for the betterment of those around you.

REFLECTIVE QUESTION
How can you use your gifts to serve others and bring glory to God?

Clothed in Compassion and Kindness

Therefore, as the elect of God, holy and beloved,
put on tender mercies, kindness, humility,
meekness, longsuffering.

COLOSSIANS 3:12

IMAGINE A PERSON WHO consistently demonstrates compassion and kindness in their interactions with others. They offer a listening ear to a friend in need, show empathy towards a struggling coworker, and extend a helping hand to a stranger. These acts of compassion and kindness have the power to transform lives and bring healing to broken hearts.

Reflecting on Paul's words, we are reminded that as followers of Christ, we are called to imitate His character and display these virtues in our daily lives. When we clothe ourselves with compassion and kindness, we become a source of light and encouragement to those around us.

Today, take a moment to consider how you can demonstrate compassion and kindness in practical ways. It could be as simple as offering a word of encouragement, showing empathy towards someone going through a difficult season, or performing a random act of kindness for a stranger. These small acts can have a profound impact and reveal the love of Christ to those around us.

As you go about your day, intentionally seek opportunities to extend compassion and kindness to others. Remember, you are God's chosen and dearly loved child, and by embodying these virtues, you can bring hope and joy to those who need it most.

REFLECTIVE QUESTION

How can you demonstrate compassion and kindness to others today?

Finding Rest in God's Presence

And He said, 'My Presence will go with you,
and I will give you rest.'

Exodus 33:14

THINK OF A PERSON who finds solace in spending time alone with God, away from the noise and distractions of the world. They carve out moments each day to sit in His presence, to seek His guidance, and to find refreshment for their soul. In the midst of life's challenges and uncertainties, they find true rest in the presence of their loving Creator.

Reflecting on this verse, we are reminded that in our busy lives, it is essential to prioritize spending time in God's presence. By intentionally setting aside moments for prayer, meditation, and reading His Word, we can experience the rest and peace that surpasses all understanding.

Today, consider how you can prioritize and cultivate a deeper connection with God. It may involve waking up a few minutes earlier to start the day in prayer, finding a quiet place during lunch breaks to meditate on Scripture, or dedicating a specific time in the evening to reflect on His goodness.

As you make room for God and seek His presence, you will discover that true rest is not found in external circumstances but in the intimate relationship with Him. Allow His presence to envelop you, bringing you peace, strength, and the rest your soul longs for.

REFLECTIVE QUESTION

How can you prioritize spending time in God's presence to find true rest?

Honoring God with Our Bodies

Or do you not know that your body is the temple of the
Holy Spirit who is in you, whom you have from God,
and you are not your own? For you were bought
at a price; therefore glorify God in your body
and in your spirit, which are God's.

1 CORINTHIANS 6:19-20

SOMEONE WHO VALUES THEIR body as a temple of the Holy
Spirit takes care of it by nourishing it with wholesome food,
exercising regularly, and avoiding harmful habits. They understand
that their physical well-being is an important aspect of their
spiritual journey.

Reflecting on this verse, we are reminded that as followers
of Christ, our bodies are not our own. They have been bought
with a price—the precious blood of Jesus. Therefore, it is our
responsibility to honour God with our bodies in every aspect
of our lives.

Today, consider how you can honour God with your body.
It could be by making healthy choices in your diet, engaging in
regular exercise to maintain fitness, or treating your body with
respect and modesty. Additionally, you can honour God with
your body by using your physical abilities to serve others to
bring glory to Him.

Remember, your body is a precious gift, and by treating it with
respect and gratitude, you demonstrate your love and obedience
to God.

REFLECTIVE QUESTION
How can you honour God with your body today?

Seeking and Finding God's Promises

Call to Me, and I will answer you, and show you great and mighty things, which you do not know.
JEREMIAH 33:3

IMAGINE SOMEONE WHO EARNESTLY seeks God's promises. They spend time in prayer, meditate on His Word, and seek His guidance in all aspects of their life. In their pursuit, they witness God's faithfulness and experience the fulfilment of His promises in miraculous ways.

Reflecting on this verse, we are reminded that God delights in revealing His truth and promises to those who seek Him with a sincere heart. He invites us to call upon Him, to ask Him for guidance, and to trust in His wisdom.

Today, consider how you can actively seek God's promises and experience His faithfulness. It may involve setting aside intentional time for prayer and meditation, or seeking wise counsel from fellow believers.

As you seek God's promises, be open to His leading and be attentive to the ways in which He may be speaking to you. Remember that His ways are higher than ours, and His thoughts are higher than our thoughts.

As you go about your day, be expectant of the great and unsearchable things that God wants to reveal to you. Trust in His faithfulness and believe that as you seek Him, you will find Him and experience the fulfilment of His promises in your life.

REFLECTIVE QUESTION
How can you actively seek God's promises and experience His faithfulness in your life today?

Finding Strength in Suffering

And not only that, but we also glory in tribulations,
knowing that tribulation produces perseverance;
and perseverance, character; and character, hope.

ROMANS 5:3-4

IMAGINE SOMEONE WHO FACES difficult circumstances with unwavering faith and a hopeful spirit. They understand that even in the midst of trials, there is an opportunity for growth and transformation. Through their perseverance, they develop a resilient character that trusts in God's provision and clings to the hope found in Him.

Reflecting on this verse, we are reminded that our sufferings are not in vain. They have the potential to shape us into stronger individuals, deepen our faith, and foster a sense of hope that transcends our circumstances.

Today, consider how you can embrace the challenges you are facing and allow them to strengthen your character and deepen your faith. Instead of viewing suffering as a setback, choose to see it as an opportunity for growth. Seek God's guidance and ask Him to grant you the perseverance to endure and the wisdom to learn from every trial.

As you navigate through difficult times, hold on to the hope that God's faithfulness will carry you through. Trust that He is using your experiences to mould you into the person He created you to be. Embrace the challenges, knowing that they are preparing you for a future filled with hope and purpose.

REFLECTIVE QUESTION
How can you embrace challenges and allow them to shape your character and deepen your faith?

Be Still and Know God's Sovereignty

Be still, and know that I am God;
I will be exalted among the nations,
I will be exalted in the earth!

PSALM 46:10

IMAGINE SOMEONE WHO INTENTIONALLY carves out moments of stillness in their busy life. They find solace in quiet moments of prayer and meditation, allowing themselves to be fully present in God's presence. In that stillness, they experience His peace, gain perspective, and find renewed strength to face whatever challenges lie ahead.

Reflecting on this verse, we are reminded of the importance of cultivating stillness in our lives. In the midst of a fast-paced and chaotic world, it is in the quiet moments that we can truly encounter God and recognize His authority over every situation.

Today, consider how you can create space for stillness in your life. It might involve setting aside dedicated time each day to be alone with God, finding a quiet place to pray and reflect, or simply pausing throughout the day to take a deep breath and quiet your heart.

As you cultivate stillness, embrace the opportunity to know God in a deeper way. Allow His presence to fill you with peace, calm your fears, and reassure you of His sovereignty. Trust that in the stillness, you will find strength, guidance, and a renewed sense of purpose.

REFLECTIVE QUESTION
How can you cultivate stillness in your life to experience God's presence and acknowledge His sovereignty?

Serving with Excellence for God's Glory

**And whatever you do, do it heartily,
as to the Lord and not to men,**

COLOSSIANS 3:23

IMAGINE SOMEONE WHO EMBRACES their work as an opportunity to serve God and make a positive impact. They approach each task, no matter how big or small, with dedication, integrity, and a desire to bring glory to God. Their work becomes an act of worship, an offering to the One who has given them their abilities and opportunities.

Reflecting on this verse, we are reminded that our attitude towards work should not be driven solely by external rewards or human approval. Instead, our focus should be on serving God and doing our best for His sake.

Today, consider how you can approach your work and daily tasks with a mindset of serving God. It may involve giving your best effort, maintaining a positive attitude, and treating others with kindness and respect. By doing so, you demonstrate your love for God and your commitment to living out your faith in every aspect of your life.

As you go about your day, remember that the work you do, whether in a professional setting, at home, or in your community, has the potential to bring God glory. Seek His guidance and ask Him to help you see the significance of your work and empower you to do it with excellence.

REFLECTIVE QUESTION

How can you approach your work and daily tasks with a mindset of serving God and bringing Him glory?

Overcoming Temptation

No temptation has overtaken you except such as
is common to man; but God is faithful, who will not
allow you to be tempted beyond what you are able,
but with the temptation will also make the way of
escape, that you may be able to bear it.

1 CORINTHIANS 10:13

IN OUR JOURNEY OF faith, we all face temptations. It may be the temptation to compromise our values, indulge in unhealthy habits, or succumb to worldly desires. However, we are reminded in this passage that no temptation is unique to us; it is a common struggle faced by all humanity.

The key lies in recognizing God's faithfulness. He promises that He will not allow us to be tempted beyond what we can bear. In every temptation, God provides a way out, a path of escape. It may be through the power of prayer, seeking support from a trusted friend, or immersing ourselves in His Word.

When we trust in God's faithfulness, we can find the strength to resist and overcome temptation. It is not our own willpower that enables us, but the power of God working within us. By seeking His guidance and relying on His promises, we can endure and triumph over any temptation that comes our way. With Him by our side, we can stand firm against temptations, grow in our faith, and live a life that honours and pleases Him.

REFLECTIVE QUESTION
How can we rely on God's faithfulness to overcome temptations in our lives?

Discovering Your Life Purpose

For we are His workmanship, created in Christ Jesus
for good works, which God prepared beforehand
that we should walk in them.

EPHESIANS 2:10

IN THIS VERSE, PAUL reminds us that we are God's masterpiece, created in Christ Jesus for a specific purpose. Each one of us has been uniquely designed by God, with special gifts and abilities to carry out the good works He has prepared for us.

Embracing our identity as God's masterpiece means recognizing that we are chosen, loved, and valued by Him. It means understanding that our lives have purpose and significance in His plans. As we grow in our understanding of who we are in Christ, we can confidently step into the good works God has ordained for us.

Living out our purpose involves seeking God's guidance and aligning our lives with His will. It means utilizing our gifts and talents to serve others sharing His love and grace with those around us. It also requires stepping out in faith trusting that God will equip and empower us for the tasks He has assigned.

Let us remember that we are not here by chance but by divine design. We are God's masterpiece, created with a unique purpose. As we embrace our identity in Christ and live out our calling, we bring glory to God and impact the world for His kingdom.

REFLECTIVE QUESTION

How can we embrace our identity as God's masterpiece and live out our purpose?

Wholehearted Love: Devoting Our All to God

Jesus said to him, 'You shall love the Lord
your God with all your heart,
with all your soul, and with all your mind.
MATTHEW 22:37

IN THIS VERSE, JESUS reveals the greatest commandment: to love God with all our heart, soul, and mind. This call to wholehearted devotion challenges us to surrender every aspect of our lives to Him and prioritize our relationship with Him above all else.

To demonstrate wholehearted love for God, we must first cultivate intimacy with Him through prayer, worship, and studying His Word. As we spend time in His presence, our love for Him deepens, and we become more attuned to His will.

Furthermore, our actions should align with our love for God. We should seek to honour Him in our relationships and decisions. By loving our neighbours, showing kindness, and seeking justice, we reflect God's love to the world.

In our daily lives, it is important to examine our hearts and ask ourselves if we are truly giving our all to God. Are there areas where we hold back? Are we placing other things or people above Him?

Let us strive to love God wholeheartedly, allowing Him to be the centre of our lives. When we love Him with all our heart, soul, and mind, we experience the depth of His love and walk in alignment with His purposes.

REFLECTIVE QUESTION
How can we demonstrate wholehearted love for God in our daily lives?

Living with a Purposeful Perspective

**So teach us to number our days
That we may gain a heart of wisdom.**
PSALM 90:12

IN THIS VERSE, THE psalmist implores God to teach us to number our days, recognizing that our time on earth is finite. This call reminds us of the importance of living with intentionality.

To cultivate a perspective that values the limited time we have, we can start by acknowledging the brevity of life and the significance of each passing day. This awareness can inspire us to prioritize what truly matters: our relationships, our purpose, and our impact on others.

Seeking wisdom is crucial in making the most of our days. We can do this by regularly spending time in Scripture, seeking guidance from God through prayer, and learning from the experiences and insights of others. Wisdom enables us to make decisions that align with God's will and have a positive influence on those around us.

Additionally, we can evaluate how we are investing our time and energy. Are we spending our days on things that bring us closer to our goals and aspirations? Are we using our talents and resources to serve others and make a difference in the world?

Let us continually seek God's wisdom and guidance as we navigate through life. We can make each moment count and leave a lasting impact for His glory.

REFLECTIVE QUESTION

How can we cultivate a perspective that values the limited time we have and seeks wisdom in our daily choices?

Embracing God's Spirit of Power, Love, and Self-Discipline

For God has not given us a spirit of fear,
but of power and of love and of a sound mind.
2 TIMOTHY 1:7

To HARNESS GOD'S SPIRIT of power, we must first recognize that it is not our own strength but a gift from Him. We can tap into this power through prayer, seeking His guidance, and trusting in His promises. With God's power within us, we can face any adversity with confidence.

God's spirit of love empowers us to love Him, others, and ourselves. Love is the foundational principle that guides our actions and relationships. When we abide in His love, we reflect His character and experience the transformative power of love in our own lives.

Self-discipline is an essential component of living a purposeful life. It involves aligning our thoughts, words, and actions with God's truth and committing to live according to His standards. By practising self-discipline, we can resist temptation, make wise choices, and pursue God's purposes for our lives.

Let us reflect on how we can embrace God's spirit of power, love, and self-discipline in our daily lives. Are fear and self-doubt hindering us from living boldly for God? By leaning on God and allowing His spirit to work within us, we can conquer fear, love abundantly, and live a purpose-driven life that brings glory to His name.

REFLECTIVE QUESTION
How can we lean on God's spirit of power, love, and self-discipline to overcome fear and live a bold, purposeful life?

Using Your Gifts for God's Glory

As each one has received a gift,
minister it to one another, as good stewards
of the manifold grace of God.

1 Peter 4:10

Discovering our gifts requires self-reflection and seeking God's guidance. We can explore our natural abilities, passions, and experiences to identify areas where we excel and enjoy serving others. God often speaks through our desires, prompting us to use our gifts to make a difference in the lives of those around us.

Utilizing our gifts to serve others requires humility and a genuine heart of compassion. When we invest our gifts in serving others, we become vessels of God's grace, reflecting His love and bringing glory to His name. It is essential to remember that our gifts are not solely for our own benefit. We are called to be faithful stewards, faithfully using what God has entrusted to us for His purposes. As we do so, we experience the joy of fulfilling our God-given purpose.

Let us take time to prayerfully reflect on our gifts and how we can use them to serve others. How can we be faithful stewards of God's grace in our various forms?

By embracing and utilizing our gifts for God's glory, we participate in His work of transforming lives and bringing His kingdom to earth.

REFLECTIVE QUESTION

How can we discover and utilize our unique gifts to serve others and bring glory to God?

Walking in Truth and Love

**I have no greater joy than to hear
that my children walk in truth.**

3 JOHN 1:4

IN THIS VERSE, THE Apostle John expresses his delight in hearing that his spiritual children are walking in the truth. Like John, our ultimate goal should be to bring joy to our heavenly Father by living lives that align with His truth and embody His love.

Walking in the truth involves aligning our beliefs, thoughts, and actions with the teachings of Christ. It requires digging deep into God's Word, allowing it to shape our worldview, and seeking to live out its principles in our daily lives. When we walk in truth, we honour God and reflect His character to the world around us.

Additionally, walking in love is an essential part of pleasing God. It entails showing compassion, kindness, and sacrificial love towards others, just as Christ demonstrated to us. Love should permeate every aspect of our lives, impacting our relationships, interactions, and decisions.

Let us reflect on our own lives and ask ourselves if we are truly walking in truth and love. Are there areas where we need to align ourselves more closely to God's truth? Are there relationships or circumstances where we need to show more love and grace?

By walking in truth and love, we bring joy to our heavenly Father, fulfil our purpose, and become powerful witnesses of His transformative love.

REFLECTIVE QUESTION
How can we bring joy to our heavenly Father by walking in truth and love?

Reaping the Blessing of Obedience

If you are willing and obedient,
you shall eat the good of the land;

ISAIAH 1:19

To CULTIVATE A WILLING heart, we can start by seeking God in prayer surrendering our own desires and plans to Him. When we surrender to His will, we allow Him to shape our hearts, aligning them with His purposes. Through a surrendered heart, we become more willing to do what He asks of us.

Obedience flows naturally from a willing heart. It requires actively seeking to know God's will through studying His Word and listening to the Holy Spirit's guidance. Obeying God often involves stepping out in faith and trusting Him, even when it may be challenging or uncomfortable. As we walk in obedience, we position ourselves to receive the fullness of God's blessings.

Let us reflect on our own lives and hearts. Are we willing to submit to God's authority and align our lives with His will? Are we actively seeking to be obedient to His commands and guidance, even when it may require sacrifice or stepping out of our comfort zones?

By cultivating a willing and obedient heart, we position ourselves to experience the abundant blessings that God has in store for us. May we joyfully surrender to His will and obediently follow Him, reaping the richness of His goodness in our lives.

REFLECTIVE QUESTION

How can we cultivate a willing and obedient heart to experience God's abundant blessings?

Cultivating a Wise Heart

But the wisdom that is from above is first pure,
then peaceable, gentle, willing to yield, full of mercy and
good fruits, without partiality and without hypocrisy.

JAMES 3:17

IN TODAY'S PASSAGE, JAMES presents a powerful description of heavenly wisdom, contrasting it with the wisdom of the world. This divine wisdom, granted to us by God, is characterized by its pure and peace-loving nature. It is considerate, submissive, and marked by mercy and good fruit. Above all, it remains impartial and sincere.

As we navigate through life's challenges and responsibilities, we often encounter various sources of wisdom. But James reminds us that true wisdom originates from heaven. To consistently manifest this wisdom, we must seek God's guidance through prayer, meditation on His Word, and cultivating a personal relationship with Him. By doing so, we open ourselves to His leading and allow His wisdom to flow through us, affecting our interactions with others and influencing our decision-making processes.

As we grow in the wisdom that comes from above, we become more peace-loving, considerate, and merciful individuals. We bear good fruit in our relationships, making impartial judgments and approaching others with sincerity. Let us seek this divine wisdom daily, inviting God to transform our hearts and minds so that we may be instruments of peace and love in a world that desperately needs it.

REFLECTIVE QUESTION

How can we seek and embrace the wisdom that comes from above in our daily lives?

The Power of Persistent Prayer

Pray without ceasing.

1 THESSALONIANS 5:17

IN JUST THREE WORDS, the Apostle Paul delivers a profound imperative to the Thessalonians and to us: "Pray continually." This simple yet powerful instruction reminds us of the importance of maintaining a vibrant and unceasing connection with God through prayer.

Prayer is not limited to specific times or places; it is an ongoing conversation with our Heavenly Father. To cultivate a life of continual prayer, we can start by setting aside dedicated times each day to intentionally seek God's presence. But beyond these focused moments, we can also develop a habit of offering up quick prayers throughout our daily activities – in the midst of work, chores, or even during a commute.

When we pray without ceasing, we invite God's presence into every aspect of our lives. We acknowledge our dependence on Him and seek His guidance, wisdom, and strength. This constant communication keeps us connected to God's heart and aligns our thoughts and actions with His will.

Let us strive to make prayer an integral part of our lives, always inviting God's presence and guidance. Through continual prayer, we can experience a deeper intimacy with our Creator and find comfort, strength, and guidance in every situation we encounter.

REFLECTIVE QUESTION
How can we develop a lifestyle of continual prayer in the midst of our daily activities?

Walking Humbly: The Call to Live Justly

He has shown you, O man, what is good;
And what does the Lord require of you
But to do justly, To love mercy, And to walk
humbly with your God?

MICAH 6:8

IN THIS POWERFUL VERSE, the prophet Micah offers a concise summary of God's expectations for His people. He calls us to live justly, to extend mercy, and to walk humbly in our relationship with God.

Living justly requires actively seeking to uphold fairness and equality in our interactions with others. It means treating everyone with dignity and respect, regardless of their background or circumstances. We can advocate for social justice, help the oppressed, and stand against injustice in our spheres of influence.

Loving mercy involves extending compassion, forgiveness, and kindness to others, even when they may not deserve it. We can choose to show grace and understanding, seeking reconciliation and healing in our relationships.

Walking humbly with God entails acknowledging our dependence on Him, recognizing His authority, and submitting to His will. It involves cultivating a heart of gratitude, humility, and obedience to God's guidance, surrendering our own pride and desires.

Let us embrace God's call to live justly, love mercy, and walk humbly, knowing that through our actions and attitudes, we can reflect His character and bring about positive change in the world around us.

REFLECTIVE QUESTION

How can we practically live out the call to act justly, love mercy, and walk humbly with God in our daily lives?

Cultivating Healthy Christian Friendships

**A friend loves at all times,
And a brother is born for adversity.**
PROVERBS 17:17

IN THIS VERSE, THE wisdom of Proverbs reminds us of the immeasurable value of true friendship. A genuine friend loves unconditionally, standing by us in every season of life, and is especially present during times of difficulty and hardship.

True friendship requires intentional effort and commitment. Firstly, we must be willing to invest time and energy into nurturing relationships with those we consider our friends. Socializing, engaging in meaningful conversations, and being present in both joyful and challenging moments are vital.

Secondly, we should strive to be trustworthy, reliable, and supportive friends ourselves. Actively listening, offering empathy and understanding, and extending grace are essential qualities in cultivating deep connections.

Lastly, we must learn to celebrate the diversity and unique qualities that each friend brings. Honouring and appreciating our friends' differences enriches our relationships and broadens our perspectives.

Let us seek to be friends who love at all times, standing by one another in both good and bad times. Through the gift of true friendship, we can experience the joys of companionship, find strength in times of adversity, and grow together in love and grace.

REFLECTIVE QUESTION
How can we cultivate and cherish deep, lasting friendships that mirror the love described in this verse?

Empowered for Purpose

"Alas, Sovereign LORD," I said,
"I do not know how to speak; I am too young."

JEREMIAH 1:6

IN THIS VERSE, WE witness Jeremiah's initial response to God's call upon his life. Despite feeling inadequate and unprepared, Jeremiah's vulnerability opens the door for God to empower him for the purpose He has in mind.

We may doubt our abilities, experience fear, or consider ourselves too young or inexperienced. However, just as God assured Jeremiah of His presence and empowerment, He also promises to equip and enable us for the tasks He sets before us.

To overcome feelings of inadequacy, we must first surrender our doubts and insecurities to God, acknowledging our need for His guidance and strength. By trusting in His wisdom and provision, we can find the courage to step out in faith.

Moreover, surrounding ourselves with a supportive community of believers can also provide encouragement and accountability, insights and reassurance.

Ultimately, embracing God's call requires a willingness to let go of our self-perceived limitations, trusting that God's power is made perfect in our weaknesses. As we yield ourselves to Him, He will work through us, accomplishing His purposes and transforming lives.

Remember, it is not our own abilities but the power of God that equips us for the path He has set before us.

REFLECTIVE QUESTION

How can we overcome our feelings of inadequacy and step into the calling and purpose that God has for us?

Growing in the Grace and Knowledge

**But grow in the grace and knowledge
of our Lord and Savior Jesus Christ.
To Him be the glory both now and forever. Amen.**

2 PETER 3:18

PETER LEAVES US WITH a powerful exhortation to continually grow in the grace and knowledge of our Lord and Savior, Jesus Christ. It is a call to ongoing spiritual growth and deepening intimacy with God.

To grow in the grace and knowledge of Christ, we must prioritize our relationship with Him. This involves dedicating time daily for prayer, studying the Scriptures, and seeking the guidance of the Holy Spirit. Engaging in fellowship with other believers, attending church, and participating in small groups can also provide opportunities for learning and spiritual growth.

In addition, we must align our actions with our beliefs, living out the principles and teachings of Christ in our daily lives. This could include practising forgiveness, showing love and compassion to others, and actively seeking ways to serve and bless those around us. Furthermore, it is crucial to remain humble and open to learning, allowing God to refine and challenge our understanding and beliefs.

Let us embrace the call to grow in the grace and knowledge of Christ, understanding that it is a lifelong journey characterized by continuous learning, transformation, and intimate communion with our Savior.

REFLECTIVE QUESTION

How can we actively grow in the grace and knowledge of Christ in our daily lives?

Surrendering to the Gentle Yoke of Christ

Take my yoke upon you and learn from Me,
for I am gentle and lowly in heart, and you will
find rest for your souls.

MATTHEW 11:29

To TAKE JESUS' YOKE means to align our lives with His teachings and ways. It involves surrendering our own self-reliance, worries, and burdens and entrusting them to Him. To effectively take His yoke, we need to cultivate a spirit of humility, acknowledging our need for His guidance, wisdom, and strength.

Learning from Jesus requires intentional study of His Word, seeking His presence through prayer, and developing a deep, personal relationship with Him. It involves adopting His character traits of gentleness and humility, allowing His transformative power to shape our attitudes and actions.

As we willingly take on Jesus' yoke, we discover a profound rest for our souls. This rest transcends physical weariness and offers spiritual rejuvenation. It is found in the assurance of His love, the peace that surpasses understanding, and the comfort of knowing we are not alone in navigating life's challenges.

Let us embrace Jesus' invitation to take His yoke, finding rest for our souls as we walk in His gentle and humble ways. In surrendering our burdens to Him and learning from His example, we experience the abundant life He promises and find true rest in His loving presence.

REFLECTIVE QUESTION

How can we effectively take Jesus' yoke and experience the rest He promises in our daily lives?

Trusting in God's Provision

**And my God shall supply all your need
according to His riches in glory by Christ Jesus.**
PHILIPPIANS 4:19

IN THIS VERSE, THE Apostle Paul assures the believers in Philippi that their faithful God will abundantly provide for all their needs. It is a reminder of God's unfailing provision and the limitless resources available to His children.

Trusting in God's provision begins with recognizing His faithfulness throughout history and in our own lives. Reflect on past experiences when God has provided in unexpected and miraculous ways. This builds our confidence in His ability to meet our current and future needs.

Next, we must align our priorities with God's kingdom and seek His guidance in managing our resources. This involves practising wise stewardship, being content with what we have, and living generously, knowing that God blesses us to be a blessing to others.

Additionally, nurturing a consistent prayer life allows us to bring our needs before God, expressing our dependence on Him and surrendering our worries and anxieties. Strengthening our faith through Scripture study and surrounding ourselves with a supportive community can also bolster our trust in God's provision.

As we cultivate a mindset of trust in God's provision, we can be rest assured that He will meet our needs according to His riches. By leaning on His unfailing love and faithfulness, we can face uncertainties with confidence.

REFLECTIVE QUESTION
How can we cultivate a mindset of trust in God's provision, even in times of uncertainty?

The Power of God's Love

Nor height nor depth, nor any other created thing,
shall be able to separate us from the love of God
which is in Christ Jesus our Lord.
ROMANS 8:39

THESE POWERFUL WORDS BY Apostle Paul remind us that God's love for us is unwavering and unshakeable, regardless of our circumstances or shortcomings.

Imagine the comfort and assurance that comes from knowing that no matter what we face – be it trials, failures, or even our own doubts – God's love remains constant. It is a love that surpasses human understanding, a love that endures all things.

When we fully grasp the depth of God's love, it transforms the way we live our lives. We can face challenges with confidence, knowing that we are not alone. We can find peace in the midst of chaos, knowing that God's love will never abandon us. We can have hope in times of despair, knowing that God's love is greater than any darkness.

So, as we reflect upon Romans 8:39, let us ask ourselves: How does knowing that nothing can separate us from the love of God impact our daily lives? How does it shape our perspective, our actions, and our relationships? May we truly embrace and live out the truth that we are unconditionally loved by our Heavenly Father.

REFLECTIVE QUESTION
How does knowing that nothing can separate us from the love of God impact your daily life?

Finding Joy in Trials

My brethren, count it all joy
when you fall into various trials.

JAMES 1:2

IN TODAY'S READING, JAMES challenges us to shift our perspective. Rather than viewing trials as burdens to be avoided, he encourages us to embrace them as opportunities for growth. When we face trials, we have the chance to develop perseverance, character, and faith.

Consider a seed that is buried deep in the ground. It undergoes immense pressure, darkness, and discomfort. Yet, these challenging conditions are necessary for the seed to sprout, grow, and bear fruit. Similarly, trials can be the catalysts that lead to personal transformation and spiritual maturity.

When we embrace a mindset of joy in the face of trials, we open ourselves up to the possibility of discovering God's faithfulness, experiencing His grace, and witnessing His power at work in our lives. We become more resilient and able to navigate life's challenges with a sense of purpose and hope.

So, let us reflect upon James 1:2 and ask ourselves: How does our perspective on trials change when we consider them as opportunities for growth and endurance? How can we cultivate a joyful attitude in the midst of difficulties? May we find strength and joy in knowing that God is with us, guiding us through each trial we encounter.

REFLECTIVE QUESTION

How does your perspective on trials change when you consider them as opportunities for growth and endurance?

Seeking God's Kingdom First

But seek first the kingdom of God
and His righteousness,
and all these things shall be added to you.

MATTHEW 6:33

IN OUR FAST-PACED AND busy lives, it's easy to get caught up in the pursuit of success, material possessions, or personal ambitions. However, Jesus calls us to prioritize seeking God's kingdom, which encompasses righteousness, justice, love, and obedience to God's will.

Seeking God's kingdom first means aligning our hearts and minds with His purposes. It involves seeking His presence, studying His Word, and living out His teachings. It means placing our trust in God's provision rather than relying solely on our own efforts or worrying about our needs being met.

When we prioritize seeking God's kingdom, we experience a transformative shift in our priorities and perspectives. Our focus shifts from worldly concerns to eternal values. We find peace in knowing that God will provide for our needs as we faithfully seek Him.

So, as we reflect upon Matthew 6:33, let us ask ourselves: How can we prioritize seeking God's kingdom above all else in our daily lives? How can we intentionally make time for prayer, reading Scripture, and serving others? May we continually seek and pursue God's kingdom, trusting in His faithfulness and experiencing the abundant blessings that come from following Him wholeheartedly.

REFLECTIVE QUESTION
How can you prioritize seeking God's kingdom above all else in your daily life?

Called to Follow

Then He [Jesus] said to them,
"Follow Me, and I will make you fishers of men.

MATTHEW 4:19

To FOLLOW JESUS MEANS more than just acknowledging him as our Savior; it involves surrendering our lives to him and aligning our actions with his teachings and example. It means embracing his mission of sharing the good news and making disciples.

Following Jesus requires a daily commitment to walk in his footsteps, imitating his love, compassion, and selflessness. It means seeking opportunities to share our faith and serve others, just as Jesus did during his earthly ministry.

In our everyday lives, we can respond to Jesus' call to follow by prioritizing our relationship with him. We can dedicate time for prayer, studying His Word, and cultivating intimacy with him. We can actively seek ways to bring others closer to Jesus through our words, actions, and testimonies.

So, let us reflect upon Matthew 4:19 and ask ourselves: How can we respond to Jesus' call to "follow me" in our everyday lives? How can we live as fishers of people, intentionally sharing the gospel and inviting others into a relationship with Jesus? May we wholeheartedly embrace the call to follow Jesus, allowing his transformative love to shape every aspect of our lives.

REFLECTIVE QUESTION
How can you respond to Jesus' call to "follow me" in your everyday life?

Drawing Near to God

Draw near to God and He will draw near to you.
Cleanse your hands, you sinners;
and purify your hearts, you double-minded.

JAMES 4:8

THE WORDS IN JAMES 4:8 convey a powerful truth – when we draw near to God, seeking Him with a sincere heart, we can expect to experience His presence and receive His blessings.

Drawing near to God requires intentionality and a desire for intimacy with Him. It involves setting aside time for prayer, worship, and reading His Word. It means cultivating a heart that is sensitive to His leading, His voice, and His will.

As we actively pursue a closer relationship with God, we create space for Him to work in and through us. We open ourselves up to His transformative power, His guidance, and His love. We become more attuned to His presence, finding solace, strength, and wisdom in His nearness.

So, let us reflect upon James 4:8 and ask ourselves: How can we actively pursue a closer relationship with God and experience His presence in our daily lives? How can we make room for Him in our schedules and prioritize spending time with Him? May we continually seek after God's heart, knowing that as we draw near to Him, He will faithfully draw near to us.

REFLECTIVE QUESTION

How can you actively pursue a closer relationship with God and experience His presence in your daily life?

Growing in Christ-Like Character

> But the fruit of the Spirit is love, joy,
> peace, patience, kindness, goodness,
> faithfulness, gentleness, self-control.
> GALATIANS 5:22-23

AS FOLLOWERS OF CHRIST, we are called to actively cultivate these fruits in our daily interactions with others. Love compels us to show compassion and kindness. Joy enables us to rejoice with others in their victories and find hope in challenging times. Peace guides us to be peacemakers, seeking reconciliation and harmony. Patience and forbearance help us to extend grace and understanding, even when it's difficult.

Goodness, faithfulness, gentleness, and self-control shape our character and influence how we treat others. They enable us to serve with integrity, speak with kindness, and exercise self-discipline.

To cultivate these fruits, we must be intentional. We can pray for God's help and guidance, asking Him to transform our hearts and mould us into vessels of His love. We can study Scripture to understand how Jesus embodied these virtues and learn from His example. We can actively seek opportunities to practice these traits, allowing the Spirit to work through us.

So, let us reflect upon Galatians 5:22-23 and ask ourselves: How can we actively cultivate the fruits of the Spirit in our interactions with others? How can we intentionally demonstrate love, joy, peace, forbearance, kindness, goodness, faithfulness, gentleness, and self-control? May we strive to embody these virtues, bringing glory to God and blessing those around us.

REFLECTIVE QUESTION

How can you actively cultivate the fruits of the Spirit in your interactions with others?

Living in the Present

Therefore do not worry about tomorrow,
for tomorrow will worry about its own things.
Sufficient for the day is its own trouble.

MATTHEW 6:34

OFTEN, OUR MINDS ARE consumed with worries about the future – what will happen, how things will turn out. Yet, Jesus encourages us to release our anxieties and focus on the present. He assures us that God's grace is sufficient to meet our needs as they arise.

Living in the present requires trust in God's sovereignty and provision. It involves surrendering our worries and fears consciously choosing to place our faith in Him. It means seeking His guidance and direction for each step, relying on His wisdom and strength.

When we practice living in the present, we can fully embrace the opportunities, blessings, and challenges of each day. We can find peace and contentment, knowing that God is with us in every moment. We can be more attentive to the needs of others, sharing God's love and grace in tangible ways.

So, as we reflect upon Matthew 6:34, let us ask ourselves: How can we practice living in the present and trusting God's provision for each day? How can we let go of worries and anxieties about the future and instead focus on what God has placed in front of us? May we cultivate a mindset of faith and gratitude, fully embracing the gift of each day.

REFLECTIVE QUESTION

How can you practice living in the present and trusting God's provision for each day?

Growing in Maturity and Love

When I was a child, I spoke as a child,
I understood as a child, I thought as a child;
but when I became a man, I put away childish things.

I CORINTHIANS 13:11

PAUL'S WORDS REMIND US that love is not merely a feeling or emotion but a choice and a way of life. This love is characterized by selflessness, patience, kindness, and forgiveness. It is a love that seeks the good of others above our own desires.

To embrace maturity and love, we must examine our thoughts, words, and actions. How do we communicate with others? Are our words uplifting and encouraging? Do we allow love to guide our interactions, even in challenging circumstances? Are we patient and understanding, even when it's difficult?

Maturity and love require us to let go of selfishness, and pride. It means humbling ourselves, seeking reconciliation, and extending forgiveness. It also means pursuing unity and peace.

So, let us reflect upon 1 Corinthians 13:11 and ask ourselves: In what areas of our lives do we need to embrace maturity and allow love to guide our thoughts, words, and actions? How can we grow in selflessness, kindness, and patience towards others? May we continually strive to put away the ways of our past and embrace the transformative power of love in all aspects of our lives.

REFLECTIVE QUESTION

In what areas of your life do you need to embrace maturity and allow love to guide your thoughts, words, and actions?

Shining Light in a Dark World

Walk in wisdom toward those who are outside,
redeeming the time. Let your speech always be
with grace, seasoned with salt, that you may know
how you ought to answer each one.

Colossians 4:5-6

In Colossians 4:5-6, the Apostle Paul encourages the believers in Colossae to be wise in their interactions with outsiders. He tells them to make the most of every opportunity and to let their speech always be gracious, seasoned with salt.

The Bible often uses the metaphor of light to describe the influence of believers in the world. Just as light dispels darkness, our words and actions can bring hope and truth to those around us.

Being wise in our interactions means considering the needs of others and being sensitive to their perspectives. We should seek to build bridges of understanding rather than erecting walls of judgment. When we speak, our words should be gracious, uplifting, and respectful, reflecting the love of Christ.

Seasoning our speech with salt implies that our communication should be relevant. Just as salt enhances the flavour of food, our words should add value and bring out the best in others.

As we navigate through a world filled with differing beliefs and values, let us remember that our purpose is to reflect God's love and truth to those around us. May our interactions be marked by grace and wisdom as we shine the light of Christ in the darkness.

REFLECTIVE QUESTION
How can we effectively maintain our Christian values in our engagements?

Armor Up with Intercession

Praying always with all prayer and supplication in the Spirit, being watchful to this end with all perseverance and supplication for all the saints—

EPHESIANS 6:18

PRAYER IS NOT JUST a passive religious duty; it is a powerful means of communication with God. It is through prayer that we equip ourselves with the spiritual armour needed to stand against the enemy's schemes.

To cultivate a consistent and powerful prayer life, we must first prioritize our relationship with God. This involves setting aside daily time for communion with Him, seeking His guidance, and presenting our requests with a heart of surrender.

Staying alert means being aware of the spiritual battles that surround us. We must actively intercede for ourselves and fellow believers, lifting up their needs, struggles, and victories before God.

Perseverance in prayer means not giving up, even when answers are delayed or not as we expect. It is a reminder of our dependence on God and His perfect timing.

Supplication for all the saints reminds us of the unity of the body of Christ. We are called to pray for our brothers and sisters, bearing their burdens and interceding for their spiritual growth and well-being.

Let us armour up with the power of intercession, being diligent and consistent in our prayers. Through prayer, we access the supernatural strength and wisdom we need to navigate life's challenges.

REFLECTIVE QUESTION

How can we cultivate a consistent and powerful prayer life?

Living Out Faith in the Workplace

**And whatever you do, do it heartily,
as to the Lord and not to men.**
COLOSSIANS 3:23

AS BELIEVERS, OUR WORK is not merely a means of earning a living or achieving personal success. It is an opportunity to glorify God and reflect His character in all that we do.

When we approach our work with excellence, giving our best effort, we demonstrate our commitment to honouring God. Whether we are in a professional role, serving others, or completing daily tasks, we can offer our work as an act of worship to the Lord.

Working with all our hearts means investing our time, skills, and talents wholeheartedly. It involves having a positive attitude, being diligent, and striving for excellence in both big and small tasks.

By shifting our perspective and understanding that our work is ultimately for the Lord, we can find purpose and meaning in even the most mundane of tasks. We can approach our work with gratitude, knowing that it is a privilege to contribute to God's kingdom in whatever capacity we are in.

So, let us work with all our hearts, seeking to honour God in everything we do. May our dedication, integrity, and excellence serve as a testimony of our love and devotion to Him.

REFLECTIVE QUESTION
**How can we approach our work or daily tasks
with a mindset that honours God?**

The Unfailing Word

So shall My word be that goes forth from My mouth;
It shall not return to Me void, but it shall
accomplish what I please, and it shall prosper
in the thing for which I sent it.

ISAIAH 55:11

THE WORDS OF GOD hold immense power and authority. When He speaks, His Word is certain to fulfil its intended purpose. This verse reminds us of the unwavering reliability and effectiveness of God's promises.

Knowing that God's Word will not return empty assures us of His faithfulness and trustworthiness. It instils confidence in His plans for our lives and gives us the assurance that His promises will always come to pass.

When we encounter challenges or uncertainties, we can rest in the fact that God's Word will accomplish what He has purposed in our lives. We can trust that His promises, spoken through Scripture or whispered to our hearts, will not fail.

We are encouraged to align our lives with God's Word and to cling to His promises. It reminds us to live with hope, knowing that the words spoken by our Heavenly Father will bring about the fulfilment of His divine plans and purposes.

So, let us place our trust and faith in the unfailing Word of God. May we find comfort, guidance, and strength in the assurance that His Word will accomplish what He has spoken.

REFLECTIVE QUESTION
How does knowing that God's Word is unfailing impact our trust and faith in Him?

Embracing Victory through Christ

And they overcame him by the blood of the Lamb and by the word of their testimony...
REVELATION 12:11

TO EXPERIENCE VICTORY, WE must fully embrace the power of the blood of the Lamb. It is through His blood that we are cleansed, made righteous, and set free from the chains of sin and death. By placing our faith in Jesus and confessing Him as our Lord and Savior, we are covered by His precious blood.

Additionally, our testimony plays a significant role in our victory. Sharing how God has transformed our lives and brought us through trials strengthens our faith and encourages others. Our testimony becomes a powerful weapon against the enemy, as it declares the redemptive power of Jesus' blood.

Lastly, we are called to love, not our lives, even unto death. This means surrendering our own desires and ambitions to the will of God, living sacrificially, and being willing to lay down our lives for His sake. When we prioritize the eternal and live for God's purposes, we experience true victory.

So, let us daily embrace the power of the blood of the Lamb and testify to His saving grace. By loving God more than our own lives, we can conquer the enemy and walk in the victory that Jesus has already won for us.

REFLECTIVE QUESTION
How can we experience victory in our spiritual battles through the power of the blood of Jesus Christ?

Submission to God

Therefore submit to God.
Resist the devil and he will flee from you.
JAMES 4:7

SUBMISSION TO GOD IS an act of humility and surrender. It involves recognizing His authority over our lives, aligning our will with His, and trusting in His wisdom and guidance. When we submit to God, we position ourselves under His protection and care.

Practically, submission to God begins with cultivating a relationship with Him through prayer, studying His Word, and seeking His guidance in all aspects of our lives. It means obeying His commands and following the example of Jesus Christ.

In addition to submission, we are called to resist the devil. This involves actively and intentionally standing against his temptations, lies, and schemes. We resist the enemy by grounding ourselves in the truth of Scripture, relying on the power of the Holy Spirit, and putting on the armour of God (Ephesians 6:10-18).

As we submit to God and resist the devil, we experience the freedom and victory that comes from living in alignment with God's will. The devil, who seeks to steal, kill, and destroy, will flee from us when we stand firm in our faith and trust in God's strength.

So, let us choose daily to submit to God, embracing humility and resisting the enemy. May our lives be characterized by a deep reverence for God and a steadfast commitment to resisting all that opposes His truth and love.

REFLECTIVE QUESTION
How can you practically submit to God and resist the devil in your daily life?

Renewed Day by Day

Therefore we do not lose heart.
Even though our outward man is perishing,
yet the inward man is being renewed day by day.

2 CORINTHIANS 4:16

AS WE JOURNEY THROUGH life, we may face various challenges, hardships, and even physical weaknesses. However, this verse reminds us not to lose heart. Though our outer selves may experience trials and decay, our inner selves can experience continuous renewal.

This inward renewal is a work of God's grace and transforming power. Through His Holy Spirit, He breathes new life into our spirits, strengthening us from within. It is in this inward renewal that we find the strength, hope, and resilience to face the outer challenges of life.

To tap into this inward renewal, we need to cultivate a close relationship with God through prayer, worship, and the study of His Word. As we surrender ourselves to Him and rely on His strength, He pours out His grace and renews our hearts and minds.

Additionally, we can find strength and encouragement in the community of believers by surrounding ourselves with fellow Christians.

So, let us not lose heart but instead find solace in the inward renewal that comes from God. May we daily seek His presence, allowing Him to restore and revitalize our inner selves, giving us the strength we need to navigate the challenges of life.

REFLECTIVE QUESTION
How can we find strength and hope in the inward renewal that comes from God?

God's Unconditional Love

We love because He first loved us.
1 JOHN 4:19

THE LOVE WE HAVE for others is not self-generated; it originates from God Himself. His love is the wellspring from which our capacity to love flows. When we realize this truth, it transforms our relationships and actions towards others.

Recognizing that God's love is the source of our ability to love humbles us and reminds us of our dependency on Him. It shifts our focus from ourselves to Him, allowing His love to flow through us to touch the lives of those around us.

Understanding that God loved us first also challenges us to extend that same love to others. It compels us to love sacrificially, unconditionally, and selflessly. We can love others not based on their merit but because we have experienced the unconditional love of God.

This truth also frees us from seeking validation or love from others. We can rest in the assurance that we are deeply loved by our Heavenly Father, which gives us the confidence to love others without expecting anything in return.

So, let us embrace the overflow of God's love as the driving force behind our relationships and actions towards others. May His love flow through us, transforming us into vessels of compassion, kindness, and grace.

REFLECTIVE QUESTION
How does recognizing that God's love is the source of our ability to love impact our relationships and actions towards others?

Beyond Words and Actions

Though I speak with the tongues of
men and of angels, but have not love, I have become
sounding brass or a clanging cymbal.

1 CORINTHIANS 13:1

THIS VERSE CHALLENGES US to examine the authenticity and motive behind our words and actions. It reminds us that love should be the driving force behind everything we say and do. Without love, our words and actions become empty and meaningless, like the noise of a gong or a clanging cymbal.

As we reflect on this verse, we are prompted to consider whether our interactions with others are rooted in genuine love. Are we speaking with kindness, compassion, and truth? Do our actions reflect a selfless and sacrificial love that seeks the best for others?

Moreover, this verse invites us to evaluate our hearts and motives. Are we seeking personal recognition or validation through our words and actions? Or are we genuinely seeking to love and serve others without expecting anything in return?

So, let us go beyond empty noise and strive to embody the true essence of love in all that we do. May our words and actions be fueled by a sincere and selfless love that reflects the heart of our Heavenly Father.

REFLECTIVE QUESTION
How does this verse challenge us to examine the authenticity and motive behind our words and actions?

Embracing Humility

For whoever exalts himself will be humbled,
and he who humbles himself will be exalted.

LUKE 14:11

IN THIS VERSE, JESUS teaches us an important lesson about humility. He reminds us that those who exalt themselves, seeking recognition and glory, will ultimately be humbled. On the other hand, those who choose to humble themselves before God and others will be exalted.

Humility is not about thinking less of ourselves but rather thinking of ourselves less. It is an attitude that acknowledges our own limitations and places our trust in God's sovereignty. It involves setting aside our pride, ego, and the need for recognition and instead focusing on serving others with genuine love and compassion.

Practicing humility allows us to build authentic relationships, fosters unity, and opens our hearts to receive God's blessings. It enables us to learn from others, grow in character, and become more like Christ.

Let us reflect on how we can actively embrace humility in our interactions with others, seeking to serve rather than be served. As we do so, we will find that God lifts us up and blesses us beyond measure.

REFLECTIVE QUESTION
How can we cultivate humility in our daily lives?

Seek Knowledge with an Open Heart

A scoffer does not love one who corrects him, nor will he go to the wise.
PROVERB 15:12

IN THIS PROVERB, WE are reminded of the danger of pride and the importance of having a teachable spirit. Those who mock and resent correction tend to distance themselves from those who are wise.

Having a humble and teachable spirit involves recognizing that we don't have all the answers and being open to receiving guidance and correction. It requires setting aside our ego, being willing to admit our mistakes, and being open to learning from others, even if their perspective challenges our own.

To cultivate a teachable spirit, we can develop habits such as seeking wisdom through reading, studying Scripture, and engaging in meaningful conversations with wise and knowledgeable individuals. We must also be willing to reflect on our own actions and attitudes and not shy away from facing areas where we need growth and improvement.

The journey of learning and growing never ends, and it is through humility and openness that we can continue to gain wisdom and be transformed into the person God wants us to be. Let us embrace correction and seek knowledge with an open heart, understanding that it is through humility that we truly grow.

REFLECTIVE QUESTION
How can we cultivate a humble and teachable spirit?

Hope in a Challenging World

Then Jesus spoke to them again, saying,
'I am the light of the world. He who follows Me
shall not walk in darkness, but have the light of life.

JOHN 8:12

IN OUR JOURNEY THROUGH life, we often find ourselves stumbling in the darkness of confusion, doubt, and fear. However, Jesus offers us a divine light that dispels all darkness. He invites us to follow Him and find the path that leads to everlasting life.

Imagine being in a dark forest, unsure of which way to go. Suddenly, a powerful beam of light appears, guiding you through the maze of trees and obstacles, leading you to safety and hope. That is the role Jesus plays in our lives. He is the light that shines in our darkest moments.

To allow Jesus to guide our steps, we must surrender ourselves to His teachings and lean on His wisdom. We can do this by spending time in prayer, studying His Word, and seeking His guidance in every decision. As we allow the light of Jesus to be the compass of our lives, we will walk confidently, knowing that we are securely on the path that leads to eternal life.

Let the Light of the World shine through you today, illuminating the lives of others and leading them to the hope and joy found in Jesus.

REFLECTIVE QUESTION

**How can you allow Jesus, the Light of the World,
to guide your steps and illuminate your path today?**

Committing Our Plans

Commit your works to the Lord,
and your thoughts will be established.
PROVERBS 16:3

IMAGINE A SKILLED ARCHER meticulously aiming for a target. They don't hastily release the arrow but take their time to adjust their aim, ensuring that they are aligned with the bullseye. Similarly, when we commit our plans to the Lord, we seek His guidance, align our desires with His will, and actively involve Him in every decision we make.

Cultivating a habit of committing our plans to the Lord begins with an attitude of humility and surrender. We acknowledge that God's ways are higher than our ways and that His wisdom surpasses our own. Spending time in prayer, seeking His guidance, and studying His Word are essential practices that align us with His perfect plan.

By committing our actions to the Lord, we acknowledge that our success ultimately depends on Him. We trust in His divine guidance, knowing that He will direct our steps and lead us on paths of righteousness. As we faithfully commit our plans to Him, we can rest assured that our actions are aligned with His purpose and that He will bring success in His perfect timing.

Let us be individuals who commit our plans to the Lord, seeking His guidance and trusting in His faithfulness. Through our commitment, we will experience His provision, guidance, and the fulfilment of His plans in our lives.

REFLECTIVE QUESTION
How can you cultivate a habit of committing your plans and actions to the Lord?

The Lord is My Light

**The Lord is my light and my salvation;
Whom shall I fear? The Lord is the strength of my life;
Of whom shall I be afraid?**

PSALM 27:1

IMAGINE WALKING THROUGH A pitch-black room, unsure of what lies ahead. Suddenly, a beam of light illuminates the path before you, providing clarity and safety. The Lord is the light that guides us through the darkness. He reveals the way we should go and assures us that we have nothing to fear.

To live with the assurance that the Lord is our light and salvation, we must nurture a deep relationship with Him. This involves spending time in prayer, seeking His presence, and studying His Word. As we draw near to Him, we will discover His faithfulness, love, and strength that enable us to face our fears with confidence.

When fear attempts to grip our hearts, we can find strength in the Lord, our stronghold. He is our refuge and fortress, ready to protect and shield us from harm. By placing our trust in Him, we can overcome fear and walk in the assurance of His presence and protection.

Let us be individuals who declare with confidence that the Lord is our light and salvation and find strength in Him to face our fears. Through His guidance and strength, we can live victoriously.

REFLECTIVE QUESTION

How can you live with the assurance that the Lord is your light and salvation and find strength in Him to overcome fear?

Transformed by Renewed Thinking

**Do not be conformed to this world,
but be transformed by the renewing of your mind.**
ROMANS 12:2

IMAGINE A GARDEN THAT has been overgrown with weeds, obscuring the beauty and potential of the plants within. To restore the garden to its intended state, diligent effort is required to remove the weeds, nourish the soil, and cultivate growth. In the same way, renewing our minds involves intentionally uprooting negative thoughts, nourishing our minds with God's Word, and cultivating a mindset that aligns with His will.

Actively renewing our minds begins with immersing ourselves in Scripture, meditating on its truths, and seeking the Holy Spirit's guidance in understanding and applying God's Word to our lives. Prayer, worship, and fellowship with other believers also contribute to the renewal process. As we engage in these practices, our thinking is transformed, enabling us to discern and align ourselves with God's good, pleasing, and perfect will.

Living a transformed life requires a constant dedication to renewing our minds. It means consciously choosing to reject the patterns of this world and allowing God's Word and Spirit to shape our thoughts, desires, and actions. By doing so, we gain a clearer perspective on what is truly important.

Let us be individuals who actively engage in the process of renewing our minds, seeking to align our thoughts and desires with God's perfect will.

REFLECTIVE QUESTION
How can you actively renew your mind to align your thoughts and desires with God's perfect will?

The Nearness of a Faithful God

The Lord is near to all who call upon Him,
to all who call upon Him in truth.
PSALM 145:18

IMAGINE HAVING A CLOSE friend whom you can call at any time, knowing they will listen, understand, and provide support. That is the kind of relationship we can have with God. He is always ready to listen to our prayers, understand our deepest needs and desires, and provide comfort, guidance, and strength.

Cultivating a genuine and earnest relationship with God begins with an open heart and a sincere desire to seek Him. We can do this through prayer, spending intentional time in His presence, studying His Word, and actively living out our faith. It is through these practices that we deepen our connection with God and experience the reality of His nearness.

As we seek God in truth, we come to understand His character and His faithfulness. We learn to trust Him more fully, knowing that He is attentive to our prayers and intimately involved in every aspect of our lives. In turn, this knowledge strengthens our faith and encourages us to continually draw near to Him.

REFLECTIVE QUESTION
How can you cultivate a genuine and earnest relationship with God, knowing that He is near and attentive to those who seek Him?

The Power of a Simple 'Yes' or 'No'

But let your 'Yes' be 'Yes,' and your 'No,' 'No.' For whatever is more than these is from the evil one.

MATTHEW 5:37

IN A WORLD WHERE promises are easily broken, and words can be deceptive, Matthew 5:37 reminds us of the importance of integrity and consistency in our communication. Jesus encourages us to let our "Yes" mean yes and our "No" mean no, embracing truthfulness and sincerity in all our interactions.

Cultivating integrity and consistency begins by seeking God's guidance in every aspect of our lives, including our speech and actions. Through prayer, studying His Word, and relying on the Holy Spirit's guidance, we can align our thoughts and desires with God's truth. As we surrender to His wisdom, His truth seeps into our hearts and transforms our words and actions.

Letting our "Yes" be yes and our "No" be no requires a commitment to living honestly and authentically. It means being accountable for our words and actions, taking ownership of our commitments, and honouring our promises. By doing so, we reflect the character of a reliable and trustworthy God.

Let us be individuals who cultivate integrity and consistency in our words and actions, aligning them with God's truth. Through our commitment to truthfulness and sincerity, we become vessels of His grace, love, and reliability to a world in need of authentic examples of faith.

REFLECTIVE QUESTION

How can you cultivate integrity and consistency in your words and actions?

Rooted and Built Up in Christ

As you therefore have received Christ Jesus the Lord,
so walk in Him, rooted and built up in Him and
established in the faith, as you have been taught,
abounding in it with thanksgiving.
COLOSSIANS 2:6-7

IN OUR JOURNEY OF faith, it is crucial to not only receive Christ Jesus as Lord but also to continue living our lives in Him. Colossians 2:6-7 reminds us to be deeply rooted in Christ, allowing our lives to be built upon His truth and love. As we do so, we are strengthened in our faith and become sources of overflowing thankfulness.

Living a life rooted and built up in Christ involves daily seeking His presence through prayer, studying His Word, and actively applying His teachings in our lives. It means surrendering our will and desires to His lordship, trusting in His guidance, and relying on His strength. As we do so, our faith is strengthened, and we experience the transformative power of His love and grace.

Overflowing with thankfulness is a natural response to a life rooted in Christ. When we recognize His goodness, faithfulness, and blessings in our lives, gratitude overflows from our hearts. Gratitude not only changes our perspective but also inspires others to seek a relationship with the One who is the source of all blessings.

REFLECTIVE QUESTION
How can you actively live a life that is rooted and built up in Christ, strengthened in faith and overflowing with thankfulness?

Fear Not

Fear not, for I am with you; be not dismayed,
for I am your God. I will strengthen you,
Yes, I will help you, I will uphold you with
my righteous right hand.

ISAIAH 41:10

IN THIS POWERFUL VERSE, God assures us of His unending presence and support in our lives. He encourages us to let go of fear and discouragement, for He is our God and will be there for us, offering strength and assistance whenever we need it.

Remember, when we face challenges, it is easy to become anxious and overwhelmed. However, Isaiah 41:10 reminds us that God's promise to strengthen us is unwavering. We have a divine ally who will uplift us and carry us through the storms of life.

In times of fear and uncertainty, we can turn to God through prayer, seeking His guidance, and finding solace in His word. Take a moment to reflect on a recent experience where you felt God's strength and support. What steps can you take to increase your reliance on His promise in the future?

May this verse serve as a constant reminder of God's unfailing love and power in our lives, providing us with the strength and courage to face any situation that comes our way.

REFLECTIVE QUESTION
How can you lean on God's promise of strength in times of fear and uncertainty?

Build a Solid Faith Foundation

**If the foundations are destroyed,
what can the righteous do?**

PSALMS 11:3

THE IMAGERY OF FOUNDATIONS being destroyed refers to the challenges, doubts, and trials that can shake our faith. Yet, the verse also emphasizes that even in these moments, there is hope for the righteous.

Just as a building needs a strong foundation to withstand storms, our faith requires a solid base. We can establish this by nourishing our relationship with God through prayer, studying His Word, participating in worship, and surrounding ourselves with fellow believers who encourage and support us. These practices help us deepen our understanding of God's character, His promises, and His unchanging love.

When we build our faith on these enduring foundations, it becomes resilient to the doubts and uncertainties that may seek to undermine it. Our faith becomes a source of refuge, providing us with strength and guidance even in the darkest of times.

So, let us examine the foundations upon which our faith stands. Are they firm and unshakeable, or are they susceptible to the winds of adversity? By intentionally fortifying our faith, we can navigate life's challenges with confidence and find solace in God's unwavering presence.

REFLECTIVE QUESTION

How can we ensure that our faith is built on solid foundations?

Embracing Forgiveness

Bearing with one another, and forgiving one another,
if anyone has a complaint against another;
even as Christ forgave you, so you also must do.

COLOSSIANS 3:13

FORGIVENESS IS A CORNERSTONE of our faith, as it mirrors God's forgiveness towards us. By extending forgiveness to others, we not only reflect Christ's love but also experience freedom from the burden of resentment and grudges.

Cultivating a spirit of forgiveness begins with recognizing the great forgiveness we have received through Christ. When we grasp the enormity of our own forgiven sins, it becomes easier to extend forgiveness to others. We can also seek guidance from the Holy Spirit, who empowers us to forgive and heal broken relationships.

Additionally, it is important to remember that forgiveness does not mean condoning or forgetting the wrongdoing. It is a conscious decision to release the anger and bitterness, allowing God's grace to work in both our hearts and the hearts of those we forgive.

By embracing forgiveness, we become agents of reconciliation and witness to the transformative power of Christ. As we release the burden of unforgiveness, we can experience the peace and joy that comes from living in harmony with others.

So, let us reflect on our own capacity for forgiveness. Are there any grievances we need to release? May we embrace the call to forgive as the Lord forgave us and experience the freedom and restoration that forgiveness brings.

REFLECTIVE QUESTION
**How can we cultivate a spirit of forgiveness
in our lives?**

We Need Each Other

*That is, that I may be encouraged together
with you by the mutual faith both of you and me.*
ROMANS 1:12

IN ROMANS 1:12, THE Apostle Paul expresses his desire to visit the Church in Rome to encourage them and be encouraged by their faith. This verse highlights the importance of community and the impact it can have on our spiritual journey.

Living in a community with fellow believers provides an opportunity for us to grow in our faith and draw strength from one another. When we surround ourselves with people who share a common goal of following Christ, we can inspire and motivate one another to stay faithful and persevere through challenges.

Whether it's attending church services, joining a small group, or participating in service projects, engaging with a community of believers allows us to share our joys, struggles, and questions. Through our interactions, we can offer support, wisdom, and encouragement to one another.

By investing in relationships within our faith community, we create a space where we can be vulnerable, celebrated, and uplifted. Together, we can face life's trials, celebrate triumphs, and ultimately grow in our faith journey.

So, take the step today to actively participate in a community of faith. Not only will you be mutually encouraged, but you will also have the opportunity to encourage and uplift others in their walk with God.

REFLECTIVE QUESTION

How can you actively participate in a community of faith to mutually encourage and be encouraged by others?

Living with Purpose

But none of these things move me; nor do I count my life
dear to myself, so that I may finish my race with joy, and
the ministry which I received from the Lord Jesus,
to testify to the gospel of the grace of God.

ACTS 20:24

LIVING WITH PURPOSE MEANS seeking God's will for our lives
and actively pursuing the tasks He has assigned us. It involves
recognizing that our lives have a greater meaning beyond our
personal ambitions and desires. Just as Paul dedicated himself to
the task of testifying to God's grace, we, too, are called to share
the good news with those around us.

To align our lives with God's mission, we can start by seeking
His guidance and spending time in prayer and studying His Word.
By surrendering our plans and desires to Him, we open ourselves
up to His leadership and direction. We can also ask ourselves
how we can be a vessel of grace and love to those around us.

Living with purpose requires intentionality and a willingness
to let go of our own agendas. When we align our lives with God's
mission, we find true fulfilment and joy in knowing that we are
part of something greater than ourselves.

So, let us embrace God's mission in our lives today, seeking
ways to testify to His grace and share the good news with those
around us.

REFLECTIVE QUESTION
**What steps can you take today to align your life
with God's mission and testify to His grace?**

Serving with Faithfulness

Having then gifts differing according to the grace
that is given to us, let us use them: if prophecy,
let us prophesy in proportion to our faith;

ROMANS 12:6

IDENTIFYING OUR GIFTS BEGINS with prayerful reflection and seeking God's guidance. We can examine the areas in which we feel passionate, skilled, and energized. Our gifts may be in areas such as teaching, leadership, craftsmanship, creativity, compassion, or administration. It's important to remember that our gifts are not for our own glory but to build up the Church and bring glory to God.

Once identified, we can begin using our gifts by serving others within our Church, community, and the world at large. This may involve volunteering, mentoring, using our talents in worship services, organizing events, or contributing to ministries that align with our gifts.

Faithfulness in using our gifts means being consistent and steadfast, even when the tasks seem small or go unnoticed. It means using our gifts with integrity, humility, and a genuine love for others. When we faithfully use our gifts, we participate in God's work, and He can accomplish mighty things through us.

Let us embark on a journey of discovering and utilizing our God-given gifts, serving others faithfully with the unique abilities He has blessed us with. May our lives be a testament to His grace and love, bringing transformation, hope, and joy to those around us.

REFLECTIVE QUESTION

How can you identify and use your God-given gifts to serve others faithfully?

A New Thinking Pattern

Casting down arguments and every high thing
that exalts itself against the knowledge of God,
and bringing every thought into captivity
to the obedience of Christ.

2 CORINTHIANS 10:5

TAKING CAPTIVE OUR THOUGHTS involves being intentional about what we allow to occupy our minds. It means recognizing and rejecting thoughts that contradict the knowledge of God and His Word. We can accomplish this by immersing ourselves in Scripture, meditating on its truth, and seeking the guidance of the Holy Spirit.

Paying attention to our thought patterns and being aware of negative or harmful thoughts allows us to replace them with thoughts that are true, noble, right, pure, lovely, admirable, excellent, and praiseworthy (Philippians 4:8). We can also seek accountability and surround ourselves with fellow believers who can help us stay focused on Christ.

Renewing our minds is a continuous process. It requires discipline, prayer, and surrendering our thoughts to God. As we align our thinking with His truth, we experience transformation, growth, and a deeper intimacy with Him.

Let us be proactive in taking captive our thoughts, ensuring they are obedient to Christ. As we guard our minds and renew them in His truth, we can live victoriously, with minds focused on God's purposes and filled with His peace.

REFLECTIVE QUESTION
**How can you actively take captive your thoughts
and align them with the truth of Christ?**

Watchful and Prayerful

Watch and pray, lest you enter into temptation.
The spirit indeed is willing, but the flesh is weak.
MATTHEW 26:41

TO CULTIVATE WATCHFULNESS, we need to be aware of our surroundings and the potential triggers that may lead us astray. It involves being mindful of the influences we allow into our lives, such as media, relationships, or habits that may have a negative impact on our faith. Regular self-examination and accountability can help us identify areas of weakness and take necessary precautions.

Prayer becomes our lifeline in the battle against temptation. By committing our struggles, fears, and desires to God in prayer, we invite His presence and guidance into our lives. We can ask Him for strength, wisdom, and discernment to navigate the temptations that come our way.

Creating a habit of prayer and developing a personal relationship with God equips us with the spiritual armour necessary to resist temptation. Through prayer, we draw closer to God, and His power strengthens us, enabling us to overcome the fleshly desires that seek to pull us away from Him.

Heed Jesus' admonition to watch and pray. With vigilant hearts and a commitment to prayer, we can find strength in our weaknesses and victory over temptation, relying on God's grace and guidance each step of the way.

REFLECTIVE QUESTION
How can you cultivate a lifestyle of watchfulness and prayer to guard against temptation?

Embracing God's Guidance

**Happy is the man who finds wisdom
and the man who gains understanding.**
PROVERBS 3:13

SEEKING GOD'S WISDOM BEGINS with a posture of humility and a willingness to acknowledge our need for His guidance. We can cultivate this through regular prayer, study of Scripture, and seeking wise counsel from mature believers.

Applying God's wisdom involves aligning our thoughts, actions, and decisions with His principles and truth. It means seeking His perspective before making choices, seeking to understand His will instead of relying solely on our own understanding. As we do this, we experience the fruit of wisdom in our lives and find ourselves walking in alignment with God's purposes.

Wisdom is not merely intellectual knowledge but also the ability to discern and apply that knowledge in practical ways. It impacts how we navigate relationships, make decisions, manage our time, handle conflicts, and pursue our goals.

When we actively seek and apply God's wisdom, we experience a life that is marked by blessings, peace, and fulfilment. We gain a deeper understanding of God's character and purposes, and we are better equipped to navigate the complexities of life with His guidance.

Embrace the blessing of wisdom by seeking, gaining, and applying God's wisdom in every area of our lives. May your pursuit of wisdom reflect your desire to honour God and draw closer to Him each day.

REFLECTIVE QUESTION
How can you actively seek and apply God's wisdom in your daily decisions and interactions?

Blossom Where You are Planted

Then Isaac sowed in that land,
and reaped in the same year a hundredfold;
and the Lord blessed him.

GENESIS 26:12

ISAAC'S STORY TEACHES US the importance of obedience and faith in God's promises. He trusted in God's guidance and chose to sow seeds, even when it seemed illogical in the midst of a famine. This demonstrates the power of stepping out in faith, believing that God can bring abundant fruit even in seemingly unfavourable situations.

Trusting in God's provision requires surrendering our plans and desires to His will. It means seeking His guidance and relying on His wisdom instead of relying solely on our own understanding. It involves being open to unexpected directions and opportunities that He may present to us.

In challenging seasons, our faith is tested. Yet, by trusting in God's sovereignty and leaning on His promises, we can take courageous steps. We can sow seeds of faith, kindness, and generosity, knowing that God's blessing is not limited by external circumstances.

As we faithfully follow God's lead, we may experience His provision and blessings in ways we never imagined. Like Isaac, we can flourish even in the midst of seemingly barren times.

Let us trust in God's provision and faithfully follow His lead, believing that He can bring abundance even in the most challenging seasons of our lives. May we sow seeds of faith, knowing that God's blessing awaits us.

REFLECTIVE QUESTION

How can you trust in God's provision and follow His lead, even in challenging seasons?

Embracing Our Identity

For you did not receive the spirit of bondage
again to fear, but you received the Spirit of adoption
by whom we cry out, "Abba, Father."

ROMANS 8:15

EMBRACING OUR IDENTITY AS children of God starts with renewing our minds and aligning our thoughts with the truth of Scripture. We must let go of the lies and fears that try to separate us from God's love and instead embrace the reality that we are deeply loved and accepted by Him.

Daily prayer and intimate communion with God enable us to experience His love and presence in our lives. By cultivating a personal relationship with Him, we can confidently approach Him as our loving Father, knowing that He desires a closeness with us.

Living out our identity involves walking in the freedom that Christ has provided. This means letting go of the burdens of guilt, shame, and self-condemnation and receiving the forgiveness and grace offered to us through Jesus. As children of God, we are empowered to live with confidence, purpose, and hope.

Let us fully embrace our identity as children of God, living in the freedom and love that comes from our Heavenly Father. May we walk confidently, knowing that we are deeply loved and accepted, and may our lives reflect the joy and transformation that can only come from being in His family.

REFLECTIVE QUESTION
How can you embrace your identity as a child of God and experience the freedom and love that comes with it?

Finding Strength in the Wilderness

Now when the tempter came to Him (Jesus),
he said, "If You are the Son of God, command that
these stones become bread.
MATTHEW 4:3

THE WILDERNESS REPRESENTS A period of struggle, isolation, and vulnerability. Just as Jesus found himself in the wilderness, we, too, may face difficult seasons in our lives. The devil's temptation reminds us that we may be tempted to compromise our values and seek immediate gratification when we encounter hardship.

However, Jesus responds to the devil's temptation by relying on God's Word, saying, "Man shall not live by bread alone, but by every word that comes from the mouth of God." This teaches us the importance of grounding ourselves in Scripture and seeking spiritual nourishment during times of trial.

By following Jesus' example, we can find strength in the wilderness. Instead of succumbing to temptations, we can draw closer to God, trust in His promises, and rely on His guidance. In doing so, we will emerge from the wilderness with a deeper understanding of God's faithfulness and a strengthened spirit.

Through this passage, we are encouraged to persevere, hold firm to our beliefs, and seek sustenance from God's Word when faced with challenges.

REFLECTIVE QUESTION
How can we use this passage to navigate our own temptations and find strength in challenging times?

Ask, Seek and Knock

Ask, and it will be given to you;
seek, and you will find; knock,
and it will be opened to you.

MATTHEW 7:7

JESUS ENCOURAGES US TO approach God with confidence, knowing that He delights in hearing and answering our prayers. The verbs "ask," "seek," and "knock" suggest an active and persistent engagement with God. Through prayer, we have the privilege of communing with the Creator of the universe, pouring out our hearts and presenting our needs before Him.

This passage reminds us that prayer is not just a mere request for material blessings but a means of deepening our relationship with God. It is through persistent prayer that we draw closer to Him, seek His will, and align our desires with His purposes.

As we persistently pray, we not only experience answers to our specific requests but also grow in faith, trust, and dependence on God. We learn to surrender our will to His and to seek His guidance in all aspects of our lives.

By embracing the promise of persistent prayer, we invite God to work in and through us, transforming our lives and bringing us into a deeper relationship with Him.

REFLECTIVE QUESTION
How can we apply this promise of persistent prayer to our own lives and deepen our relationship with God?

Seeking Wisdom Above All Else

And Solomon loved the Lord,
walking in the statutes of his father David,
except that he sacrificed and burned incense
at the high places.

1 KINGS 3:3

THIS VERSE HIGHLIGHTS SOLOMON'S desire to follow in his father's footsteps, but it also reveals a flaw. Despite his devotion to God, he continued the practice of offering sacrifices in the high places, which was not in accordance with God's instructions. However, this verse is just the beginning of Solomon's journey, and we see his growth and wisdom develop throughout the rest of the chapter.

As we reflect on Solomon's journey, it challenges us to evaluate our own lives and the areas where we may be compromising our commitment to God. It reminds us that seeking wisdom, above all else, is essential in our pursuit of spiritual growth.

Let us learn from Solomon's example and seek God's wisdom in every decision we make. Through prayer, reading Scripture, and seeking wise counsel, we can align our lives with God's instructions and experience the blessings that come from walking in obedience. May our love for the Lord be evident in every aspect of our lives as we strive to follow His ways wholeheartedly.

Remember, seeking wisdom is a lifelong journey, and each day is an opportunity to grow closer to God. So, let us commit ourselves to seek His wisdom above all else.

REFLECTIVE QUESTION

Are there any areas in your life where you may be compromising your commitment to God's instructions?

Favour With God and Men

**And the child Samuel grew in stature,
and in favour both with the Lord and men.**
1 SAMUEL 2:26

SAMUEL'S EXAMPLE INSPIRES US to prioritize our relationship with God and invest in our personal development. Just as Samuel continues to grow in stature and favour, we, too, can cultivate a strong bond with God and build healthy relationships with those around us.

To grow in favour with God, we must devote time to prayer, study the Scriptures, and seek His guidance in all aspects of our lives. Our commitment to living according to His principles and seeking His will leads to spiritual growth and favour in His eyes.

In building favour with others, we can practice love, kindness, and empathy. By treating others with respect, serving selflessly, and fostering positive relationships, we can create a ripple effect of goodwill and gain favour in the eyes of our fellow humans.

Let us follow Samuel's example and strive to grow in favour with God and others. As we invest in our relationship with God and prioritize building healthy connections with those around us, we can experience a life of fulfilment, impact, and blessing. Remember, each day is an opportunity for growth and favour.

REFLECTIVE QUESTION
In what ways can you intentionally grow in favour with God and others?

Seeking God's Strength in Our Weakness

For the eyes of the Lord run to and fro throughout the whole earth to show Himself strong on behalf of those whose heart is loyal to Him. In this you have done foolishly; therefore from now on you shall have wars.

2 CHRONICLES 16:9

ARE WE FULLY DEVOTED to God, or are there areas of our lives where we are holding back? Surrendering our hearts completely to God allows us to experience His strength and provision in our times of weakness.

In our weaknesses, we often find ourselves turning to our own abilities or seeking help from others. While it is vital to seek support from trusted friends and mentors, we must never forget that true strength comes from God alone. He is the one who can provide us with the resilience, wisdom, and guidance we need.

Let us strive to be individuals whose hearts are fully committed to God. By placing our trust in Him, we can receive His strength and be empowered to face any challenge that comes our way. As we lean on His power rather than our own, we can experience the abundant life He has promised us.

Remember, God's eyes are constantly searching for those who are fully committed to Him. Let us be that person and allow His strength to be made perfect in our weakness.

REFLECTIVE QUESTION

How can you deepen your commitment to God and open yourself to His strength in your weakness?

Created For His Purpose

**You are worthy, O Lord, to receive glory and honour
and power; for you created all things,
And by Your will they exist and were created.**
REVELATION 4:11

THIS VERSE INVITES US to reflect on the immense power and glory of God as the Creator of all things. It reminds us that everything exists because of His will and purpose. In our daily lives, it is essential to recognize and honour God's majesty and authority.

We can honour and worship God by acknowledging His sovereignty, expressing gratitude for His creation, and living in accordance with His will. Our actions and attitudes should reflect our understanding of God's power and the privilege we have to exist in His creation.

Let us contemplate the following: How can we actively incorporate an attitude of worship and honour towards God in our everyday lives? How can we intentionally praise Him for His creations and acknowledge His authority in all areas of our existence?

Take a moment today to offer a prayer of praise and thanksgiving to the Creator of all things, and seek His guidance on how to honour Him more fully each day.

REFLECTIVE QUESTION
How can we honour and worship God in our daily lives?

Abundance

You crown the year with your goodness,
And Your paths drip with abundance.
PSALMS 65:11

PSALM 65:11 REMINDS US that God is a generous provider who blesses us with abundance. He crowns each year with His goodness and fills our lives with His overflowing bounty. Reflecting on this truth, we are called to cultivate a heart of gratitude for the blessings God bestows upon us.

Often, it's easy to take these blessings for granted or overlook them amidst the busyness of life. However, when we intentionally focus on the numerous ways God has provided for us, gratitude flows naturally from our hearts.

Today, let's contemplate how we can cultivate a heart of gratitude. Consider keeping a gratitude journal, where you can jot down daily blessings and express appreciation to God. Take time to reflect on the specific ways God has blessed you recently and offer a prayer of gratitude.

Furthermore, an attitude of gratitude prompts us to share our blessings with others. How can we extend God's abundant blessings to those in need? Reflect on ways to be a channel of His love and provision to others.

Let the words of Psalm 65:11 inspire you to seek the richness of God's blessings and foster an attitude of gratitude in your daily life.

REFLECTIVE QUESTION
How can we cultivate a heart of gratitude for the abundant blessings God provides?

Make Your Next Move a Spirit Move

For as many as are led by the Spirit of God,
these are sons of God.

ROMANS 8:14

AS BELIEVERS, WE HAVE been adopted into God's family. Through Christ, we are no longer slaves to fear or sin but children of the Most High. With this new identity, we are called to live in a way that reflects our Father's character and love.

Embracing our identity as children of God transforms the way we view ourselves and the world around us. It means we can approach each day with confidence, knowing that we are loved, accepted, and guided by our Heavenly Father.

Living as children of God involves following the leading of the Holy Spirit. Through prayer and the study of God's Word, we can discern His voice and allow Him to guide our thoughts, words, and actions. We can experience the freedom and joy that come from living in alignment with our divine inheritance.

So, let us strive to embrace our identity as children of God today and every day. Let us walk in the Spirit, allowing His guidance to shape our lives and bring glory to our Heavenly Father.

REFLECTIVE QUESTION

How can you intentionally live as a child of God today? What steps can you take to seek the leading of the Holy Spirit in your daily life?

Longing for Intimacy

Draw me away! We will run after you.
The king has brought me into his chambers.
We will be glad and rejoice in you. We will remember
your love more than wine. Rightly do they love you.
SONG OF SOLOMON 1:4

HAVE YOU EVER FELT a longing deep within your soul for profound intimacy? The Shulammite woman's desire to be drawn close to her beloved speaks to our own longing for a deep and meaningful connection. In our spiritual journey, we seek a closeness with God that fulfils our deepest needs and desires.

Just as the Shulammite woman desires to be brought into the chambers of her king, we, too, yearn to be drawn into the presence of our heavenly King. We long for a sacred space where we can experience the fullness of God's love and grace.

Take a moment to reflect on your own longing for intimacy with God. How can you draw closer to Him? Is there anything holding you back from entering into a deeper relationship with Him?

Let this verse remind you of the invitation to run after God, seeking His presence and allowing Him to draw you close. May you find the fulfilling intimacy your soul desires as you pursue a deeper relationship with the King of Kings.

REFLECTIVE QUESTION
How does the Shulammite woman's longing for intimacy with her beloved reflect our own longing for a deeper relationship with God?

A Heart Transformed

I will give you a new heart and put a new spirit
within you; I will take the heart of stone out of your
flesh and give you a heart of flesh.

EZEKIEL 36:26

HAVE YOU EVER FELT as though your heart has become hardened
by the challenges and trials of life? The promise in Ezekiel 36:26
gives us hope that God can transform our hearts and make them
soft and receptive to His love and guidance.

A heart of stone is unyielding and resistant to change, but a
heart of flesh is tender, compassionate, and open to the work
of the Holy Spirit. When we surrender our hearts to God, He
begins the beautiful process of transforming them.

Take a moment to reflect on your own heart. Are there areas
where you feel hardness or resistance? Are there areas where you
need God's transformative touch?

Allow this verse to remind you of God's unconditional love and
grace. His desire is to remove the hardness from your heart and
replace it with a heart that is responsive to His leading. May you
experience the transforming power of God's love as He shapes
your heart into one that reflects His character.

REFLECTIVE QUESTION
**How does the transformation of a heart of stone
into a heart of flesh remind us of God's love and
grace in our lives?**

Running the Race

Do you not know that those who run in a race all run,
but one receives the prize? Run in such a way
that you may obtain it.

1 CORINTHIANS 9:24

LIFE CAN SOMETIMES FEEL like a race, filled with challenges, obstacles, and the need for endurance. The analogy that Paul presents in this verse reminds us of the importance of staying focused and committed to our spiritual journey.

Just as runners train diligently, sacrifice their comfort, and push through fatigue, we, too, are called to persevere in our walk of faith. The prize that awaits us is not a temporary earthly reward but an eternal one – the crown of righteousness and life in Christ.

Reflect on your own spiritual race. Are there moments where you feel weary or discouraged? Are there areas in your life where you need to renew your commitment to Christ?

As you run the race of faith, remember to rely on God's strength, not your own. Embrace discipline, perseverance, and a deep devotion to your relationship with God. With His help, you can overcome any obstacle and obtain the eternal prize that awaits. Keep running with endurance, my friend, and fix your eyes on Jesus, the ultimate prize.

REFLECTIVE QUESTION

How can we apply the principles of perseverance and discipline from running a physical race to our spiritual lives?

Strength in Weakness

And He said to me, "My grace is sufficient for you,
for My strength is made perfect in weakness...

2 CORINTHIANS 12:9

IN A WORLD THAT often celebrates strength and self-sufficiency, the concept of finding power in weakness may seem counterintuitive. However, the truth of God's Word reveals that it is in our weakness that His strength is most prominently displayed.

By acknowledging our own limitations and embracing our weaknesses, we position ourselves to experience the fullness of God's grace. It is in these moments of vulnerability and dependency that we can truly rely on His power and allow Him to work in and through us.

Take a moment to reflect on areas of your life where you may feel weak or inadequate. How can you surrender those areas to God and invite His power to be manifested?

Remember, it is not our own strength or abilities that bring about transformation; it is God's grace working in us. As we humble ourselves and rely on Him, His power is made perfect in our weakness. May you find comfort and strength in knowing that God's grace is sufficient for you and that His power is available for you in every circumstance.

REFLECTIVE QUESTION

How can embracing our weaknesses and relying on God's grace allow His power to be manifested in our lives?

Counting the Cost

**For which of you, intending to build a tower,
does not sit down first and count the cost,
whether he has enough to finish it.**

LUKE 14:28

FOLLOWING JESUS IS A journey that requires commitment and sacrifice. Just as a wise builder counts the cost before constructing a tower, we, too, must evaluate the cost of discipleship and faithfully consider the implications of committing our lives to Christ.

Jesus calls us to follow Him wholeheartedly, surrender our will, and align ourselves with His purpose. As we count the cost, we must be willing to let go of our own desires, lay down our ambitions, and embrace a life of selfless service to God and others.

Take a moment to reflect on your own commitment to following Jesus. Are there areas where you need to count the cost anew? Are there sacrifices you need to make or areas of your life that need to be surrendered?

Remember, the cost of following Jesus is high, but the rewards are immeasurable. When we willingly count the cost and lay our lives before Him, we experience the joys of knowing Him intimately, walking in His purpose, and receiving eternal life. May you wholeheartedly count the cost and follow Jesus with unwavering commitment and devotion.

REFLECTIVE QUESTION

How can the principle of counting the cost of building a tower be applied to our spiritual lives and commitment to following Jesus?

A Firm Foundation

Nevertheless, the solid foundation of God stands,
having this seal: "The Lord knows those who are His,"
and, "Let everyone who names the name of
Christ depart from iniquity.
2 TIMOTHY 2:19

IN A WORLD THAT is constantly shifting and changing, it is comforting to know that our faith has a solid foundation in Jesus Christ. God's firm foundation stands unshakable and secure, providing us with stability, assurance, and a sense of belonging.x

Knowing that the Lord knows those who are His brings a deep sense of comfort and security. We are not just nameless faces in the crowd but cherished and known by the Creator of the universe. This knowledge should shape our actions, choices, and priorities.

Reflect on your own life. How does the understanding of being known by God impact your decisions and behaviour? Are there areas where you need to align your life more closely with His will?

As we embrace the reality of God's firm foundation in our lives, we are called to depart from iniquity and live in a way that reflects our identity as His children. May you find strength and confidence in knowing that you are firmly rooted in Christ, navigating life's challenges with faith and obedience.

REFLECTIVE QUESTION
How does the understanding of God's firm foundation impact the way we live and navigate the challenges of this world?

Don't Give Up

**But you, be strong and do not let your hands be weak,
for your work shall be rewarded!**

2 CHRONICLES 15:7

THERE ARE TIMES IN life when we may feel overwhelmed, discouraged, or weary in our faith journey. In those moments, we can find solace and inspiration in the words spoken by Azariah. We are reminded to take courage, to strengthen our resolve, and to persevere in the work set before us.

It is essential to remember that our efforts in serving God and living out our faith will not go unnoticed or unrewarded. God sees our faithfulness, our obedience, and our labour of love. He promises to reward us, whether in this life or the next.

Reflect on your own life and the challenges you may be facing. How can you take courage and strengthen your hands in the work God has called you to do? Are there areas where you need to renew your trust in His promises?

May the words of Azariah echo in our hearts as an encouragement to press on, to not grow weary, and to remain steadfast in our service to God. Let us take courage, knowing that our work, done with love and faithfulness, will be rewarded by the One who sees and values our efforts.

REFLECTIVE QUESTION

How does the encouragement to take courage and not let our hands be weak resonate with you in your current circumstances?

Cast Your Burdens on Him

Cast your burden on the Lord,
and He shall sustain you; He shall never
permit the righteous to be moved.

PSALM 55:22

LIFE OFTEN PRESENTS US with burdens and challenges that can weigh us down and leave us feeling overwhelmed. In these moments, the psalmist encourages us to cast our burdens onto God, knowing that He will sustain us with His unfailing strength and unending love.

Reflect on the burdens you are carrying today. Are there worries, anxieties, or difficult circumstances that you are holding onto? Take a moment to release them into God's capable hands, allowing Him to bear the weight.

As we cast our burdens upon the Lord, we experience the freedom and peace that come from trusting in His provision. He promises to sustain us through every trial and difficulty, providing us with the strength we need to endure.

Remember, the Lord will never allow the righteous to be moved. As you entrust your burdens to Him, allow His presence to bring stability to your life, knowing that He is faithful to carry you through.

May you find solace and strength in the promise of Psalm 55:22, and may you experience the sustaining power of God as you cast your burdens upon Him.

REFLECTIVE QUESTION
What burdens are you carrying today that you need to release and entrust to the Lord? How can you experience His sustaining power in the midst of your challenges?

Unveiled Faces

Therefore, since we have such hope,
we use great boldness of speech—
2 CORINTHIANS 3:12

AS BELIEVERS IN CHRIST, we have a living hope that transcends the difficulties and uncertainties of this world. This hope is not based on our own achievements or merits but on the finished work of Jesus on the cross. It is this hope that gives us the confidence to live boldly and authentically.

When we understand and embrace our identity as children of God, we are liberated from the pressure of trying to earn His love or approval. We can approach Him with unveiled faces, fully known and fully accepted.

Reflect on your own life. How does the hope you have in Christ impact the way you live and interact with others? Are there areas where you can be bolder in sharing your faith or stepping out in obedience?

As we cultivate a deep sense of hope in Christ, we are emboldened to live as authentic witnesses of His goodness and grace. We can walk confidently, knowing that His love covers us and empowers us to impact the world around us. May you embrace the hope you have in Christ and live boldly, shining His light in every area of your life.

REFLECTIVE QUESTION

How does the hope we have in Christ empower us to live boldly and authentically in our faith?

Growing in Grace

But grow in grace, and the knowledge of our
Lord and Saviour Jesus Christ. To him be glory
both now and forever. Amen.

2 PETER 3:18

AS FOLLOWERS OF CHRIST, our journey is not just about accepting His grace but also about growing in it. In 2 Peter 3:18, we are encouraged to continually expand in both the grace and knowledge of our Lord and Savior Jesus Christ. Just as a tree grows by absorbing nutrients from the soil, our spiritual growth is fueled by immersing ourselves in God's grace.

Is there an area of your life where you need to rely more on His grace and let go of self-reliance? Growing in grace means deepening our understanding of God's love, mercy, and forgiveness. It involves allowing His grace to shape our attitudes, actions, and relationships. It also means extending that grace to others, just as Christ has extended it to us.

Finding time for personal reflection and study, joining a Bible study group, or seeking guidance from a mentor can all aid in nurturing our growth in grace. Additionally, embracing a spirit of humility and seeking God's presence through prayer and meditation can help us grow in our relationship with Him.

Let us pursue this journey of growing in grace, knowing that as we grow nearer to Him, we will experience His transformative power in our lives.

REFLECTIVE QUESTION
How can you actively pursue growth in God's grace today?

Choosing the Path of Blessing

Blessed is the man who walks not in the counsel
of the ungodly, Nor stands in the path of sinners,
Nor sits in the seat of the scornful.

PSALMS 1:1

THIS VERSE INVITES US to reflect on the choices we make in our daily lives. It highlights theo path of blessing, emphasizing the importance of avoiding the influence of the wicked, sinners, and mockers. But what does it mean to walk in step with the wicked, stand in the way of sinners, or sit in the company of mockers?

Walking in step with the wicked refers to aligning ourselves with values and actions that are contrary to God's principles. Standing in the way of sinners implies actively participating in sinful activities while sitting in the company of mockers suggests surrounding ourselves with those who scorn or belittle spiritual matters.

To cultivate a life rooted in God's Word, we must be intentional about the company we keep, the choices we make, and the priorities we set. It involves seeking God's guidance through prayer, studying His Word, and surrounding ourselves with like-minded individuals.

Take a moment to reflect on the choices you make in your daily life. Are they aligning with God's Word? How can you further cultivate a life rooted in His truth?

Remember, choosing the path of blessing involves daily decisions that align with God's truth.

REFLECTIVE QUESTION
How can I cultivate a life that is rooted in God's Word?

Prosperity in Integrity

When his master saw that the Lord was with him and that the Lord gave him success in everything he did...

EPHESIANS 2:10

JOSEPH FOUND HIMSELF IN a foreign land as a slave, serving in the house of Potiphar. However, he didn't allow his circumstances to define him. He chose to trust in God's plan and maintain his integrity, regardless of the challenges that came his way.

Despite being a slave, Joseph experienced God's presence and favour in his life. His unwavering faithfulness and commitment to righteousness led to his promotion and success in everything he did.

In our own lives, we often encounter difficult situations that test our integrity and trust in God. It can be tempting to compromise our values or take matters into our own hands. However, just like Joseph, we are called to remain steadfast and trust in God's plan.

Trusting God's plan doesn't mean that everything will go smoothly or that we will be exempt from trials. It means surrendering our desires and relying on God's wisdom and guidance

So, let us reflect on this: How can you trust God's plan and maintain integrity in the face of adversity? How can you seek His wisdom and guidance in every decision you make? Remember that God's ways are higher than ours, and He is faithful to provide and prosper us when we align our lives with His perfect plan.

REFLECTIVE QUESTION
How can you trust God's plan and maintain integrity in challenging situations?

Guarding the Heart

Grace be with you all.

HEBREWS 13:25

THE BOOK OF HEBREWS concludes with a benediction: "Grace be with you all." These simple words carry profound meaning and serve as a reminder of the eternal grace we have in Christ.

Devotional:

In our fast-paced and ever-changing lives, it's easy to lose sight of the significance of God's grace. But when we pause and reflect on the immense love and unmerited favour that God has bestowed upon us through His Son, our perspective shifts.

God's grace is a constant presence, sustaining us in times of difficulty and empowering us to live lives that honour Him. It is His unmerited favour that allows us to approach His throne confidently, knowing that we are forgiven and dearly loved.

As we go about our daily routines, let us remember the depth of God's grace and allow it to permeate every aspect of our lives. May it shape our attitudes, guide our actions, and inspire us to extend grace to others.

Embrace the reality of God's grace today. Let it be your anchor in the storms of life, your source of strength when you are weak, and your motivation to live a life that reflects His love. And may His grace be with you always.

REFLECTIVE QUESTION
How does the assurance of God's grace impact your daily life?

Contentment in God's Faithfulness

...For He (God) has said,
"I will never leave you nor forsake you.
HEBREWS 13:5

IN A WORLD THAT constantly tells us we need more to be happy and fulfilled, contentment can be challenging to find. Yet, the writer of Hebrews urges us to free ourselves from the love of money and instead find contentment in God's presence and promises.

Contentment doesn't mean settling for less or being complacent. Rather, it is an attitude of gratitude and trust in God's provision. When we realize that our ultimate source of security and satisfaction is found in Him, we can let go of the constant pursuit of material possessions and find true contentment.

God's promise to never leave or forsake us is a powerful reminder of His unwavering presence in our lives. No matter what we face, we can find comfort and assurance in His faithfulness.

Today, take a moment to reflect on your own pursuit of contentment. Are you placing your trust in possessions, achievements, or relationships? Or are you finding true contentment in God's presence and provision? Trust in His promises, and may you experience the deep contentment that comes from knowing His everlasting faithfulness.

REFLECTIVE QUESTION
How can you cultivate contentment in your life, trusting in God's provision and faithfulness?

Finding Stability in God's Presence

**I have set the Lord always before me;
Because He is at my right hand I shall not be moved.**
PSALM 16:8

LIFE IS FILLED WITH ups and downs, uncertainties, and challenges. In the midst of it all, Psalm 16:8 offers a powerful reminder to keep our eyes steadfastly fixed on the Lord. When we make God our priority and allow His presence to guide us, we find stability and strength even in the most turbulent times.

Keeping our eyes on the Lord means seeking Him daily, aligning our thoughts and desires with His will, and relying on His wisdom and guidance. It involves being intentional about spending time in prayer, meditating on His Word, and seeking His face in all areas of our lives.

When we make God our constant companion, we can face whatever comes our way with confidence. His presence brings stability, peace, and an unwavering assurance that we are not alone. No matter what challenges arise, we can trust that He is with us, providing us with the strength we need.

So, today, let us make a conscious effort to keep our eyes always on the Lord. May His presence be our anchor, our source of stability, and our guiding light. In doing so, we will find the strength to navigate life's uncertainties and live with unwavering faith.

REFLECTIVE QUESTION
How can you continually keep your focus on God, finding stability and strength in His presence?

Finding Comfort in the Valley

Yea, though I walk through the valley of the shadow
of death, I will fear no evil; for You are with me;
Your rod and Your staff, they comfort me.

PSALM 23:4

LIFE IS FULL OF valleys—darkness, uncertainty, and fear. In these moments, Psalm 23:4 offers us a powerful reminder that we are not alone. God is with us, providing comfort, guidance, and protection.

When we face difficulties or walk through the darkest valley, it is natural to feel afraid. However, the psalmist declares his faith and trust in God's presence. He recognizes that even in the midst of challenges, God's loving presence brings comfort and security.

God's rod and staff are symbols of His protection and guidance. They represent His watchful care over us, ensuring that we are led in the right direction and kept safe from harm. When we embrace the reality of His presence in our lives, fear loses its power and is replaced by unwavering faith.

Today, take a moment to reflect on the difficult situations you may be facing. How does the knowledge of God's presence bring you comfort? How does it strengthen your faith? Trust in His loving presence even in the darkest valley, and allow His rod and staff to guide you. May His presence be your source of comfort, and may your faith be deepened as you walk with Him through every season of life.

REFLECTIVE QUESTION
How does the knowledge of God's presence bring you comfort and strengthen in difficult times?

Renewed Strength

**He gives power to the weak, And to those who
have no might, He increases strength.**

ISAIAH 40:29

LIFE CAN BE DRAINING, and we often find ourselves feeling weary and weak. But Isaiah 40:29 offers us a beautiful promise: God gives strength to the weary and increases the power of the weak.

Our own strength may fail us, but when we turn to God and rely on His power, an incredible transformation takes place. He has an unlimited source of strength that He graciously makes available to us. When we acknowledge our weaknesses and surrender them to Him, He fills us with His power and renews our spirits.

To tap into God's strength, we need to cultivate a deep dependence on Him through prayer, studying His Word, and seeking His guidance. We must let go of self-reliance and humbly lean on Him for every step we take.

Today, take a moment to reflect on the challenges you're facing. Are you trying to overcome them in your own strength, or are you leaning on God and trusting in His power? Surrender your weaknesses to Him, and allow Him to fill you with renewed strength. May His power empower you to face each day with courage and perseverance.

REFLECTIVE QUESTION

**How can you rely on God's strength and find renewed
energy to face the challenges in your life?**

Divine Help

**God is our refuge and strength,
an ever-present help in trouble.**

PSALM 46:1

LIFE CAN OFTEN FEEL overwhelming, filled with challenges and uncertainties. In the midst of these storms, Psalm 46:1 reminds us that God is our refuge and strength. He is our safe haven, a source of unwavering support and help in times of trouble.

When we encounter difficulties, God invites us to turn to Him and find solace in His presence. He is not a distant or aloof God but an ever-present help, ready to assist and comfort us. In His presence, we find strength and courage to face the trials that come our way.

To experience God as our refuge and strength, we must cultivate a close relationship with Him. Spend time in His presence through prayer, meditate on His Word, and seek His guidance. Trust in His promises, knowing that He is faithful to provide for our every need.

Today, as you encounter challenges, remember that God is your refuge and strength. Lean on Him, find shelter in His unfailing love, and allow His strength to sustain you. May you experience His presence as an ever-present help, bringing you peace and confidence in the midst of life's storms.

REFLECTIVE QUESTION
How can you experience God as your refuge and strength in the midst of life's challenges?

The Unchanging Word

For assuredly I say unto you,
Till heaven and earth pass, one jot or one tittle
shall in no wise pass from the law, till all be fulfilled.

MATTHEW 5:18

IN A WORLD OF constant change, it is comforting to know that God's Word remains steadfast and unchanging. Matthew 5:18 assures us that every word, down to the smallest detail, will endure until everything is accomplished.

This eternal truth reminds us that God's promises are sure and His guidance is trustworthy. His Word provides a solid foundation upon which we can build our lives, and through it, we can find direction, wisdom, and comfort.

In times of uncertainty or doubt, we can turn to the unchanging truth of the Scriptures for assurance. We can trust that God's Word stands firm, even when everything else seems to be shifting. It is in His Word that we find the timeless principles and promises that give us hope and anchor our souls.

Today, reflect on the impact of God's eternal Word in your life. Are you confident in His promises, even amidst the challenges and changes? Are you seeking guidance from His unchanging truth? Trust in His Word, for it is a lamp to your feet and a light to your path. Embrace the consistency of His promises, and find comfort in His eternal faithfulness.

REFLECTIVE QUESTION
How does the eternal nature of God's Word impact your trust in His promises and guidance?

Nothing is Impossible

For with God nothing will be impossible.
LUKE 1:37

LIFE IS OFTEN FILLED with challenges that seem insurmountable. In times of difficulty, we may question if there is a way forward or if our circumstances can change. But Luke 1:37 reminds us of a powerful truth: nothing is impossible with God.

God is the ultimate source of power and possibility. He is not limited by human constraints or circumstances. He has the ability to bring about extraordinary breakthroughs and accomplish what seems impossible to us.

When we internalize this truth, it transforms our faith and perspective. We realize that no situation is too daunting for God to handle. We can approach life's challenges with confidence, knowing that He is capable of turning the impossible into the possible.

Today, reflect on your current circumstances or challenges. Are there areas in your life where you have limited God's power? Surrender those areas to Him and trust in His limitless possibilities. Embrace the truth that nothing is impossible with God, and allow His power to work in and through your life. May your faith be strengthened as you place your trust in His unwavering ability to accomplish the impossible.

REFLECTIVE QUESTION
How does the truth that nothing is impossible with God impact your faith and perspective on life's challenges?

Sowing Tears, Reaping Joy

Those who sow in tears shall reap in joy.

PSALM 126:5

THIS POWERFUL VERSE REMINDS us that life is often filled with seasons of sorrow and joy. Sometimes, we may find ourselves facing trials, hardships, or moments of deep sadness. However, even in our tears, there is hope for a brighter future.

Just as a farmer sows seeds with tears, knowing that they will eventually reap a bountiful harvest, we, too, can have faith that our tears and sorrows will not last forever. In difficult times, it's important to remember that our pain is not in vain. We can choose to sow our tears, trusting that God will bring about a harvest of joy and restoration in due time.

When we face challenging circumstances, it can be difficult to imagine a future filled with joy. But the promise of Psalm 126:5 encourages us to hold on to hope. God sees our tears and will turn them into songs of joy. Though we may not understand the timing or the ways in which our sorrows will be redeemed, we can trust that God is faithful to His promises.

So, let us find solace in knowing that our tears are not wasted. Through seasons of sorrow, we can cling to the hope of a future where our tears and pain will transform into songs of joy, and God's abundant blessings.

REFLECTIVE QUESTION

How can you find strength in moments of sorrow and trust in the promise of joy?

Confident in His Work

*...Being confident of this very thing,
that He who has begun a good work in you will
complete it until the day of Jesus Christ.*

PHILIPPIANS 1:6

SOMETIMES, WE MAY FEEL discouraged or uncertain about our own abilities and shortcomings. However, Philippians 1:6 assures us that God is not finished with us yet. He has initiated good work in us, and He will faithfully continue to mould and shape us into the image of Christ until the day of His glorious return.

When we face challenges or struggles, it can be easy to lose sight of God's work in our lives. However, the verse reminds us to remain confident in His work. We can trust that He will use every every triumph, and even every failure for our growth and His glory.

Knowing that God is actively involved in our lives should bring us reassurance and hope. He is with us, guiding us, teaching us, and transforming us. Even when we stumble or face obstacles, we can rely on His strength and His promise that He will complete what He started.

Let us find comfort and encouragement in the knowledge that God is faithful. He will not abandon us or leave us unfinished. With confidence, let us surrender ourselves to His work in our lives, eagerly anticipating the day when we will be fully complete in Christ.

REFLECTIVE QUESTION
How does knowing that God will complete the good work He began in you bring you reassurance and hope?

Faith Makes All Things Possible

So Jesus said to them, "Because of your unbelief;
for assuredly, I say to you, if you have faith as
a mustard seed, you will say to this mountain,
'Move from here to there,' and it will move;
and nothing will be impossible for you.

MATTHEW 17:20

FAITH IS NOT ABOUT the size or quantity but rather the quality and depth of our trust in God. Even the smallest amount of genuine faith can have a profound impact. Just as a tiny mustard seed can grow into a large tree, our faith has the power to move mountains and overcome seemingly impossible obstacles.

Cultivating and strengthening our faith requires intentional steps. We can nourish our faith by immersing ourselves in God's Word, spending time in prayer, surrounding ourselves with a supportive community of believers, and stepping out in obedience to God's leading.

As we deepen our relationship with God, our faith grows stronger. It becomes rooted in the assurance of His love, His faithfulness, and His power. Our confidence in God increases, allowing us to step out in boldness and witness His miraculous work in our lives.

In moments of doubt or when facing insurmountable challenges, let us remember the words of Jesus in Matthew 17:20. No matter how small our faith may feel, we can trust that God is able to do the impossible through us.

REFLECTIVE QUESTION
How can we cultivate and strengthen our faith to experience the power of God in our lives?

God Answers Prayers

Therefore I say to you, whatever things you ask
when you pray, believe that you receive them,
and you will have them.

MARK 11:24

PRAYER IS A DIRECT line of communication with our Heavenly Father, an opportunity to pour out our hearts and seek His guidance, provision, and intervention. However, along with praying, we are called to believe and have faith that God will hear and answer our prayers according to His perfect will.

Developing a deep trust in God's faithfulness and the effectiveness of prayer comes through cultivating a close relationship with Him. As we spend time in His Word, meditate on His promises, and witness His faithfulness in our lives, our belief in prayer's power is strengthened. Additionally, seeking the guidance of the Holy Spirit helps us align our prayers with God's will, increasing our confidence in His answers.

While it's important to believe that God will answer our prayers, it's crucial to remember that His answers may not always align with our desires or expectations. Sometimes, God's answer may be different or come in a way we don't anticipate. Yet, we can trust that His wisdom and love surpass our limited understanding.

As we deepen our trust in His faithfulness, we are transformed, and our prayers become a powerful channel through which God's purposes are fulfilled.

REFLECTIVE QUESTION

How can we deepen our trust in God's faithfulness and believe that He will answer our prayers?

Putting on the New Self

Do not lie to one another, since you have put off
the old man with his deeds, and have put on the
new man who is renewed in knowledge according to
the image of Him who created him.

COLOSSIANS 3:9-10

WHEN WE ACCEPT JESUS as our Savior, we are called to leave behind our old ways and seek to align ourselves with His character and teachings. This involves intentionally letting go of dishonesty, anger, malice, and all other practices that are contrary to the nature of Christ.

To live out our new identity, we need to nurture our relationship with God, allowing His Word to renew our minds and transform our hearts. Through continuous growth in knowledge and understanding, we become more like our Creator, reflecting His image in our thoughts, words, and actions.

Putting on the new self also involves practical actions. We can actively seek opportunities to show love, kindness, patience, forgiveness, and compassion to others. We can choose to speak truthfully, even when it's not easy. We can embrace humility and seek reconciliation in broken relationships.

As we daily live out our new identity in Christ, we become living testimonies of His grace and power. The world around us will witness the difference He has made in our lives, drawing them closer to the truth of the Gospel.

REFLECTIVE QUESTION

What are some practical ways we can actively live out our new identity in Christ and reflect His image to the world?

Rooted and Built Up in Christ

*Rooted and built up in Him and established
in the faith, as you have been taught,
abounding in it with thanksgiving.*
COLOSSIANS 2:7

JUST AS A STURDY tree draws strength and sustenance from its roots, we, too, need to cultivate deep spiritual roots in Christ. This begins by immersing ourselves in God's Word, spending time in prayer, and seeking His presence daily. As we meditate on His teachings and allow His truth to penetrate our hearts, our faith grows stronger, providing a solid foundation for our lives.

To be built up in Christ, we also need the support and encouragement of a community of believers. Surrounding ourselves with fellow Christians who can strengthen and challenge us in our walk with Christ is crucial. Through fellowship, discipleship, and accountability, we can grow together in faith and knowledge.

Additionally, an attitude of gratitude is essential in our journey of faith. When we recognize and appreciate God's blessings in our lives, our hearts overflow with thankfulness. Gratitude fosters humility, contentment, and an increased awareness of God's goodness, enabling us to navigate challenges with hope and trust.

Prioritize deepening your spiritual roots, building up your faith, and cultivating a heart of thankfulness.

REFLECTIVE QUESTION

How can we deepen our spiritual roots and strengthen our foundation in Christ, enabling us to grow and thrive in our faith?

Love: The Way to Victory

Love never fails…
1 CORINTHIANS 13:8

IN THE MIDST OF life's struggles, especially within families and close relationships, the power of love often becomes the most effective tool for victory. While prayer is vital in spiritual warfare, its efficacy is greatly enhanced with a heart filled with love. Perhaps you've been praying and fasting for a change, yet the situation remains unchanged. This could indicate that what's missing is the element of love.

The devil is well aware of the transformative power of love, so he strives to prevent believers from fully embracing and expressing God's love.

Love is a formidable weapon against the enemy's influence over your family. For instance, winning over a rebellious child is not just about what you say but more about showing them the unconditional, selfless love that reflects God's heart. This divine love is boundless, unconditional, and altruistic. It forgives without limit, gives generously without expecting anything in return, and never repays evil with evil.

To bring about real and lasting victory in your life and within your family, commit to loving the way God intends. Let this pure, selfless love infuse your actions, words, and prayers. This kind of love has the power to break down barriers, heal wounds, and put an end to the enemy's schemes. It will transform your life and the lives of those around you.

REFLECTIVE QUESTION
How can you cultivate a love that transcends time, endures challenges, and reflects the eternal nature of God?

Confession of Faith

(As it is written, "I have made you a father of many
nations") in the presence of Him whom he believed —
God, who gives life to the dead and calls those
things which do not exist as though they did.
ROMANS 4:17

THE WORLD'S SYSTEM ADMONISHES you to believe only what
you see. But the reserve is the case in God's kingdom. God wants
you to see what you believe. This is what is called faith. Nothing
is impossible with your faith in God through Jesus Christ. Faith
is the currency in this kingdom to access all that God has said
concerning you. But you need first to see it in God's word.

Whatever you believe in God's word is yours. There is no
reason to doubt the possibility. God said it. You believe it, and
it is yours. But then, how do you possess what you believe? It's
simple: Your words are the keys to establishing what you believe
by faith. Speak faith-filled words over your life situation, and you
will be amazed at the massive turnaround.

Never let your situation make you say things contrary to your
belief in God's word. However, challenges around you might
negate what you saw in God's word. Nevertheless, do not stop
confessing your faith in His word. Whatever you see will be
yours. What would you say today?

REFLECTIVE QUESTION
**How does the concept of God 'calling into existence
things that do not exist' impact your faith journey?**

God's Purpose in Hard Times

Many are the afflictions of the righteous,
But the Lord delivers him out of them all.

PSALM 34:19

REJOICE, FOR TODAY MAY be the day of an extraordinary encounter with the Lord. If you're feeling overwhelmed, heartbroken, or on the brink of giving up, this message is for you.

God has a purpose for your life, which is often revealed through a challenging process. While this process may be arduous and trying, remember that it strengthens you and prepares you for what lies ahead.

The hardships and trials you face are not meant to defeat you; they are tools in God's hands, shaping and moulding you for greater things. Believe that God works actively in your life, even if His handiwork isn't immediately visible. Though you may not see it now, trust that He is guiding you towards a place of safety and blessing.

So hold on to faith, even in the midst of trials. God's plans for you are filled with hope and a promise of a better future.

You are being prepared for something wonderful, and in due time, you will see the fruit of your perseverance. Stay strong in faith, for your journey leads you to the fulfilment of God's great purpose in your life. Amen.

REFLECTIVE QUESTION

Think about a difficult situation you have faced recently. How did you handle it? Did you find strength in your faith or from other sources?

Living By God's Word

For if anyone is a hearer of the word and not a doer,
he is like a man observing his natural face in a mirror;
for he observes himself, goes away, and immediately
forgets what kind of man he was.

JAMES 1:23-24

JAMES URGES US TO not only listen to God's Word but also to embody it in our lives. Just as we observe our reflection in a mirror and make adjustments accordingly, we are called to reflect upon and act upon the truths we find in Scripture. However, if we merely listen to God's Word without allowing it to change us, we become like forgetful person who quickly forgets their own appearance after glancing in a mirror.

As we encounter God's Word, we are invited to go beyond passive hearing and delve into active participation. Embracing God's Word involves internalizing its wisdom, aligning our behaviour with its teachings, and allowing it to shape our character. By cultivating a responsive and obedient heart, we can truly become doers of the Word, experiencing personal growth and reflecting God's transformative power in our lives.

Take a moment to reflect on James 1:23-24 and consider how you can apply the truths of Scripture in tangible ways that bring about positive change in your life and the lives of those around you.

REFLECTIVE QUESTION

The last time you encountered a message or teaching from God's Word, did it lead to any changes in your attitudes, actions, or thoughts?

God is Faithful

"Then I said to you, 'Do not be terrified or afraid
of them. The LORD your God, who goes before you,
He will fight for you, according to all He did
for you in Egypt before your eyes."
DEUTERONOMY 1:29-30

JUST AS THE ISRAELITES faced uncertainties and challenges
upon entering the Promised Land, we also encounter moments
in life that evoke fear and trepidation. However, Deuteronomy
1:29-30 reminds us that when we trust in God's strength and
guidance, we can face these obstacles with confidence, knowing
that He is with us.

Often, fear can paralyze us and hinder our faith. It can cloud
our judgment and prevent us from fully embracing the plans
and blessings God has for us. Yet, when we choose to place our
trust in God, we tap into His power and provision. We can move
forward with courage, knowing that He is going before us, fighting
on our behalf, and leading us on the right path.

Today, if you find yourself in a position of fear or uncertainty,
take comfort in the promise of Deuteronomy 1:29-30. Rather than
allowing fear to hold you back, choose to trust in God's provision,
strength, and faithfulness. Reflect on His past faithfulness in
your life and allow it to bolster your faith.

REFLECTIVE QUESTION
**Think about a situation in your life where you felt
fearful or intimidated. How did you handle it? Did you
trust in God's provision and guidance, or did fear hinder
your faith?**

God's Time

For the vision is yet for an appointed time;
But at the end it will speak, and it will not lie.
Though it tarries, wait for it;
Because it will surely come, It will not tarry.

HABAKKUK 2:3

AS HUMAN BEINGS, WE often find waiting to be challenging and frustrating. We yearn for immediate answers, quick resolutions, and the fulfilment of our deepest desires. However, Habakkuk 2:3 teaches us the importance of patience and unwavering hope in God's promises.

Just as a farmer eagerly waits for the crops to grow, we must trust that God's plans for our lives are unfolding at the perfect time. Even when it seems like our dreams and prayers are taking longer than expected, we can find solace in the knowledge that God's timing is always impeccable. His promises are true, and He will fulfil them in His appointed time.

Rather than allowing doubt and impatience to cloud our hearts, let us choose to wait with hope and trust in God's faithfulness. Embrace the waiting period as an opportunity for growth, surrender, and deepening our relationship with Him. Know that as we remain steadfast, God's promises will come to pass, and His faithfulness will shine brighter than ever before.

REFLECTIVE QUESTION

Think about a desire or dream you have been waiting to see fulfilled. How have you approached the waiting period? Have you maintained hope and trust in God's timing, or has impatience and doubt crept in?

Comfort in Times of Trial

Who comforts us in all our tribulation that we
may be able to comfort those who are in any trouble,
with the comfort with which we
ourselves are comforted by God.

2 CORINTHIANS 1:4

LIFE OFTEN PRESENTS US with various trials and hardships
that can leave us feeling overwhelmed and in need of comfort.
However, 2 Corinthians 1:4 offers us the assurance that God
is not only present in our distress but also actively working to
provide us with solace and support.

God's comfort is not solely for our benefit. It is meant to flow
through us to others who are in need. As we experience His
comfort in our lives, we are called to extend that same love, empathy,
and consolation to those around us who are also facing trials.
By sharing our own journey of receiving God's comfort, we can
offer hope and encouragement to others who may be struggling.

Take a moment to reflect on 2 Corinthians 1:4 and consider
how you can be a vessel of God's comfort in the lives of those
around you. Embrace the opportunity to be both comforted by
God's love and a comforter to others, knowing that through these
acts, His divine compassion is revealed.

REFLECTIVE QUESTION
How can you show empathy, offer a listening ear, or
provide practical support to someone who is going
through a challenging time?

Strength for the Journey

They go from strength to strength;
each one appears before God in Zion.

PSALMS 84:7

LIFE IS OFTEN FILLED with ups and downs, and there are times when we may feel weary and weak on our journey. However, Psalms 84:7 reminds us that when we place our trust in God, He empowers us to go from strength to strength. He grants us the resilience to overcome obstacles, the courage to face adversity, and the endurance to continue pressing forward.

God's strength is not limited or finite; it is limitless and ever-present. As we rely on Him, He infuses us with His power and grace, enabling us to navigate life's challenges with steadfastness and unwavering faith.

When we encounter moments of weakness or uncertainty, we can draw strength from knowing that God is with us every step of the way. We can find comfort in His promises and find solace in His unchanging character. His strength sustains us and propels us forward until we reach the ultimate destination of appearing before Him in Zion.

Trust that as you surrender to His guidance, He will provide the strength needed to carry you through every season of life.

REFLECTIVE QUESTION

Think about a time in your life when you felt God's strength and provision carrying you through a challenging season. How did that experience shape your faith and trust in Him?

The Power of Persistent Prayer

Then He spoke a parable to them,
that men always ought to pray and not lose heart.

LUKE 18:1

PRAYER IS A POWERFUL means of communication with God, allowing us to express our thoughts, concerns, and desires. Luke 18:1 teaches us that prayer should not be a one-time event but rather a continuous and unwavering practice in our lives. Through the parable of the persistent widow, Jesus emphasizes the importance of persisting in prayer and not giving up.

When we face challenges or desires that seem unanswered, it is easy to become discouraged and tempted to abandon our prayers. However, the parable reminds us that God is attentive to our cries and invites us to persistently seek Him, trusting in His perfect timing and wisdom.

Persistent prayer deepens our dependence on God and strengthens our faith. It aligns our hearts with His will, fosters intimacy with Him, and allows us to witness His faithfulness. Even when we do not see immediate results, we can find comfort in knowing that our prayers are heard and that God is actively working behind the scenes.

Trust that as you persistently seek God in prayer, He will shape and transform your heart, and His answers will unfold according to His perfect plan.

REFLECTIVE QUESTION
How can you develop a habit of consistent and unwavering prayer?

Faithful Stewardship

And to one he gave five talents, to another two,
and another one, to each according to his own ability;
and immediately he went on a journey.

MATTHEW 25:15

EACH ONE OF US has been uniquely gifted by God with talents, abilities, and resources. As Matthew 25:15 illustrates, these gifts are distributed according to our abilities. Our responsibility as faithful stewards is to recognize and utilize these gifts for the glory of God and the benefit of others.

God entrusts us with various talents, not for our own personal gain or comparison with others, but to be used in service to Him and His Kingdom. Whether it be our skills, time, finances, or influence, it is important to cultivate a heart of stewardship, ensuring that we invest and multiply what God has given us.

Fear, comparison, and complacency can often hinder us from fully embracing our stewardship responsibilities. However, when we trust in God's provision and step out in faith, we unlock our true potential and contribute to His purposes in meaningful ways.

Take a moment to reflect on Matthew 25:15 and assess your stewardship. Embrace the call to be a faithful steward, knowing that as you utilize your gifts for His glory, you will experience the joy of participating in God's work and making a positive impact in the lives of others.

REFLECTIVE QUESTION

Are you using your gifts fully and wisely? Are there areas where you can step out in faith and invest what God has given you?

The Everlasting Word

The grass withers, the flower fades,
but the word of our God stands forever."
ISAIAH 40:8

AS WE NAVIGATE THROUGH the ups and downs of life, it is easy to find ourselves seeking permanence and stability. We crave something solid, unchanging, and everlasting.

The world around us is in a constant state of flux, and even the most beautiful and vibrant things eventually fade away. However, God's Word remains unchanging and eternal. It provides us with a firm foundation, a source of wisdom and truth that we can rely on in every circumstance.

When we face uncertainty or challenges, we can turn to Scripture for guidance and encouragement. The Word of God offers timeless principles, promises, and instructions that provide comfort in times of sorrow, direction in times of confusion, and hope in times of despair.

Knowing that God's Word stands forever reminds us of His faithfulness and the reliability of His promises. It assures us that amidst the changing tides of life, we have a sure and steadfast anchor in God's unchanging truth.

Take comfort in the fact that the Word of God endures through all generations. Let it shape your thoughts, guide your decisions, and bring you closer to the everlasting God who loves you unconditionally.

REFLECTIVE QUESTION
How does the eternal nature of God's Word provide comfort and guidance in your daily life?

In the Midst of Trials

**I have not departed from the commandment
of His lips; I have treasured the words of His mouth
more than my necessary food.**

JOB 23:12

LIFE IS A JOURNEY that often presents us with trials and difficulties. In the midst of our struggles, it is natural to question God's presence and purpose.

Job, a man who faced unimaginable suffering and loss, recognized the immeasurable worth of God's Word. Despite his anguish, Job held tightly to the promises, teachings, and wisdom found within Scripture. He understood that during the darkest moments, the Word of God brings hope, comfort, and guidance.

In the midst of our own trials, we can find solace and strength in Job's example. When our hearts are heavy and our circumstances overwhelming, we can turn to God's Word. It reminds us of His faithfulness, His unchanging love, and His ultimate plan for our lives.

When we prioritize the Word of God, even above our physical sustenance, we acknowledge its transformative power. It feeds our spirits, nourishes our souls, and provides us with the wisdom and perspective needed to navigate life's challenges.

In the midst of your own trials, treasure the words of God. Allow it to sustain you, guide you, and give you hope. As you lean on His promises, you will find that His presence and purpose are steadfast, even in the most difficult seasons of life.

REFLECTIVE QUESTION
How does the value and impact of God's Word become more evident during times of adversity?

Judging with Compassion

Judge not, that you be not judged. For with what judgment you judge, you will be judged; and with the measure you use, it will be measured back to you."

MATTHEW 7:1-2

JESUS'S WORDS REMIND US of the essence of examining our own hearts before hastily passing judgment on others. It is easy to point out flaws, or shortcomings in people, but true compassion calls us to seek understanding and empathy.

While it is necessary to discern right from wrong and make wise decisions, we must do so with a heart filled with love and understanding. Rather than judging others from a place of self-righteousness, we are called to view them through the lens of compassion.

When we choose compassion over judgment, we create space for growth, forgiveness, and reconciliation in our relationships. We recognize that we, too, are imperfect and in need of grace. By extending that same grace to others, we demonstrate the transformative power of Christ's love.

Let us remember that our judgments of others are not without consequence. When we treat others with harshness or condemnation, we invite the same treatment upon ourselves. Conversely, when we offer understanding and compassion, we open the door for the same measure of grace in return.

Therefore, strive to judge with compassion. Seek to understand rather than condemn, and let the love of Christ guide your interactions; thereby, creating an environment of acceptance, healing, and transformation.

REFLECTIVE QUESTION

How can we cultivate a heart of compassion and understanding while maintaining discernment in our interactions with others?

Don't Give Up, Keep Sowing

And let us not grow weary while doing good,
for in due season we shall reap if we do not lose heart.
GALATIANS 6:9

IN A WORLD THAT often values instant results and immediate gratification, it can be disheartening when our efforts to do good seem to go unnoticed or without impact. We may become weary and tempted to give up.

However, Paul reminds us to persevere. He assures us that our labour in doing good is not in vain. Though we may not see the harvest immediately, God promises that in due time, we will reap the rewards of our faithfulness.

When we feel weary, it is essential to find strength in God's promises and draw upon His limitless resources. We can seek nourishment through regular prayer, studying His Word, and connecting with fellow believers who can offer support and encouragement.

Additionally, shifting our perspective can help us find renewed motivation. Rather than focusing solely on the outcome, we can learn to find joy in the process of doing good. Every act of kindness, every word of encouragement, every expression of love brings us closer to the likeness of Christ and impacts the lives of others.

Choose to persevere, knowing that God sees and values every effort we make in His name. Keep sowing seeds of goodness, and trust that in His perfect timing, the harvest will come.

REFLECTIVE QUESTION

How can we find strength to persevere in doing good even when we feel weary?

Fixing Our Eyes on Jesus

Looking unto Jesus, the author and finisher of our faith,
who for the joy that was set before Him endured the
cross, despising the shame, and has sat down at the
right hand of the throne of God.

HEBREWS 12:2

IN A WORLD THAT constantly pulls our attention in various directions, it is crucial to have a steadfast focal point. Jesus, the author and perfecter of our faith, serves as our unwavering foundation. When we fix our eyes on Him, we find strength, guidance, and encouragement to press on.

Keeping our focus on Jesus helps us to navigate life's trials and temptations in several ways. Firstly, it reminds us of His example – His love, grace, and sacrificial life. By studying His teachings and observing His actions, we gain insights into how to live a life pleasing to God.

Secondly, fixing our eyes on Jesus provides us with hope. His resurrection assures us of life beyond death and the promise of eternity with Him. In times of despair or difficulty, we can find solace in His unchanging love and the victory He has already won.

Lastly, focusing on Jesus enables us to receive His strength and empowerment. We surrender our desires, fears, and burdens to Him, knowing that He is faithful to provide us with the wisdom, courage, and endurance needed to persevere.

REFLECTIVE QUESTION
How does keeping our focus on Jesus empower us to navigate the trials and temptations of life?

God's Partnership With Us

Now God worked unusual miracles by the hands of Paul,
so that even handkerchiefs or aprons were brought from
his body to the sick, and the diseases left them
and the evil spirits went out of them.

ACTS 19:11–12

THIS PASSAGE CHALLENGES US to examine our faith and ask ourselves if we truly believe in the power and authority of God. It invites us to trust Him to do the extraordinary in our own lives, regardless of the circumstances we may be facing.

When we encounter sickness, brokenness, or spiritual oppression, we can look to God as the source of healing and restoration. Just as the handkerchiefs and aprons carried from Paul's body became channels of God's power, we can also be vessels for His miraculous works.

However, it is important to remember that miracles are not solely for our personal gain or comfort. They often serve a greater purpose – to bring glory to God and to draw others to Him. As we trust in His power and allow Him to work through us, we become witnesses to His love, grace, and healing in those around us.

Allow it to inspire you to trust in His miraculous work in your own life and to be open to being used as His instrument. Embrace the opportunity to bring glory to God through your faith and obedience.

REFLECTIVE QUESTION

How does the example of God's extraordinary power in Acts 19:11-12 inspire and challenge you to trust in His miraculous work in your own life?

It is Worth the Wait

Behold, I send the promise of my Father upon you.
But tarry in the city of Jerusalem until you endure
with power from on high.

LUKE 24:49

THE PROMISE OF BEING clothed with power from on high points to the coming of the Holy Spirit upon the disciples. Jesus knew that they needed supernatural strength and guidance to fulfil the mission He entrusted to them.

Likewise, as believers today, we have access to the same empowering presence of the Holy Spirit. The Holy Spirit equips us with spiritual gifts, wisdom, and boldness to live out and proclaim the gospel message to a broken world.

Being clothed with power reminds us that we are not alone in our journey of faith. The Holy Spirit dwells within us, giving us the strength and wisdom we need to navigate the challenges and uncertainties of life.

Furthermore, this power is not meant to be kept to ourselves. It is meant to propel us into action, to go out and make disciples of all nations. The Holy Spirit empowers us to bear witness to Christ's love and gift of salvation with others.

Embrace the mission of spreading the gospel, knowing that you are clothed with power from on high, and let the Holy Spirit work through you to bring light, hope, and transformation to the world.

REFLECTIVE QUESTION

How does the promise of being endued with power from on high impact your understanding of the Holy Spirit's role in your life and the mission of spreading the gospel?

Step Out in Faith

To you, O Lord, I lift my soul.
PSALM 25:1

DAVID'S PRAYER IN PSALM 25:1 encapsulates a posture of complete trust and surrender to God. When we lift up our souls to the Lord, we acknowledge His sovereignty and wisdom. We release our worries, fears, and desires into His capable hands.

Seeking the Lord's guidance requires an open and receptive heart. When we surrender our soul, we declare our willingness to submit to His will and follow His ways. In doing so, we position ourselves to receive His direction with humility and trust.

Lifting up our soul is an act of faith. It is an acknowledgement that God knows what is best for us, even when we cannot see the way ahead. In this surrender, we find peace and assurance, knowing that God is faithfully leading and guiding us.

Trusting in God's guidance does not mean that our path will always be easy or clear. However, it means that we can rest in the knowledge that He is with us every step of the way. He promises to guide us along the right path, to teach us His ways, and to reveal His truth to those who seek Him.

Seek His presence and allow Him to lead you on the path of righteousness. In doing so, you will experience the peace and assurance that comes from relying on His perfect guidance.

REFLECTIVE QUESTION
How does trusting in and surrendering to the Lord bring you peace and assurance in seeking His guidance?

Running the Race

Do you not know that those who run in a race all run,
but only one receives the prize?
Run in such a way that you may obtain it.

1 CORINTHIANS 9:24

THE APOSTLE PAUL COMPARES the Christian life to a race. He writes, "Do you not know that in a race, all the runners run, but only one receives the prize? So run that you may obtain it."

Just like in a race, the Christian journey requires endurance, discipline, and a focus on the ultimate goal. We are called to run with perseverance, continually striving to grow in our relationship with God and fulfil His purposes for our lives.

Think about how you can prioritize your spiritual growth, such as reading Scripture regularly, spending time in prayer, and seeking fellowship with other believers. Consider areas where you may need to cultivate discipline or remove distractions that hinder your progress.

Remember, the race isn't about comparison or competition with others; it's about personal growth and pursuing God's calling for your life. Let us all run our race with determination, fixing our eyes on Jesus, the ultimate prize and finisher of our faith (Hebrews 12:1-2).

May you be encouraged to run the race set before you, knowing that God is with you every step of the way.

REFLECTIVE QUESTION
**What steps can you take today to ensure that you are
running the Christian race with endurance and purpose?**

Seeking God's Presence

**Then he said to Him, if your presence does not
go with us, do not bring us up from here.**
EXODUS 33:15

EXODUS 33:15 HOLDS A profound moment in the life of Moses,
where he implores the Lord, saying, "If your presence does not
go with me, do not bring us up from here."

Moses recognized the significance of God's presence in his life
and understood that without it, all other blessings would pale in
comparison. He desired an intimate relationship with God, one
that would guide and empower him in every step of his journey.

Consider the importance of cultivating a close relationship with
the Lord, seeking His presence above all else. Reflect on whether
you have been prioritizing this connection or have drifted into a
transactional approach with God. Are you seeking Him earnestly,
desiring to know Him more intimately?

Take the time to evaluate your heart and renew your commitment
to seeking God's presence. Set aside dedicated moments each day
for prayer, meditation, and reading His Word. Cultivate a spirit
of gratitude and dependency on Him, acknowledging that His
presence is the ultimate blessing.

Remember that God is always ready to meet with you to guide
and comfort you. Seek Him with all your heart, and you will find
Him (Jeremiah 29:13).

May you embrace the beauty of seeking God's presence, knowing
that it is in His presence where you will find true fulfilment and
purpose.

REFLECTIVE QUESTION
**Do you genuinely seek God's presence in your life,
or are you primarily focused on His blessings and
provisions?**

Restoring What was Lost

So I will restore to you the years that the
swarming locust has eaten, and the crawling locust,
The consuming locust, And the chewing locust,
My great army which I sent among you.

JOEL 2:25

IN THIS VERSE, THE prophet Joel speaks to a community that has experienced devastation and loss. But God, in His faithfulness and mercy, promises to restore what was taken away. He assures them that He can redeem the time and bring forth abundance in the midst of barrenness.

Take a moment to reflect on the losses and hardships you may have faced – whether in relationships, career, health, or personal dreams. Surrender them to God and seek His guidance and provision. Ask Him to bring restoration and renewal into these areas.

Remember, God is not restricted by time or circumstances. He is able to transform the brokenness and make something beautiful out of it. Trust in His perfect timing and His ability to turn your mourning into dancing (Psalm 30:11-12).

May you find hope in the promise of restoration, knowing that God is faithful to heal, revive, and bring new life to every area of your existence. Trust in His sovereignty and cling to His unfailing love.

REFLECTIVE QUESTION
What areas of your life do you feel have been devastated or stripped away? Can you trust God's promise of restoration in those areas?

Fervent in Spirit

Not lagging in diligence,
FERVENT IN SPIRIT,
serving the Lord.
ROMANS 12:11

AS FOLLOWERS OF CHRIST, we are called to live with passion and purpose. This verse reminds us to be diligent and enthusiastic in our devotion to God. We are to serve Him wholeheartedly, allowing our spirits to burn brightly for His glory.

Consider the areas of your life where you may have become complacent or lukewarm in your faith. Are there any distractions or obstacles that have hindered your fervour? Reflect on what steps you can take to rekindle your passion for serving God.

Seek to know Him more intimately through prayer, studying His Word, and cultivating a vibrant relationship with Him. Surround yourself with fellow believers who inspire and challenge you to grow in your faith. Engage in acts of service and selflessness, allowing the love of Christ to flow through you to others.

Remember, our zeal for God is not dependent on circumstances but is fueled by the indwelling presence of the Holy Spirit. Allow the fire of the Spirit to ignite your soul and empower you to live a life that is pleasing to God.

May you be encouraged to embrace a fervent spirit, serve the Lord with enthusiasm, and experience the joy and fulfilment that comes from wholeheartedly following Him.

REFLECTIVE QUESTION
How can you cultivate a fervent spirit and maintain zeal in your walk with the Lord?

Listening to God's Voice

*Your ears shall hear a voice behind you, saying,
this is the way, walk in it, whenever you turn to the
right hand or whenever you turn to the left.*

ISAIAH 30:21

GOD, OUR LOVING FATHER, desires to guide and direct us in every step of our journey. He promises to speak to us, leading us on the path of righteousness. Amidst the noise and chaos of life, He offers His still, small voice to guide us toward His perfect will.

Consider the busyness and distractions that often drown out God's voice. Are there areas of your life where you need to intentionally create quietness and solitude to seek His presence? Reflect on how you can align your heart and mind with His, allowing Him to speak and direct your steps.

Take time each day to be still before the Lord, offering Him your undivided attention. Meditate on His Word and pray, inviting Him to speak into your life. Be open and attentive to His promptings, trusting that He will guide you according to His perfect wisdom and love.

Remember, God is ever-present, always ready to guide you. Tune your ears and heart to His voice, for He will show you the way to walk. Trust in His guidance and follow Him with confidence.

May you experience the joy and peace that comes from hearing and obeying God's voice. Trust that He will lead you into His perfect plan for your life, step by step.

REFLECTIVE QUESTION

How can you create space to hear Him more clearly?

Jehovah Jireh
— The Lord Provides

And Abraham called the name of the place,
THE LORD-WILL PROVIDE; as it is said to this day,
in the mount of the Lord it shall be provided.

GENESIS 22:14

THIS PASSAGE SHOWCASES GOD'S faithfulness in providing for His people, even in the most challenging circumstances. It reminds us that God is our ultimate provider, meeting our needs according to His perfect plan.

Consider the areas where you may struggle to fully trust God's provision. Are there financial worries, career uncertainties, or relational needs that cause anxiety or doubt? Reflect on how you can surrender these concerns to God and place your trust in His faithfulness.

Allow your faith in God's provision to shape your mindset and actions. Seek His wisdom in managing your resources, talents, and time. Cultivate a heart of gratitude, recognizing that every good thing comes from Him (James 1:17).

Remember, God's ways and timing are often different from ours, but He never fails to provide according to His purpose and love for us. Hold on to His promises and trust in His provision in all circumstances.

May you find peace and reassurance in knowing that Jehovah Jireh is your faithful provider. Trust in His provision and continue to walk in obedience, knowing that He will always take care of you.

REFLECTIVE QUESTION
Do you trust God as your Jehovah Jireh (Provider)? How can you deepen your reliance on His provision in every aspect of your life?

Guarding Against Lukewarmness

**I know your works, that you are neither cold nor hot.
I could wish you were cold or hot.**

REVELATION 3:15

REVELATION 3:15 WARNS AGAINST the danger of being lukewarm. These words from Christ remind us of the importance of wholehearted devotion and passion in our relationship with Him.

Take a moment to examine your heart and assess your spiritual fervour. Are there times when you find yourself going through the motions of faith without genuine passion? Are there areas where you have become spiritually apathetic or complacent?

For instance, it might be in your prayer life, spending time in God's Word, or engaging in worship and fellowship with other believers. Identify these areas of lukewarmness and invite God to ignite a fresh fire within you.

Remember, our love and devotion to Christ should never stagnate. He desires a fervent, wholehearted pursuit from us. Repentance and surrendering these areas to Him will allow Him to revive and renew your love for Him, empowering you to walk in obedience and intimate fellowship.

May today be a day of rekindling the flame of passion for God in every aspect of your life, ensuring that your devotion remains steadfast and ablaze.

REFLECTIVE QUESTION

In what areas of your life have you allowed complacency to creep in, causing your love and zeal for God to grow lukewarm?

Chosen and Set Apart

But you are a chosen generation, a royal priesthood,
a holy nation, His own special people, that you
may proclaim the praises of Him who called you
out of darkness into His marvellous light.

1 PETER 2:9

TAKE A MOMENT TO reflect on the incredible privilege and responsibility that comes with being chosen by God. As His special possession, you have been set apart to declare His praises and reflect His light to the world.

Consider how this truth informs your actions and attitudes. Does it impact the way you make decisions, treat others, or view your purpose in life? Does it give you confidence and assurance in your worth and significance?

Knowing that God has called you out of darkness can give you hope and strength during difficult times. Understanding that you are set apart for His purposes can inspire you to live a life that honours Him in every aspect.

Embrace your identity as a chosen and set-apart individual. Let it shape your thoughts, guide your actions, and infuse your life with purpose. By doing so, you will not only experience the joy of living in God's wonderful light but also inspire others to discover the transformative power of His love.

REFLECTIVE QUESTION
How does understanding your identity as a chosen and set-apart individual impact the way you live your life?

Let God Build Your House

Unless the Lord builds the house, they labor in vain
who build it; unless the Lord guards the city,
the watchman stays awake in vain.

PSALMS 127:1

IN THE HUSTLE AND bustle of our fast-paced lives, finding true
rest can be a challenge. We often seek rest in various ways – a
vacation, a day off, a good night's sleep – but these forms of rest
can only provide temporary relief. In Psalm 127:1, we are reminded
of a deeper source of rest.

This verse encourages us to place our trust in God's provision
rather than relying solely on our own efforts. When we try to
build our lives and secure our future without God's guidance and
help, our labour becomes futile. We may achieve material success,
but our souls can still feel restless and unsatisfied.

True rest is found when we surrender control and trust in God's
plan for our lives. It means acknowledging that our achievements
and worldly accomplishments are ultimately meaningless if they
are not aligned with God's purpose. Resting in God's provision
involves seeking His presence, relying on His strength, and finding
peace in His promises.

As we meditate on Psalm 127:1, let us reflect on the areas in
our lives where we may be striving in vain. May we find rest by
surrendering our desires, hopes, and dreams to God, trusting that
His wisdom and provision are far greater than our own efforts.

REFLECTIVE QUESTION

**How can we find true rest in God's provision as we
navigate the challenges of daily life?**

Choosing Holiness over Temptation

Therefore, my beloved, FLEE FROM IDOLATRY.
1 CORINTHIANS 10:14

IN A WORLD FILLED with countless temptations, it can be challenging to live a life that is pleasing to God. This verse encourages us to actively resist the allure of sin and make choices that align with God's desires for our lives.

Temptations come in various forms – from the subtle enticements of material possessions to the allure of fleeting pleasures. It is important for us to recognize that giving in to these temptations ultimately leads us away from God's purpose for us. Instead, we are called to flee from idolatry and pursue holiness.

Choosing holiness over temptation requires both intentionality and vigilance. We must be aware of the things that lead us astray and consciously make choices that honour God. This involves seeking His guidance through prayer and studying His Word, surrounding ourselves with fellow believers who can support and hold us accountable, and relying on the power of the Holy Spirit to help us resist temptation.

As we reflect on 1 Corinthians 10:14, let us examine our lives and identify the areas where we may be vulnerable to temptation. May we find the strength and courage to flee from idolatry and embrace the path of holiness. Remember, even when faced with temptation, we can rely on God's grace and guidance to lead us to a life that is pleasing to Him.

REFLECTIVE QUESTION
How can we resist the pull of temptation and choose holiness in our daily lives?

Extending Love and Kindness

Whoever shuts his ears to the cry of the poor
Will also cry himself and not be heard.

PROVERBS 21:13

IN PROVERBS 21:13, WE are reminded of the importance of extending compassion towards others. This verse serves as a powerful reminder that God calls us to actively care for the needs of those around us, especially the poor and marginalized.

Compassion is more than just feeling sympathetic towards someone's situation; it involves taking action to alleviate their suffering. It is about extending love, kindness, and tangible support to those who are in need. When we shut our ears to the cries of the poor, we not only ignore their immediate needs but also hinder our own ability to receive help from God when we cry out.

Cultivating a heart of compassion starts with opening our eyes and ears to the struggles of those around us. It involves actively seeking opportunities to meet the needs of others, whether through acts of charity, volunteering, or simply offering a listening ear and a helping hand. Compassion allows us to reflect God's love and mercy in a broken world.

As we reflect on Proverbs 21:13, let us examine our own hearts and actions. Are we shutting our ears to the cry of the poor? Are we willing to extend compassion and care to those in need?

REFLECTIVE QUESTION
How can we cultivate a heart of compassion and actively care for the needs of others, as highlighted in Proverbs 21:13?

Hope for the Future

For surely, there is a hereafter,
and YOUR HOPE WILL NOT BE CUT OFF.

PROVERBS 23:18

LIFE CAN BE UNPREDICTABLE, and at times, it may seem as if our dreams and aspirations are being cut off or delayed. However, Proverbs 23:18 reminds us that our hope is anchored in God's unfailing faithfulness. He has a plan and purpose for each one of us, and He will not let our hope be extinguished.

Finding hope in God's promise for the future requires us to trust in His sovereignty and timing. It means surrendering our worries and anxieties and, instead, fixing our eyes on the promises found in His Word. It involves seeking His guidance through prayer and allowing His Holy Spirit to renew our strength, courage, and perseverance.

As we meditate on Proverbs 23:18, let us reflect on where we are placing our hope. Are we relying solely on our own abilities and circumstances, or are we trusting in God's unchanging promises? May this verse serve as a reminder to hold onto hope, knowing that God is faithful and His plans for us are good. Let us embrace His promise for the future with unwavering faith and anticipation for what He has in store for us.

REFLECTIVE QUESTION

How can we find hope and encouragement in God's promise for the future, as emphasized in Proverbs 23:18?

God's Discipline

But if you are without chastening,
of which all have become partakers,
then you are illegitimate and not sons.
HEBREWS 12:8

GOD'S DISCIPLINE IS ROOTED in His love for us. It is not meant to be punitive or harsh but rather a means of correction, growth, and refinement. Similar to a loving parent who disciplines their children for their own good, God's discipline is a sign of His care and desire to mould us into the image of Christ.

Embracing God's discipline involves a humble and teachable heart, recognizing that we are not perfect and in need of His guidance. It requires us to surrender our will to His, trusting that His ways are higher and better than our own. In moments of discipline, we can seek His forgiveness, learn from our mistakes, and allow Him to shape our character and faith.

As we reflect on Hebrews 12:8, let us examine our response to God's discipline. Do we resent it or see it as an opportunity for growth? Are we willing to learn and change through His correction? May this verse encourage us to embrace God's loving discipline, knowing that it is a sign of His love and a pathway to spiritual maturity. Let us humbly submit to His guidance, growing in character and faith as we strive to become true sons and daughters of a loving Heavenly Father.

REFLECTIVE QUESTION
How can we embrace God's discipline as a means of growing in character and faith?

Living as a Beacon of Hope

Let your light shine before men so they may
see your good works and glorify
your Father in Heaven.

MATTHEW 5:16

TO SHINE THE LIGHT of Christ means more than simply professing our faith with words; it involves living out our beliefs through our actions. It means being kind, compassionate, and serving others selflessly. When our lives reflect the character of Christ, we become a source of hope, inspiration, and encouragement to those who may be searching for meaning and truth.

Effectively shining the light of Christ requires us to be intentional in our thoughts, words, and actions. It means choosing to respond with love instead of anger, forgiveness instead of resentment, and generosity instead of selfishness. It means being a living testimony of God's transforming power and grace.

As we meditate on Matthew 5:16, let us reflect on how we are currently shining the light of Christ in our daily lives. Are there areas where we can be more intentional and consistent in displaying His love and mercy? May this verse inspire us to let our light shine brightly so that others may come to know the goodness of our Heavenly Father. Let our actions draw others closer to Him and bring glory to His name.

REFLECTIVE QUESTION

How can you effectively shine the light of Christ in our daily lives, as emphasized in Matthew 5:16?

Trusting God's Ways

For My thoughts are not your thoughts,
nor are your ways my ways, says the Lord.

ISAIAH 55:8

As HUMANS, WE OFTEN try to understand and control our circumstances, but God's ways are higher and more profound than we can comprehend. While we may not always understand His purposes, we can find peace and assurance in knowing that His wisdom surpasses our own limited understanding.

Trusting in God's unlimited wisdom means surrendering our desire for control and humbly acknowledging that His perspective extends beyond our own. It involves embracing the truth that He knows what is best for us and that His plans are ultimately for our good, even if they may be difficult or challenging in the moment.

As we reflect on Isaiah 55:8, let us examine our trust in God's wisdom. Are there areas in our lives where we struggle to let go of control? How can we intentionally cultivate a deeper trust in His ways? May this verse serve as a reminder of God's sovereignty and His unfathomable wisdom. Let us release our concerns, surrender to His guidance, and trust that His ways will lead us to abundant life and eternal purposes.

REFLECTIVE QUESTION

How can we cultivate trust in God's unlimited wisdom, even when His ways seem different from ours, as highlighted in Isaiah 55:8?

Embrace Humility

But He gives more grace.
Therefore He says: God resists the proud,
but GIVES GRACE TO THE HUMBLE.
JAMES 4:6

IN JAMES 4:6, WE are reminded of the significance of humility in our relationship with God.

Humility involves recognizing our dependence on God acknowledging that we are not self-sufficient or in control of our own destinies. It requires us to surrender our pride and submit ourselves to God's authority. When we embrace humility, we open ourselves up to receiving God's abundant grace.

One practical way to cultivate humility in our daily lives is through prayer. Taking time each day to humbly come before God, expressing our gratitude, confessing our weaknesses, and seeking His guidance helps us to maintain a humble posture before Him.

Additionally, serving others with a humble heart can also foster humility. By putting others' needs before our own and seeking to serve them selflessly, we learn to set aside our pride and focus on the well-being of others.

Remember, humility is not a one-time achievement but a lifelong journey. May we continually seek to embrace humility, knowing that through it, we receive the grace of God abundantly.

REFLECTIVE QUESTION

How can you cultivate a humble heart in your daily life?

The Blessings of Diligence

Wealth gained by dishonesty will be diminished,
But he who gathers by labor will increase.

PROVERBS 13:11

THIS PROVERB HIGHLIGHTS THE contrast between dishonest gain, which ultimately fades away, and the value of steady, honest effort. It teaches us that diligent work produces lasting blessings, while shortcuts or deceitful ways lead to empty outcomes.

Cultivating diligence in our pursuits requires discipline, perseverance, and a focus on long-term goals. It involves consistently investing our time, energy, and skills into a task, even when obstacles arise.

Building a habit of diligence starts with setting clear and achievable goals. Break down larger tasks into smaller, manageable steps, and celebrate each milestone along the way. Hold yourself accountable and resist the temptation to take shortcuts or give in to procrastination.

Seeking wisdom and guidance from others who have shown diligence in their lives can also be immensely beneficial. Surround yourself with mentors and like-minded individuals who inspire and encourage you to stay committed to your endeavours.

Remember, success is not always measured by immediate results but by the effort and dedication put into achieving a goal. May we embrace the blessings that come from diligence as we journey through life.

REFLECTIVE QUESTION
How can you cultivate diligence in your pursuits?

It's Your Season of Laughter

When the Lord brought back the captivity of Zion,
we were like them who dream. Then was our mouth
filled with laughter, and our tongues with singing.
Then they said among the nations,
The Lord has done great things for them.

PSALM 126:1

THIS PSALM REFLECTS A moment of great rejoicing when God's people witnessed the restoration of their land and fortunes. It serves as a reminder that God is a restorer, and He brings about transformation and renewal in our lives.

To cultivate a heart of gratitude for God's restoration work, we can start by reflecting on the areas of our lives that He has already redeemed. Consider moments when God has turned ashes into beauty, brought healing into brokenness, or provided unexpected blessings. Take time to express thankfulness for those restorative moments.

Prayer is another powerful tool for nurturing gratitude. Spend time in prayer, acknowledging God's faithfulness and His restoration in your life. Offer praise and thanksgiving for the ways He has redeemed and transformed your circumstances.

Sharing your testimony of God's restoration with others can also cultivate gratitude. By sharing the story of how God has worked in your life, you not only inspire others but also reinforce your own gratitude for His faithfulness.

May we continually cultivate a heart of gratitude for the restoration work of God, knowing that He is always faithful to bring beauty from ashes.

REFLECTIVE QUESTION
How can you cultivate a heart of gratitude for the restoration work of God in your life?

Mercy

The Lord is merciful and gracious, slow to anger,
and abounding in mercy.
PSALM 103:8

THE COMPASSION OF GOD is a beautiful and comforting attribute that influences our relationship with Him and others. It signifies His deep empathy and tender care for His creation. God's compassion compels Him to act on behalf of His people, expressing His love and mercy.

When we truly grasp the depth of God's compassion, it has the power to transform our view of ourselves and others. It reminds us that we are deeply loved, valued, and understood by our Heavenly Father. This understanding fosters an intimate and trusting relationship with Him.

God's compassion also challenges us to extend the same love and understanding to those around us. It inspires us to treat others with kindness, forgiveness, and empathy, reflecting the heart of our compassionate God.

Reflecting on God's compassion in our own lives can cultivate a spirit of gratitude and humility. Take time to consider instances when God has shown His compassion towards you, even when you may not have deserved it. How does this knowledge of God's compassion impact how you view yourself?

Consider how you can demonstrate God's compassion to others today. Is there someone in your life who needs a word of encouragement, a listening ear, or a helping hand? How can you extend compassion and love in practical ways?

REFLECTIVE QUESTION
How does the compassion of God impact your relationship with Him and others?

Diligence

The hand of the diligent will rule,
but the lazy man will be put to forced labour.

PROVERBS 12:24

THIS PROVERB HIGHLIGHTS THE importance of a diligent work ethic in our lives. It reminds us that consistent effort and dedication lead to success and influence, while laziness brings about unwanted consequences.

Cultivating a mindset of diligence begins with recognizing the value of the tasks entrusted to us, whether big or small. When we approach our work and responsibilities with a sense of purpose and commitment, we position ourselves to excel and make a positive impact.

One practical way to cultivate diligence is by setting clear goals and prioritizing them. Break down larger tasks into smaller, manageable steps, and stay focused on the task at hand. Celebrate each milestone achieved along the way, knowing that diligence requires perseverance.

Seeking accountability from others can also aid in developing a diligent mindset. Share your goals and aspirations with a trusted friend or mentor who can provide support, encouragement, and gentle reminders of the importance of diligence.

Reflect on the consequences of laziness and the benefits of a diligent approach. Consider areas in your life where you may have been tempted to procrastinate or become complacent. How can you reframe your mindset to embrace diligence and the rewards it brings?

REFLECTIVE QUESTION
How can you cultivate a mindset of diligence in your work and responsibilities?

God, the Ultimate Judge

For exaltation comes neither from the east nor
from the west nor from the south. But God is the judge:
He puts one down, And He exalts another.

PSALM 75:6-7

IN A WORLD FILLED with injustice and inequality, it can be easy to become discouraged and lose faith. However, this psalm reassures us that God is the ultimate authority and holds the power to bring justice and righteousness.

Trusting in God's timing and justice requires a surrendering of our desire for control and a firm belief in His wisdom. Even when circumstances seem unfair, or when we face trials, we can find comfort in knowing that God sees all and will ultimately bring about justice.

Reflect on moments in your life where you may have questioned God's timing or doubted His justice. How did those experiences shape your faith? How can you cultivate a greater trust in God's perfect timing and justice moving forward?

Prayer is a powerful way to surrender our concerns and doubts to God, placing our trust in His hands. Spend time in prayer, seeking His guidance and strength to trust in His timing and justice, even when it's difficult.

REFLECTIVE QUESTION
How can you trust in God's timing and justice in your own life?

Crossing the Jordan

And Joshua said to the people,
SANCTIFY YOURSELVES, for tomorrow the
LORD will do wonders among you.

JOSHUA 3:5

THIS VERSE MARKS A significant moment in the Israelites'
journey as they prepared to cross the Jordan River and enter
the Promised Land.

Consecration is the act of setting oneself apart for a holy purpose.
Just as the Israelites were called to consecrate themselves before
crossing the Jordan, we, too, are called to prepare ourselves for
the extraordinary work God wants to do in our lives.

Consecration involves surrendering our desires and aligning
our hearts with God's will. It means seeking Him wholeheartedly,
repenting of any sins, and renewing our commitment to follow
Him faithfully.

When we consecrate ourselves, we position ourselves to
experience the amazing things God has planned. As we cross our
personal "Jordan Rivers," facing challenges and uncertainties, we
can trust that God will part the waters and lead us into a land
of blessings and fulfilment.

Take time today to reflect on how you can consecrate yourself
and prepare to receive the amazing things God wants to do in
your life. Seek His guidance, surrender your plans, and commit
to following Him wholeheartedly.

REFLECTIVE QUESTION
**How can you consecrate yourself and prepare for
the amazing things that God has in store for you?**

A Friend That Sticks Closer

...But there is a friend
who sticks closer than a brother.

PROVERBS 18:24

IN A WORLD FILLED with temporary relationships, true and loyal friends are a rare treasure. While we may have many acquaintances, it is the friend who stands by us during both joyous and challenging times that truly matters. Such a friend is a gift from God.

This verse invites us to reflect on the quality of our friendships. It reminds us that it is better to have one loyal friend than many superficial companions. True friends are there to support, encourage, and uplift us, even in our darkest moments. They provide a safe space for vulnerability, understanding, and growth.

To cultivate and cherish such a friendship, we must invest time and effort. It requires being faithful and trustworthy friends ourselves, offering support and love without expecting anything in return. Additionally, it involves nurturing open communication, demonstrating empathy, and being present in each other's lives.

Take a moment to reflect on the friends you have and the depth of those relationships. If you have a friend who sticks closer than a brother, express gratitude for their presence and strive to deepen that bond. If you don't have such a friend, pray that God will bring one into your life and be open to cultivating meaningful connections with others.

REFLECTIVE QUESTION

Do you have a friend who sticks closer than a brother? How can you cultivate and cherish such a friendship?

A Living Sacrifice

I beseech you therefore brethren,
by the mercies of God, that you present your bodies
A LIVING SACRIFICE, holy, acceptable to God,
which is your reasonable service.

ROMANS 12:1

AS BELIEVERS, OUR LIVES should be marked by a deep sense of gratitude for God's mercy and love. This verse reminds us that offering ourselves as living sacrifices is the most appropriate response to His abundant grace. It's not about animal sacrifices or external rituals but about our hearts and daily choices.

To live as a living sacrifice means to surrender our desires, ambitions, and will to God. It involves aligning our thoughts, words, and actions with His truth and purpose. It means seeking to honour Him in everything we do, whether it's at home, work, school, or in our relationships.

We can offer ourselves as living sacrifices by seeking to love and serve others selflessly, by pursuing holiness and righteousness, by using our gifts and talents to build up the body of Christ, and by being intentional about our relationship with God through prayer, Bible study, and worship.

Take a moment to reflect on your life. Are there areas where you are holding back from fully surrendering to God? How can you offer yourself as a living sacrifice in those areas? Ask God to guide and empower you to live a life that is pleasing to Him, one that reflects the gratitude and love you have for Him.

REFLECTIVE QUESTION
In what ways can you offer yourself as a living sacrifice to God in your daily life?

The Power of God's Rescue

**I shall not die, but live,
and declare the works of the Lord.**

PSALMS 118:17

WE ALL EXPERIENCE MOMENTS of physical, emotional, or spiritual distress. In those moments, we may feel hopeless and overwhelmed. But this verse reminds us that God is the source of life and healing. He has the power to restore and renew us.

When we are touched by God's healing hand, it is natural to respond with thanksgiving and praise. We are called to proclaim what the Lord has done for us, bearing witness to His faithfulness and goodness.

So, let us reflect on this: In what ways has God brought healing into your life? How can you offer thanksgiving and praise for His healing power?

Whether it is healing from physical ailments, emotional wounds, or spiritual brokenness, God's healing is worth celebrating and sharing. As we declare His works and give thanks, we not only strengthen our own faith but also encourage others to seek healing from the Great Physician.

Today, let us gratefully proclaim what the Lord has done, giving Him the glory for His mighty acts of healing in our lives.

REFLECTIVE QUESTION

How has God rescued you in the past? How can you proclaim His goodness and faithfulness to others?

Choosing Companions Wisely

Do not be deceived:
Evil company corrupts good habits.
1 CORINTHIANS 15:33

THE COMPANY WE KEEP plays a significant role in shaping our thoughts, attitudes, and behaviours. When we surround ourselves with individuals who are negative, immoral, or ungodly, we are susceptible to being influenced by their ways. Conversely, when we choose companions who are virtuous, wise, and passionate about their faith, they can inspire and encourage us on our spiritual journey.

As believers, it is important to evaluate our friendships and relationships. Are there individuals who hinder our growth or lead us astray? Are there toxic influences that need to be addressed or removed?

Cultivating healthy relationships involves seeking out companions who share our values, challenge us to grow, and support us in our pursuit of God. These are individuals who will pray for us, speak truth into our lives, and hold us accountable.

Reflect on the friendships and relationships in your life. Are there any adjustments you need to make? Pray for discernment in choosing companions who will positively impact your character and draw you closer to God. Remember that through intentional and loving connections, you can both bless and be blessed on your spiritual journey.

REFLECTIVE QUESTION
**Are the people you surround yourself with positively impacting your character and spiritual growth?
How can you cultivate relationships that align with your values and draw you closer to God?**

Nature's Response to God's Presence

The mountains skipped like rams.
O little hills like lambs.

PSALM 114:4

NATURE HAS A WAY of revealing the majesty and splendour of God. The psalmist uses poetic language to depict the mountains and hills leaping and skipping like joyful creatures in the presence of the Almighty. This metaphor captures the profound impact that God's presence has on creation.

When we witness the wondrous beauty of nature, whether it's the majestic mountains, the serene lakes, or the delicate petals of a flower, it can evoke a sense of awe and remind us of the greatness of our Creator. It serves as a tangible reminder that the same God who formed the earth and its grandeur is also intimately involved in our lives.

Take a moment to reflect on your experiences in nature. How has witnessing the marvels of creation reminded you of God's power and presence? How can you cultivate a deeper appreciation for His handiwork and allow it to draw you closer to Him?

As you spend time in nature, take the opportunity to thank God for His marvellous creation and allow its beauty to deepen your awareness of His power and presence in your life. Let nature be a source of inspiration and a reminder of the wonders God can accomplish both in the world around us and within us.

REFLECTIVE QUESTION

How does witnessing the grandeur of nature remind you of God's power and presence in your own life?

Giving and Receiving Abundantly

Give, and it will be given to you: good measure,
pressed down, shaken together, and running over
will be put into your bosom. For with the same measure
that you use, it will be measured back to you.

LUKE 6:38

IN A WORLD THAT often encourages self-centeredness and accumulation, this verse invites us to embrace a different perspective. It calls us to give freely, generously, and without expecting anything in return. When we open our hearts and hands to give, whether it's our time, resources, or love, we position ourselves to experience the overflowing blessings of God.

Generosity goes beyond monetary giving; it encompasses acts of kindness, compassion, forgiveness, and love. It involves sharing our talents, serving those in need, and being mindful of the opportunities to make a difference in the lives of others.

As we give, we can trust that God will bless us abundantly. He promises to pour out His blessings, pressed down, shaken together, and running over. However, our mindset should not be solely focused on receiving but rather on the act of giving itself as an expression of gratitude and love for God and others.

Are there opportunities to share your resources or serve others selflessly? Embrace a spirit of generosity, knowing that as you give, God will pour out His blessings upon you in ways that exceed your expectations.

REFLECTIVE QUESTION
How can you cultivate a spirit of generosity in your life? In what areas can you give freely and expectantly, trusting in God's promise of abundant blessings?

Faith that Overcomes

But He answered and said, "It is not good to take
the children's bread and throw it to the little dogs.

MATTHEW 15:26

IN THIS PASSAGE, THE Canaanite woman faced many obstacles.
She was not from the Jewish community and encountered
resistance from Jesus. However, her faith was undeterred. Instead
of being discouraged, she persisted in her belief that Jesus could
heal her daughter.

This woman's example challenges us to examine our own faith.
Do we trust in God's goodness, even when our prayers seem
unanswered or when we face trials and setbacks? Do we have
the perseverance to press forward in our belief that God is able
to work miracles in our lives and the lives of others?

Cultivating a faith that overcomes requires a deep-rooted trust
in God's character. It means surrendering our doubts and fears
and holding onto the promises of His word. It involves seeking
Him in prayer, studying His word, and relying on the Holy Spirit
for guidance and strength.

How can you cultivate a faith that perseveres, trusting in God's
goodness and power to work in your life? Remember, like the
Canaanite woman, your persistent faith can lead to miraculous
breakthroughs in your life and the lives of those around you.

REFLECTIVE QUESTION

**How can you cultivate a faith that perseveres through
challenges and believes in the goodness of God even
in difficult circumstances?**

Standing Firm in God's Promises

No weapon formed against you shall prosper,
and every tongue which rises against you in judgment
You shall condemn. This is the heritage of
the servants of the Lord, and their
righteousness is from Me, Says the Lord.

ISAIAH 54:17

THIS VERSE REMINDS US that, as believers, we are under God's divine protection. No matter what challenges or opposition we may face, God is our shield and defender. He promises to thwart any weapon formed against us and to silence every false accusation made against us. This assurance should give us great confidence and peace, knowing that we are secure in His loving care.

In our daily lives, this truth should shape how we approach difficult situations. Instead of being overwhelmed by fear or anxiety, we can trust in God's faithfulness, knowing that He will deliver us. It should also impact the way we respond to accusations and criticism. Rather than being consumed by self-doubt or wanting to retaliate, we can find our vindication in God alone, entrusting ourselves to His judgment.

As you meditate on Isaiah 54:17, take comfort in the promise of God's protection and reflect on how this truth can transform your mindset and choices. Trust in His unfailing promises and walk confidently in the knowledge that you are covered by His mighty hand.

REFLECTIVE QUESTION

How does knowing that God promises to protect you from the weapons and accusations of your enemies impact your mindset and choices in your daily life?

Finding Joy in the Morning

For His anger is but for a moment,
His favour is for life; Weeping may endure
for a night, but joy comes in the morning.

PSALMS 30:15

LIFE IS FULL OF ups and downs, seasons of weeping and seasons of rejoicing. In this verse, David acknowledges that there will be times of weeping, moments when sorrow seems overwhelming. However, he confidently declares that joy will come in the morning.

Through this verse, we are reminded that our trials and hardships are not permanent. Weeping and sorrow may endure for a night, but they are not the end of our story. God promises that joy will break through the darkness and bring a new day filled with hope and rejoicing.

This promise of joy in the morning offers us hope and strength to persevere during difficult times. It reminds us that our current struggles are temporary and that God is working behind the scenes to bring about restoration and renewal. Even in the midst of sorrow, we can hold onto the promise that God will bring joy and relief.

Consider how this promise impacts your perspective during times of weeping. How does knowing that joy will come in the morning shape your response to adversity? May you find comfort and hope in the assurance that God's joy is always waiting for you, just beyond the night of weeping.

REFLECTIVE QUESTION

How does the promise of joy coming in the morning give you hope during seasons of weeping and sorrow in your own life?

God Cares

But He was in the stern, asleep on a pillow.
And they awoke Him and said to Him,
"Teacher, do You not care that we are perishing?"

MARK 4:38

IN THIS PASSAGE, WE witness the disciples' great fear as they face the raging storm. In their desperation, they wake Jesus, questioning His care for their safety. However, what we see next reveals Jesus' unwavering power and authority over all circumstances.

Jesus rises and speaks to the wind and waves, commanding them to be still. The storm immediately ceases, leaving the disciples in awe of His power. Jesus then gently reminds them of their doubt and lack of faith.

This story reminds us that even when life's storms threaten to overcome us, Jesus is present and in control. It can be easy to question His care for us, especially when we are faced with seemingly insurmountable challenges. However, Jesus assures us that He is with us in the storm, ready to bring peace and calm.

Consider your own doubts and fears. How does this story challenge you to trust in Jesus' power and care? How can you find peace in knowing that He is in control, even in the midst of life's storms? May you find solace in the knowledge that Jesus can calm the most turbulent of seas and bring comfort to your soul.

REFLECTIVE QUESTION

How does Jesus' response to the disciples' fear and question speak to your own doubts and fears in the midst of life's storms?

Finding Strength in God's Righteousness

**You shall increase my greatness,
And comfort me on every side.**
PSALMS 71:21

IN PSALM 71:21, THE psalmist declares, "You will increase my greatness and comfort me again." This verse reminds us of the unwavering strength and comfort we can find in the presence of God, regardless of our circumstances.

Life is full of ups and downs, and sometimes we may find ourselves feeling weak, overwhelmed, or discouraged. However, when we turn to God and seek His presence, we tap into an endless source of strength and hope.

God desires to increase our greatness, not in terms of worldly success or material possessions, but in our spiritual growth and character. He longs to comfort us with His love, peace, and reassurance, especially when we face trials and challenges.

In times of difficulty, let us remember that God is always with us. He is our refuge and strength, and His presence can empower us to face any obstacle with courage and resilience. By seeking Him through prayer, meditation, and studying His Word, we can draw closer to Him and experience the fullness of His strength and comfort.

So today, let us invite God into every aspect of our lives. Let us trust in His promises and find solace in His presence, knowing that He will increase our greatness and comfort us again.

REFLECTIVE QUESTION
How can we find strength and hope in God's presence, even in difficult times?

Discovering the Wisdom and Guidance of God

If they obey and serve Him, They shall spend their days in prosperity, And their years in pleasures.

JOB 36:11

IN THE BOOK OF Job, we witness a man who faces unimaginable suffering. Yet, amidst his anguish, Job clung to his faith and sought understanding from the Almighty.

This verse reminds us that when we align ourselves with God's will, He promises to guide us and bring prosperity into our lives. However, it is crucial to remember that prosperity does not necessarily mean material wealth but encompasses spiritual growth, emotional well-being, and a deep sense of contentment.

When facing challenging times, it is easy to question God's wisdom and guidance. But let us not forget that God's perspective is much broader than our own. He sees the bigger picture, and His plans for us far exceed our limited understanding.

To trust in God's wisdom and guidance, we must cultivate a close relationship with Him through prayer, meditation, and study of His Word. By surrendering our desires and seeking His will, we open ourselves up to the profound blessings and guidance that He has in store for us.

As we navigate life's challenges, let us find solace in the truth that God's wisdom and guidance are available to us. May we remain steadfast in our faith, trusting that His plans are always for our ultimate good.

REFLECTIVE QUESTION

How can we trust in God's wisdom and guidance in challenging times?

Feeding Our Souls

But He answered and said, "It is written, 'Man shall not live by bread alone, but by every word that proceeds from the mouth of God.
MATTHEW 4:4

IN THE GOSPEL OF Matthew, we find Jesus in the midst of His wilderness temptation. Satan, attempting to sway Jesus from His mission, tempts Him to turn stones into bread. In response, Jesus utters a powerful statement in Matthew 4:4: "Man shall not live by bread alone, but by every word that proceeds out of the mouth of God."

These words remind us of the vital importance of spiritual nourishment. Just as our bodies require physical sustenance, our souls long for the nourishment of God's Word. The words of Scripture have the power to strengthen, guide, and transform us.

In our fast-paced lives, it can be tempting to prioritise material needs and neglect the feeding of our souls. Yet, Jesus teaches us that the spiritual aspect of our existence should never be overlooked. To prioritise the nourishment of our souls, we must make time for regular Scripture reading, meditation, and prayer.

Just as we make time to eat physical meals, let us also carve out moments in our day to feast on the eternal truths found within God's Word. By doing so, we open ourselves up to a deeper understanding of God's love, His will for our lives, and the wisdom we need to navigate the challenges we face.]

REFLECTIVE QUESTION
How can we prioritise the spiritual nourishment of our souls through the word of God?

Excellence

Do you see a man who excels in his work?
He will stand before kings;
He will not stand before unknown men.
PROVERBS 22:29

EXCELLENCE IS NOT ABOUT perfection or comparison to others but rather about stewarding our God-given abilities to the best of our abilities. Whether it be in our professions, relationships, or hobbies, God calls us to strive for excellence in all we do.

When we approach our tasks with a spirit of excellence, we honour God and reflect His character. We go beyond the minimum requirements and wholeheartedly give our best to glorify Him. This mindset not only impacts our own lives but also influences those around us.

To cultivate a spirit of excellence, we must embrace a growth mindset that seeks continuous improvement. It involves setting high standards for ourselves, maintaining a strong work ethic, and being open to learning and refining our skills. It requires discipline, perseverance, and a willingness to go the extra mile.

Today, let us reflect on our own areas of influence and consider how we can cultivate a spirit of excellence. How can we honour God through our work, our relationships, and our pursuits? By nurturing the potential within us and living with excellence, we can make a lasting impact in the world around us and fulfil God's purpose for our lives.

REFLECTIVE QUESTION
How can we cultivate a spirit of excellence in everything we do?

Healing for the Broken Hearted

He heals the brokenhearted
and binds up their wounds.

PSALMS 147:3

LIFE IS FILLED WITH experiences that can leave us brokenhearted. Loss, betrayal, rejection, and disappointment can leave deep wounds within us. However, we find solace in knowing that our Heavenly Father is both willing and able to heal our brokenness.

God's healing begins with His unconditional love and understanding. He empathises with our pain and offers us the peace that surpasses all understanding. His healing touch brings restoration to our hearts, renewing our hope and faith in Him.

To experience God's healing, we must first acknowledge our brokenness and bring our pain before Him in prayer. We can pour out our hearts to Him, trusting that He listens and cares. As we meditate on His Word, we find wisdom, comfort, and guidance that lead us towards healing and wholeness.

Let us reflect on the areas of brokenness in our lives and invite God to bring His healing touch. How can we surrender our pain to Him and allow His love to bind up our wounds? May we find solace in the truth that God is near, ready to restore and heal our broken hearts, bringing us toward a place of healing, wholeness, and joy once again.

REFLECTIVE QUESTION
How can we find solace and healing in God's ability to mend broken hearts?

Embracing God's Generosity

And he said to him, "Every man at the beginning
sets out the good wine, and when the guests
have well drunk, then the inferior.
You have kept the good wine until now!
JOHN 2:10

IN JOHN 2:10, WE witness the miracle of Jesus turning water
into wine at the wedding in Cana. This miraculous act reveals
God's abundant generosity and His desire to bless His children.

This verse reminds us that God's blessings surpass our
expectations and are often given in abundance. God delights in
blessing His children, not only with that which is necessary but
with an overflow of His goodness. He provides beyond what we
think we need or deserve.

To experience the overflowing abundance of God's blessings,
we must first cultivate an attitude of gratitude and trust in His
provision. We can align ourselves with God's will by seeking His
guidance in our decisions and relying on Him as our source of
strength and provision.

Additionally, we can demonstrate stewardship by managing the
blessings we have been given with integrity and generosity. As we
share our resources, time, and talents with others, we participate
in God's generosity and create a ripple effect of blessings in the
lives of those around us.

May we embrace the truth that our Heavenly Father delights in
blessing us and experience the joy of His overflowing abundance
in our lives.

REFLECTIVE QUESTION
**How can we experience the overflowing abundance
of God's blessings in our lives?**

Be Strong and Courageous

Be strong and of good courage, for to this people
you shall divide as an inheritance the land which
I swore to their fathers to give them.

JOSHUA 1:6

IN JOSHUA 1:6, WE find a powerful encouragement from God to
Joshua as he prepares to lead the Israelites into the Promised Land.

Just as Joshua faced numerous challenges and uncertainties,
we, too, encounter obstacles on our own journey of faith. Yet, in
the face of fear and uncertainty, God calls us to be strong and
courageous. He reminds us that He is faithful to His promises
and will provide the strength and guidance we need to overcome
any obstacles.

To cultivate strength and courage, we must rely on God's
presence and His Word. By meditating on His promises and
seeking His wisdom, we align our hearts and minds with His
will. Prayer becomes an essential source of strength, allowing
us to surrender our fears and anxieties into God's loving hands.

As we trust in God's promises, we can step out in faith, knowing
that He goes before us. We can face challenges with resilience,
knowing that He will never leave us nor forsake us. In our moments
of weakness, His strength becomes our own.

May we embrace the call to be strong and courageous, knowing
that in God's strength, we can overcome any obstacle and inherit
the abundant life He has promised us.

REFLECTIVE QUESTION

**How can we cultivate strength and courage to trust in
God's promises, as encouraged by Joshua 1:6?**

Unlimited Strength

I can do all things through
Christ which strengthens me.
PHILIPPIANS 4:13

IN A WORLD OFTEN filled with limitations and self-doubt, this verse offers a powerful truth: we are not alone, and we have access to a source of strength that knows no bounds. Through Christ, we have unlimited resources at our disposal.

To tap into this unlimited strength, we must first acknowledge our dependence on God. We recognise that our strength is not derived from our own efforts alone but comes through a vibrant connection with the One who is mighty and all-sufficient.

Prayer and the study of God's Word become essential in this process. As we spend time in His presence, seeking His guidance and wisdom, we are infused with His strength and empowered to face any challenge that comes our way. We realise that we are not limited by our own abilities but rather by the limitless power of Christ working within us.

Today, let us reflect on the areas of our lives where we may feel weak or inadequate. How can we tap into the unlimited strength and empowerment that comes from Christ? May we trust in His promise and rely on His Spirit to guide us, strengthen us, and enable us to walk in victory, knowing that in Him, we can do all things.

REFLECTIVE QUESTION
How can we tap into the unlimited strength and empowerment that comes from Christ?

Meditate and Prosper

This Book of the Law shall not depart from your mouth,
but you shall meditate in it day and night, that you may
observe to do according to all that is written in it.
For then you will make your way prosperous,
and then you will have good success.

JOSHUA 1:8

THIS VERSE HIGHLIGHTS THE transformative power of God's
Word. It invites us to cultivate a habit of meditating on His
teachings, not just reading them superficially but delving deep into
their meaning. Through intentional reflection and pondering, we
open ourselves up to a profound understanding of God's truth.

As we meditate on God's Word, we gain insights and wisdom
that guide our actions and decisions. It shapes our thinking, aligns
our hearts with God's will, and brings about transformation in
our lives. We begin to understand His principles for success and
prosperity, which go beyond material possessions to encompass
spiritual growth, emotional well-being, and flourishing relationships.

To cultivate the habit of meditating on God's Word, we can set
aside dedicated time each day to study and reflect on Scripture.
Journaling, prayer, and participating in Bible study groups can also
enrich our understanding and lead to life-changing insights. By
integrating God's Word into our thoughts and actions, we open
ourselves up to a life filled with purpose, prosperity, and success.

REFLECTIVE QUESTION

**How can we cultivate a habit of meditating on God's
Word to experience prosperity and success?**

The Lord Saves

Then they cried out to the Lord in their trouble,
And He saved them out of their distresses.

PSALM 107:13

LIFE IS FULL OF trials and challenges that can leave us feeling overwhelmed and powerless. But the beauty of Psalm 107:13 is that it offers hope and reassurance. It encourages us to cry out to the Lord, knowing that He hears us and is ready to save us from any distress we face. This verse reminds us that even in our darkest moments, we have a God who listens to our cries and delivers us from our troubles.

Think about a time when you felt hopeless and cried out to God for help. Perhaps it was a difficult relationship, a health crisis, or a financial struggle. Reflect on how God answered your prayers and brought you through that challenging situation. Remembering these moments can strengthen your faith and remind you of God's faithfulness.

No matter what you're going through today, take comfort in knowing that you have a God who is there for you. Trust in His unfailing love and keep seeking His guidance as you navigate life's ups and downs.

REFLECTIVE QUESTION
Have you experienced a situation where you cried out to God in your distress and felt His saving grace?

The Secret Place of Prayer

But you, when you pray, go into your room,
and when you have shut your door, pray to your Father
who is in the secret place; and your Father who sees
in secret will reward you openly.

MATTHEW 6:6

AS FOLLOWERS OF CHRIST, we are called to seek the quiet solitude of prayer. In our busy and noisy lives, it can be challenging to find a moment of stillness, but that is precisely what Jesus encourages us to do. He invites us to enter into a secret place, a physical or metaphorical room where we can offer our prayers to God.

This secret place is not about hiding from others or seeking recognition. It is about finding a space that allows us to focus solely on our relationship with God. It is a sacred space where we can pour out our hearts, share our deepest desires, and seek guidance from our Heavenly Father.

Finding this secret place can be different for everyone. It may be a designated room in your house, a favourite spot in nature, or even a quiet spot in a bustling city. The key is to intentionally set aside time and create an environment that fosters a sense of peace and connection with God.

It is in this place of vulnerability and surrender that we open ourselves to receive His rewards – peace, wisdom, comfort, and a deepening of our relationship with Him.

REFLECTIVE QUESTION
Do you have a designated place where you can retreat, shut out distractions, and commune with God in prayer?

The Power of Faith-Filled Words

For assuredly, I say to you, whoever says to this
mountain, 'Be removed and be cast into the sea,'
and does not doubt in his heart, but believes
that those things he says will be done,
he will have whatever he says.

MARK 11:23

THE WORDS WE SPEAK hold incredible power. Jesus teaches us that when we speak in faith, trusting in God's promises, mountains can be moved, and obstacles can be overcome. Our words have the ability to shape our thoughts, actions, and circumstances.

But what are the mountains in our lives? They can take various forms – challenges, struggles, doubts, fears, or even seemingly insurmountable goals. They represent the obstacles that stand between us and God's plan for our lives.

To activate the power of faith-filled words, we must align our speech with God's truth. Instead of dwelling on negative thoughts or speaking words of defeat, we are called to speak words of faith, courage, and victory. We affirm God's promises and declare His power to work in our lives.

When faced with a mountain, we can declare in faith, "I trust in God's strength to overcome this obstacle. By His power, I am more than a conqueror!" As we speak such words, we align our hearts with God's truth and open ourselves to His supernatural intervention.

Our words are an expression of our trust in God's ability to bring about the impossible. When we speak in faith, we release God's power into our situations.

REFLECTIVE QUESTION
How can you activate the power of faith-filled words to overcome them?

Aligning Desires with God's Will

**Ye ask and receive not, because ye ask amiss,
that ye may consume it upon your lust.**

JAMES 4:3

AS HUMAN BEINGS, WE are prone to seek after our own desires and pleasures. While it is not inherently wrong to have desires and ask God for specific things, our motives behind these requests must be examined.

James reminds us that our prayers may go unanswered if we ask with selfish motives. When we approach God solely for personal gain or to satisfy our own pleasures, we are not aligning ourselves with His will. Our focus becomes inward rather than outward, centred on our own desires rather than on God's glory.

To ensure our desires are aligned with God's will, we must cultivate a heart of surrender and humility. We should seek His guidance and allow His Spirit to shape our desires, aligning them with His purposes and plans for our lives.

When we come before God in prayer, it is important to examine our motives. Let us approach Him with a desire to see His kingdom come, and His will be done.

As we align our desires with God's will, we can pray with confidence, knowing that He hears us and will answer according to His perfect wisdom. Our focus shifts from selfish desires to seeking God's glory and the well-being of others.

REFLECTIVE QUESTION

How can you ensure that your requests are made with pure motives, seeking His glory above all else?

Flourishing in the Fear of the Lord

He sought God in the days of Zechariah,
who had understanding in the visions of God; and as
long as he sought the Lord, God made him prosper.

2 CHRONICLES 26:5

KING UZZIAH SERVES AS an example of someone who sought after God and embraced the fear of the Lord. He recognised the importance of seeking God's instruction and guidance, and as a result, he experienced divine favour and success.

To cultivate a heart that seeks after God, we must prioritise spending time in His presence. This can be through prayer, studying His Word, and engaging in fellowship with other believers. It is in these moments of seeking God that our hearts align with His will, and we become receptive to His leading.

Furthermore, embracing the fear of the Lord involves acknowledging His sovereignty and recognising our dependence on Him. It is not a fear characterised by terror or anxiety but rather a reverential awe and respect for the greatness of God.

When we fear the Lord, we acknowledge His holiness and align our lives with His commandments. We strive to live in a way that honours Him, seeking to please Him in all that we do.

Today, take a moment to reflect on your own pursuit of God and your attitude towards the fear of the Lord. Are you actively seeking after Him and making Him a priority in your life? Are there areas where you need to realign your heart with His will?

REFLECTIVE QUESTION
In what ways can you pursue a life marked by seeking God's guidance and presence?

Divine Justice and Deliverance

So they hanged Haman on the gallows that
he had prepared for Mordecai.
Then the king's wrath subsided.

ESTHER 7:10

THE STORY OF ESTHER is a powerful testament to God's sovereignty and His faithfulness in delivering His people. It serves as a reminder that even in the darkest of times, God is at work behind the scenes, orchestrating events for the good of His children.

Esther, in her obedience and bravery, played a pivotal role in bringing about justice and deliverance for her people. She trusted in God's guidance and was willing to risk her life for the cause of righteousness.

In our own lives, we may face circumstances that seem overwhelming and unfair. We may encounter injustice or find ourselves struggling against seemingly insurmountable odds. Yet, the story of Esther reminds us that God is always present, working in ways we cannot see.

In times of difficulty, we must place our trust in God's justice and deliverance. Just as He intervened on behalf of the Jews through Esther, He is capable of overturning evil plans and bringing about redemption in our lives.

As you walk in faith, remember that God's timing and methods may differ from our own. Trust that His plans are perfect, even if they don't align with our expectations. Rest in the assurance that He is at work, weaving together a beautiful tapestry of justice, deliverance, and redemption in your life.

REFLECTIVE QUESTION

In what areas of your life do you need to trust in God's justice and deliverance?

Soaring on Eagle's Wings

But those who hope in the Lord will renew
their strength. They will soar on wings like eagles;
they will run and not grow weary,
they will walk and not be faint.

ISAIAH 40:31

ISAIAH 40:31 IS A comforting verse that reminds us of God's promise to renew our strength and uplift us in times of weariness and despair.

Just like an eagle effortlessly soars through the sky, God promises to infuse us with renewed energy and vitality when we place our trust in Him. This verse encourages us to lean on God and trust in His power to carry us through life's challenges. When we rely on Him, we can find the strength to run our race without growing weary and to walk with unwavering faith even in the midst of trials.

In our daily lives, we can find renewed strength and hope by spending time in prayer and reading God's Word. Seeking God's guidance and relying on His wisdom can help us navigate through difficult circumstances. Additionally, surrounding ourselves with a community of believers who encourage and uplift us can also provide the support we need.

As we trust in the Lord, we can experience a transformation that enables us to soar above our circumstances and find hope even in the midst of adversity. Let us remember that our strength is not found in our own abilities but in the steadfast love and power of our Heavenly Father.

REFLECTIVE QUESTION
How can we find renewed strength and hope in our daily lives?

Trusting in the Miracle Maker

Then he said, "Go, borrow vessels from everywhere,
from all your neighbours — empty vessels;
do not gather just a few.
2 KINGS 4:3

THIS STORY TEACHES US about the power of trusting God in our times of scarcity. Despite the widow feeling overwhelmed by her circumstances, Elisha instructed her to gather empty jars, demonstrating a symbol of her faith and willingness to trust God's provision. When she poured the little oil she had left into those jars, it miraculously multiplied, filling every vessel until there were no more jars left.

In our own lives, we may face situations where resources seem scarce, and we are unsure of how to meet our needs. This story reminds us that even in our most desperate moments, God is the ultimate provider and performer of miracles. He can take what little we have and multiply it beyond our comprehension.

Trusting God to provide for our needs requires us to step out in faith and take action, just as the widow did by collecting the empty jars. It prompts us to rely on His promises and surrender our worries and fears into His capable hands. Rather than dwelling on scarcity, let us focus on God's abundance and His ability to work miracles in our lives.

Let us reflect on this story and ask ourselves, "Am I willing to trust God with my needs, even when resources seem scarce?" May we find comfort in knowing that when we place our trust in Him, He will exceed our expectations and provide abundantly.

REFLECTIVE QUESTION
How can we trust God to provide for our needs, even when resources seem scarce?

Finding Success in Surrender

When they cast you down, and you say,
'Exaltation will come!' Then He will
save the humble person.

JOB 22:29

IN THE STORY OF Job, we see a man who, despite experiencing unimaginable suffering and loss, remained faithful to God. As he faced numerous trials, Job learned that his success was not based on his own strength or achievements but on his trust in God's faithfulness. Job recognised that true success comes from aligning ourselves with God's will and relying on His guidance.

To find true success, we must surrender our plans, dreams, and desires to God. We can do this by seeking His wisdom through prayer, studying His Word, and listening to His voice. It requires humility and a willingness to let go of our own ambitions, allowing God to lead us to the path of His purpose for our lives.

When we embrace surrender, God can work miracles in our lives. He can lift us up from our lowest moments, provide us with peace and joy that surpasses all understanding, and guide us towards a life of true fulfilment. Our success is not measured by worldly standards but by our relationship with God and the impact we have on others.

May we find the courage to let go and allow God to mould us into vessels that bring glory to His name. In surrender, we discover a newfound freedom and experience the abundant life God has prepared for us.

REFLECTIVE QUESTION
How can we find true success by surrendering our plans and desires to God?

Divine Help and Guidance

Then he said, "O Lord God of my master Abraham,
please give me success this day,
and show kindness to my master Abraham.

GENESIS 24:12

IN THIS SIMPLE PRAYER, Abraham's servant demonstrates his trust in God's faithfulness to guide him in his search for Isaac's future wife.

Just as the servant relied on God for direction, we too can trust that God will guide us in our search for His will in our lives. God's faithfulness and guidance are not limited to biblical times; He continues to lead and direct His people today. We can seek His guidance through prayer, asking Him to reveal His plans and purposes for our lives.

Trusting God's guidance requires patience and a willingness to surrender our own desires and plans. We must be attentive to His voice, staying open to the ways in which He may choose to reveal Himself. Seeking wisdom from trusted mentors and studying His Word can also provide clarity and discernment as we navigate through life's decisions.

When we trust in God's guidance, He promises to show us His kindness and faithfulness. Though the path may not always be clear, we can have confidence that God is leading us in the right direction. His plans for us are good, and He desires for us to experience His abundant blessings.

REFLECTIVE QUESTION
How can we trust that God will guide us in our search for His will?

Freedom From Sin

**For the law of the Spirit of life in Christ Jesus
has made me free from the law of sin and death.**
ROMANS 8:2

THE LAW WAS NOT made for the righteous but for the unrighteous. In the Old Covenant, they make sacrifices once a year for their remission of sin. So, every year, this sacrifice would be made by the high priest on behalf of the people. However, one major limitation of this sacrifice is that it brings a remembrance of sin and does not make any of the Israelites righteous.

But there was a shift. One sacrifice was made in the new covenant, which declared you and me righteous forever. The sacrifice of Jesus on the cross made you the righteousness of God. So, whenever Jesus sees you, He no longer sees your sin but Christ in you. Isn't that amazing? Yes, I know it is.

We are declared righteous not by the law or our works but by grace through faith in Jesus Christ. Hence, we are free from sin. Nevertheless, this grace is not a yardstick to dwell in sin but the power to live a righteous life. Walk in the light of the revelation of this knowledge, and thank God always for the gift of Jesus Christ. You are redeemed! You are free from sin and death!

REFLECTIVE QUESTION
**How does living in the Spirit of Christ bring true
freedom to our lives?**

Praise Him Always

Let everything that has breath
praise the Lord. Praise the Lord.

PSALMS 150:6

IT IS EASY TO limit our praise and worship to specific occasions or designated times of prayer and worship services. However, God desires for us to cultivate a heart of praise in every aspect of our lives. Whether we are at work, spending time with loved ones, or simply going about our daily routines, we can offer heartfelt praise to our Creator.

When we recognise that every breath we take is a gift from God, we begin to see opportunities to express our gratitude and adoration. We can praise God for His faithfulness, His provision, His love, and His grace. We can worship Him through our actions, treating others with kindness and sharing His love with those around us.

Developing a lifestyle of praise requires intentional effort and a mindset of gratitude. It involves shifting our focus from our circumstances to the goodness and greatness of God. When we choose to praise Him in everything, we not only draw closer to Him but also invite His presence and blessings into our lives.

May we be reminded that praise is not limited to specific moments but is a lifestyle that invites God's presence and transforms our perspective. Let us live each day giving thanks and offering praise to our loving and deserving Heavenly Father.

REFLECTIVE QUESTION

How can we cultivate a heart of praise and worship in every aspect of our lives?

Abundant Blessings through Obedience

The Lord will open to you His good treasure,
the heavens, to give the rain to your land in its season,
and to bless all the work of your hand. You shall lend
to many nations, but you shall not borrow.

DEUTERONOMY 28:12

IN THE CONTEXT OF Deuteronomy, God was speaking to the Israelites, laying out the blessings they would receive for obeying His commands. While this was specific to them, the principle remains true for us today. When we walk in obedience to God's Word and follow His guidance, we position ourselves to receive His abundant blessings.

Obedience to God's commands includes living a life of integrity, loving others, honouring Him through our actions, and seeking His will in all things. It means prioritising our relationship with Him above everything else and aligning our desires and choices with His principles.

When we obediently follow God's commands, He opens the floodgates of His blessings. He pours out His favour, protection, and provision upon us. His abundant blessings may manifest in various ways, including physical, emotional, and spiritual blessings that bring joy, peace, and fulfilment.

May we seek to align our lives with His will and walk faithfully in His ways.

REFLECTIVE QUESTION

How does obedience to God's commands align us with His blessings and provision?

Rise and Walk in Faith

The sick man answered Him, "Sir, I have no man
to put me into the pool when the water is stirred up;
but while I am coming, another steps down before me.
JOHN 5:7

IN JOHN 5:7, WE encounter a powerful interaction between Jesus and a man who had been crippled for thirty-eight years. Despite his limitations, Jesus commanded him: "Rise, take up your bed, and walk."

This encounter teaches us the transformative power of faith in Jesus. The man's physical infirmity symbolises the spiritual brokenness we all experience. Just as Jesus offered healing to the crippled man, He offers spiritual healing and wholeness to us. When we place our faith in Him, we can experience a newness of life that transcends our circumstances.

Faith in Jesus empowers us to overcome obstacles and walk in the newness of life. It is a catalyst for transformation, enabling us to rise above our limitations and embrace the abundant life Jesus promises. As we trust in His power, His grace, and His love, we discover that nothing is impossible with Him.

Let us confidently trust in Him, allowing His transformative power to work in us and propel us forward in faith. With Jesus by our side, we can rise above our obstacles and walk confidently in the abundant life He offers.

REFLECTIVE QUESTION
How does our faith in Jesus empower us to overcome obstacles and walk in the newness of life?

Choose Today, Serve the Lord

And if it seems evil to you to serve the Lord,
choose for yourselves this day whom you will serve,
whether the gods which your fathers served that were
on the other side of the River, or the gods of the
Amorites, in whose land you dwell. But as for me
and my house, we will serve the Lord.

JOSHUA 24:15

IN JOSHUA 24:15, JOSHUA presents the people of Israel with a powerful choice. This verse encapsulates the importance of making a deliberate decision to serve God wholeheartedly.

Every day, we are faced with countless choices that shape our lives. From the mundane to the significant, our choices reflect our values and priorities. Joshua reminds us that serving the Lord is not a passive action but an intentional decision. It requires us to consciously align our thoughts, attitudes, and actions with God's will.

Consider how you can actively choose to serve the Lord in your everyday life. It may involve making time for prayer and studying His Word, seeking opportunities to show kindness and compassion to others, or making choices that align with biblical principles. By consciously choosing to serve God, we invite His presence and guidance into our lives, experiencing the blessings that come from living in obedience to Him.

May your daily choices be a testament to your commitment to follow Him wholeheartedly.

REFLECTIVE QUESTION
How can you actively choose to serve the Lord in your daily life?

Encourage Yourself in the Lord

Now David was greatly distressed, for the people spoke
of stoning him, because the soul of all the people was
grieved, every man for his sons and his daughters.
But David strengthened himself in the Lord his God.

1 SAMUEL 30:6

IN 1 SAMUEL 30:6, we find an inspiring story of David facing a moment of immense distress. The Amalekites had raided the city of Ziklag, taking captive all the women, children, and possessions. In the midst of this devastating loss, David's situation seemed utterly hopeless. However, in his moment of despair, he found strength in the Lord.

When faced with overwhelming challenges, it is easy to succumb to fear and discouragement. But David's response was different. Instead of giving in to despair, he "strengthened himself in the LORD his God." He sought solace and guidance in God's presence, finding renewed strength and courage to face the adversity before him.

In our own lives, we, too, encounter moments of difficulties and setbacks. It is during these times that we must remember to turn to God for strength and guidance. His presence is a source of comfort, peace, and wisdom. By seeking Him earnestly through prayer, meditation, and studying His Word, we tap into His divine power that can sustain us in the midst of trials.

Even in our darkest moments, God's presence can empower us to overcome the obstacles we face.

REFLECTIVE QUESTION
How can you find strength in God's presence during times of adversity?

The Power of Persistent Prayer

And when Peter had come to himself, he said,
"Now I know for certain that the Lord has sent
His angel, and has delivered me from the hand of
Herod and from all the expectation of the Jewish people.

ACTS 12:11

IN ACTS 12:11, WE witness the incredible power of persistent prayer. Peter, imprisoned by King Herod, was miraculously freed by an angel of the Lord. This passage reminds us of the significance of consistent and unwavering prayer in our own lives.

Often, we face trials and challenges that seem insurmountable. It is in these moments that prayer becomes our lifeline, connecting us to the limitless power and grace of God. Just as the early believers fervently prayed for Peter's release, we, too, are called to cultivate a persistent prayer life.

Persistent prayer involves more than simply making requests to God. It is a deepening of our relationship with Him, a conversation that allows us to align our hearts with His will. Through persistent prayer, we surrender our own desires and seek God's guidance and intervention in all aspects of our lives.

Consider how you can cultivate a deeper and more persistent prayer life. Set aside dedicated time each day to commune with God, expressing your joys, concerns, and needs. Engage in prayer not only when you are in distress but also in times of gratitude and celebration. Allow your prayer life to become a continuous dialogue with your Heavenly Father.

REFLECTIVE QUESTION

How can you cultivate a deeper and more persistent prayer life?

Becoming Agents of Generosity

If you extend your soul to the hungry
And satisfy the afflicted soul, Then your light
shall dawn in the darkness,
And your darkness shall be as the noonday.

ISAIAH 58:10

IN ISAIAH 58:10, WE are challenged to be agents of generosity and compassion: "If you spend yourselves on behalf of the hungry and satisfy the needs of the oppressed, then your light will rise in the darkness, and your night will become like the noonday."

God's heart for justice and compassion is evident throughout the Bible. Isaiah reminds us that true worship extends beyond rituals and religious practices. It involves actively caring for those in need being a light in the midst of darkness.

As followers of Christ, we are called to be reflections of God's love and compassion in the world. This requires us to step out of our comfort zones and extend a helping hand to the hungry, the oppressed, and those in need. When we invest our time, resources, and efforts in serving others, we become channels of God's grace and blessings.

Consider how you can spend yourself on behalf of the hungry and satisfy the needs of the oppressed. Embrace opportunities to extend a helping hand, show kindness, and share your resources. By becoming agents of generosity, we bring hope and healing to a broken world, reflecting God's character and love.

REFLECTIVE QUESTION
How can you actively practice generosity and serve those in need?

The Endless Cycle of Forgiveness

Then Peter came to Him and said, 'Lord,
how often shall my brother sin against me,
and I forgive him? Up to seven times?'
Jesus said to him, 'I do not say to you,
up to seven times, but up to seventy times seven.

MATTHEW 18:21-22

FORGIVENESS LIES AT THE core of the Christian faith. Just as God has extended His forgiveness to us, we are called to forgive others. But forgiveness is not always easy. It requires a deliberate choice to let go of resentment, anger, and the desire for revenge.

Jesus' response to Peter emphasises a radical truth: forgiveness knows no limits. It is not a one-time act but a continuous attitude of the heart. Cultivating a heart of forgiveness involves embracing the understanding that we have been forgiven much by God, and therefore, we can extend that same grace to others.

Reflect on your own life. Are there individuals you need to forgive or release from the burden of your anger? How can you cultivate a heart of forgiveness and extend grace to those who have hurt you?

Remember, forgiveness does not justify or condone the wrong done; rather, it breaks the chains of bitterness and allows healing and reconciliation to take place. As we walk in the freedom of forgiveness, we experience the transformative power of God's love.

REFLECTIVE QUESTION
How can you cultivate a heart of forgiveness and extend grace to others?

The Price

You were bought at a price...
1 CORINTHIANS 7:23

AS FOLLOWERS OF CHRIST, we have been set free from the bondage of sin and the expectations of the world. We are no longer slaves to human opinions or societal pressures, for our worth and identity are found in Christ alone. Our freedom stems from the sacrifice Jesus made on the cross, paying the price for our sins and offering us salvation.

Reflect on how you can fully embrace the freedom you have in Christ. Are there areas of your life where you still feel captive to the opinions of others or the ways of the world? How can you intentionally seek to live in the freedom that Christ has given you?

Living in freedom means living according to the truth and principles found in God's Word. It involves surrendering our lives to His lordship and aligning our desires and actions with His will. It means walking confidently in our identity as children of God, secure in His love and acceptance.

Embrace the freedom you have been given by Christ. Let go of the burdens that weigh you down and hold you captive. Live boldly, guided by the truth of God's Word and empowered by the Holy Spirit.

REFLECTIVE QUESTION
How can you fully embrace the freedom you have in Christ?

Tempted, Yet Without Sin

For we do not have a High Priest who can not
sympathise with our weaknesses, but was in all
points tempted as we are, yet without sin.

HEBREWS 4:15

IN OUR JOURNEY THROUGH life, we often face challenges, temptations, and struggles. It is comforting to know that our Savior, Jesus Christ, fully understands our weaknesses. He experienced the limitations and trials of human existence firsthand yet remained without sin.

Knowing that Jesus truly empathises with our weaknesses should deeply impact our relationship with Him. We can approach Him with confidence, knowing that we are not alone in our struggles. He is always there to extend His grace, offer comfort, and provide the strength we need to overcome.

Reflect on the impact of Jesus' understanding of your weaknesses. How does it change your perspective on seeking His help and guidance in times of struggle? How can you deepen your relationship with Him, knowing that He intimately knows and cares for you?

Let the knowledge of Jesus' compassion motivate you to draw near to Him, to pour out your heart in prayer, and to seek His wisdom and guidance. Through His understanding and grace, He equips us to navigate the challenges of life and grow into the people He has called us to be.

REFLECTIVE QUESTION
How does knowing that Jesus understands your weaknesses impact your relationship with Him?

Faith Over Fear

Have I not commanded you?
Be strong and of good courage; do not be afraid,
nor be dismayed, for the Lord your God
is with you wherever you go.

JOSHUA 1:9

GOD'S COMMAND TO BE strong and courageous reminds us that He is always by our side. The same assurance He gave to Joshua applies to us today. When we face trials, when fear or discouragement sets in, we can draw strength and courage from the presence of our loving and powerful God.

Reflect on how you can cultivate a mindset of strength and courage in your daily life. Are there areas where fear or discouragement has hindered your progress or caused you to hold back? How can you actively lean on God's promises and step forward with confidence?

Cultivating a mindset of strength and courage involves meditating on God's Word, filling our hearts and minds with His promises, and seeking His guidance through prayer. It means choosing to trust in His faithfulness and sovereignty, even in the face of adversity.

Remember, be strong and courageous not because of your own abilities but because of the One who walks beside you. Allow His presence to ignite a boldness within you that transcends circumstances and propels you forward in faith.

May you embrace God's command to be strong and courageous, knowing that He is with you every step of the way.

REFLECTIVE QUESTION
How can you cultivate a mindset of strength and courage in your daily life?

The Promise of the Holy Spirit

Nevertheless, I tell you the truth.
It is to your advantage that I go away; for if I do not
go away, the Helper will not come to you;
but if I depart, I will send Him to you.

JOHN 16:7

IN THIS VERSE, JESUS is speaking to his disciples, preparing them for his departure. He assures them that although he will physically leave them, he will send them the Helper, the Holy Spirit. Jesus explains that it is actually to their advantage that he goes away because the Holy Spirit will come and be with them forever.

The presence of the Holy Spirit brings comfort, guidance, and empowerment. When we embrace the Spirit's presence, we can experience a deep intimacy with God and live in alignment with His will. The Holy Spirit enables us to understand the Scriptures, helps us in prayer, convicts us of sin, and empowers us to live out our faith.

Take a moment to reflect on how the Holy Spirit impacts your walk with God. How does knowing that you have a Helper by your side change your perspective and approach to life's challenges? How can you rely on the Holy Spirit more fully in your daily life? Embrace the promise Jesus made, and invite the Holy Spirit to guide and empower you today.

REFLECTIVE QUESTION
How does knowing that Jesus sent the Holy Spirit to be with you impact your daily life and walk with God?

Set Free in Christ

**For sin shall not have dominion over you,
for you are not under law but under grace.**
ROMANS 6:14

IN THIS VERSE, THE apostle Paul reminds us of the incredible freedom we have in Christ. Through His sacrifice on the cross, Jesus has broken the power of sin over our lives. We are no longer enslaved to sin but are now under God's grace.

Understanding that we are no longer under the dominion of sin should bring great joy and gratitude to our hearts. It means that through Christ, we have been set free from the guilt, shame, and bondage that sin once held over us. We now have the power and ability to live in a way that honours God and brings Him glory.

Reflect on how this truth shapes your daily choices and actions. Are there areas in your life where you still struggle with sin? How can you rely on God's grace and the power of the Holy Spirit to overcome those areas? Embrace the freedom you have in Christ and allow His grace to transform you from the inside out.

REFLECTIVE QUESTION
How does the truth that you are no longer under the dominion of sin impact how you live your life?

The Power of God's Word

For the word of God is living and powerful,
and sharper than any two-edged sword,
piercing even to the division of soul and spirit,
and of joints and marrow, and is a discerner
of the thoughts and intents of the heart.

HEBREWS 4:12

THE AUTHOR OF HEBREWS beautifully describes the power and effectiveness of God's Word. It is not merely a collection of words on a page but a living and active force that has the ability to penetrate deep within our being. The Word of God has the power to discern our thoughts, intentions, and motives, revealing the truth of who we are before God.

Understanding that God's Word is living and active should motivate us to engage with it intentionally. It is not meant to be a passive reading but an active interaction with the very voice of God. As we spend time in His Word, it has the power to transform our hearts, renew our minds, and guide our steps.

How do you approach reading and studying the Bible? Are you seeking to truly allow it to penetrate your heart and shape your life? Embrace the power of God's Word and allow it to speak to every area of your life, bringing transformation and direction.

REFLECTIVE QUESTION
How can you cultivate a greater hunger for God's Word in your daily routine?

Fearfully and Wonderfully Made

For You formed my inward parts; You covered me in my mother's womb. I will praise You, for I am fearfully and wonderfully made; Marvelous are Your works, And that my soul knows very well.

PSALMS 139:13-14

IN THESE VERSES, THE psalmist praises God for the intricate and intentional way He formed each one of us. From the earliest stages of development in the womb, God's hand was at work, crafting and shaping us with care and purpose. The psalmist recognises the awe-inspiring nature of God's creation and acknowledges the beauty of being fearfully and wonderfully made.

Recognising that we are fearfully and wonderfully made by our Creator should fill us with a deep sense of value and worth. It reminds us that we are not accidents or mistakes but intentionally designed by God for a purpose. It also speaks to the immense love and care God has for us.

Reflect on how this truth shapes the way you view yourself and your worth. How does it influence your relationship with God and others? In what ways can you embrace and celebrate the unique way God has made you? Allow this truth to transform your perspective and cultivate a deeper appreciation for the beauty of God's work in your life.

REFLECTIVE QUESTION

How does the understanding that you are fearfully and wonderfully made impact your self-worth and relationship with God?

Transformed into His Image

But we all, with unveiled face, beholding as in
a mirror the glory of the Lord, are being transformed
into the same image from glory to glory,
just as by the Spirit of the Lord.

2 CORINTHIANS 3:18

IN THIS VERSE, THE apostle Paul speaks of the transformative power of beholding the glory of the Lord. As we fix our gaze on Him with an open and receptive heart, the Holy Spirit works within us, gradually transforming us to reflect the image of Christ. This process of transformation is ongoing, moving from one degree of glory to another.

Understanding that we are being transformed into the image of Christ should fill us with hope and purpose. It means that our lives are not stagnant or aimless but have a grand purpose of becoming more like our Savior. It also reminds us that the transformation is not achieved by our own efforts but through the work of the Holy Spirit within us.

How can you actively participate in this process of transformation? What areas of your life still need to align with the image of Christ? Surrender yourself to the work of the Holy Spirit and allow Him to mould and shape you into the person God intends you to be. Embrace the journey of transformation and trust that God is faithful to complete the work He has started in you.

REFLECTIVE QUESTION
How does the concept of being transformed into the image of Christ inspire and guide your life journey?

Be Grateful

It is good to give thanks to the Lord,
and to sing praises to your name,
O Most High.

PSALMS 92:1

THE GOODNESS OF GOD in your life cannot be overemphasised. I understand that you have other requests for what you want from God. There are many other amazing things in life you have enjoyed that you never asked for your prayers. God bless your words and thoughts. So, sometimes, He does it when you even think about it.

It will be an ungrateful attitude not to thank God for what you have while you keep asking for what you want. Gratitude takes you to a new altitude. It compels the giver to do more than you expect. Thank God for what you have while you trust Him for what you are yet to get.

Whatever is good is from God. Consider the good things around you. Look at the way God favoured you in your job. Consider how He protected you and your family. Please consider all the amazing things you have enjoyed this season. If you are thoughtful, you will be grateful.

Why do you think you deserve more from God when you have not thanked Him for what He has done? Only a grateful heart receives more from the Lord. Let your mouth be filled with songs of thanksgiving to God at all times, and you will see Him move on your behalf and in places you least expected.

REFLECTIVE QUESTION

What are three things you are thankful for today?

You are God's Handiwork

For we are His workmanship, created in Christ Jesus
for good works, which God prepared beforehand
that we should walk in them.

EPHESIANS 2:10

CREATIVE INVENTIONS BY GREAT minds got the world's technology to where it is today. The names of these men are mentioned and celebrated all over the world regarding their inventions. The beauty of life is when what you create becomes a blessing to you and the world. There is a joy that comes with this kind of achievement.

Likewise, God feels so delighted when you and I, created in His image, can do what He has ordained us on earth. God created you to show forth His pleasure to the world. Do you know what gives God pleasure? Of course, it is a life of praise for Him. Praise God with your skills and creativity. Praise Him for your purpose. Let your life reflect God's goodness because you are His handiwork.

God loves you, and He has deposited so much in you. God's investment in you is so that you will increase it and replicate it anywhere you find yourself. It will sadden God's heart when you do not live up to His investment in your life. God's investment in you is the skills, talents, and gifts you receive from Him by grace. However, what you do with God's investment will determine if you live the life He expected of you as His handiwork.

You were created for good works. Never stop living this life of goodness, love, charity, and purpose. Your purpose is tied to what you do for God and His kingdom. Start living for this purpose as of today.

REFLECTIVE QUESTION
**What good works has God specifically designed
for you to do?**

Living as Instruments of Righteousness

And do not present your members as instruments
of unrighteousness to sin, but present yourselves
as being alive from the dead, and your members as
instruments of righteousness to God.

ROMANS 6:13

THE ESSENCE OF THE creation of man is that we might give God pleasure. Your life is meant to make God's heart merry. Anything devoid of this is unrighteousness. Unrighteousness is not just living in sin but living by your will without considering God in the equation of your life. You have not truly yielded to God in righteousness until He governs your will, emotions, and actions.

God desires complete dedication of the body, spirit, and soul solely to Him. Guard against any part of your being becoming an instrument of unrighteousness. Resist allowing the devil to use your soul for lust, pride, hatred, or wickedness. Love for God should manifest in a hatred for evil. Ensure that nothing you possess becomes a tool of unrighteousness.

If you love God, you will hate evil. Let nothing that is yours become a tool of unrighteousness. Ensure your house or office does not harbour strange gods or anything you exhort above God. Set clear rules not to use your internet gadgets to view pornographic content, watch raunchy movies, or listen to songs that corrupt the heart.

Use all you have for righteousness. Let your space be God's dwelling, showcasing His works as you emulate His lifestyle. Be available to God, letting Him use you and what you have for His glory.

REFLECTIVE QUESTION

In what areas of your life do you need to offer yourself more fully to God as an instrument of righteousness?

Ask Until Your Joy is Full

**Until now you have asked nothing in my name.
Ask and you will receive, that your joy may be full.**
JOHN 16:23

WAS THERE A TIME somebody told you they were tired of giving to you? Have you ever depended on someone for a livelihood and knew it was getting the person annoyed? As someone dear to you, make you promise but end up disappointing? If any of these instances fit into your experience, it shows those people who did that to you are humans. And as humans, we are prone to mistakes, errors, and forgetfulness.

But you have a God who does not feel tired when you ask, nor does He make any mistakes concerning things that pertain to your needs. God is more interested in giving you than you desire to have it. However, the challenge has always been that we do not know how to ask. It takes faith to receive from God. When you ask, first believe you have a God willing to do what you ask.

The next step is to keep asking until you are assured that you have received it, even when you do not. This assurance is faith that produces joy in your heart about anything you ask from God. Do not give up on God because He will surely do what you ask. Sometimes, this might not be in your timing. But trust me, God will give you in His time. He makes everything beautiful in His time. Therefore, do not give up when you are yet to receive whatever you ask from God.

REFLECTIVE QUESTION
How can you deepen your prayer life and trust in the power of prayer?

What Kind of Vessel are You?

But in great house there are not only vessels of
gold and silver, but also of wood and clay,
some for honour and some for dishonour.

2 TIMOTHY 2:20

VESSELS BEFORE GOD ARE people. God seeks vessels so that He can pour Himself into them. It is not about being able to receive from God. God wants to make you a vessel that serves as well as God's deposit that flows into the world. When God sees you as a useful vessel, He makes you like Him on earth. A useful vessel before God becomes a source to others.

Today, God is looking for vessels that can be a conduit through which He can conduct His power, graces, and might. What kind of vessel are you before God? Some vessels make noise and do not impact. These are empty vessels that hold no substance. Some activities drain away God's infilling of a vessel.

Actions and habits that do not depict purity cannot hold God's outpouring. Before any vessel could be useful to God, purity is a prerequisite. God does not use a vessel that rejoices in sin and iniquity. Consecrate yourself; He will make you a vessel fit for His divine purpose.

REFLECTIVE QUESTION

How can you live your life as a vessel set apart for honourable purposes?

Write the Vision

Then the Lord answered me and said:
WRITE THE VISION and make it plain on tablets,
that he may run who reads it.
HABAKKUK 2:2

HAVE YOU EVER HAD a great idea that you did not write but later became so difficult to retrieve from your mind? Or have you ever woken up with something on your mind that you knew was great, but because you were so busy, you did not have time to write it down? If any of these two cases have been your experience, it indicates that ideas fly, and when you do not capture them by writing, you miss them.

Many wonderful thoughts, ideas, and creative powers had been lost because we could not trap them in books. The reason for writing your ideas, goals, or visions is that it strengthens you to take action about what you have written. The faintest pen is more reliable than the sharpest brain.

Some of these things could be a business idea, a strategy, or even an instruction from the Lord. Once you do not document it, you lose it. Cultivate the habit of writing. It gives you the power to take maximum action. What dream have you had today? What are some ideas that flash through your mind? Do you have specific goals for what you want to do this year? If any of these questions answer yes, I urge you to write them down now and steadily progress towards achieving them.

REFLECTIVE QUESTION
How can you actively record and share God's promises and revelations in your life?

You are Seated Above

And raised us up together, and made us sit together
in the heavenly places in Christ Jesus.
EPHESIANS 2:6

WE ARE SEATED WITH Christ in heavenly places. This is not a
fallacy but the truth. The scripture calls you co-heir with Christ
(Romans 8:17). It means you have the same access to God as Jesus
Christ. You are, interestingly, being seated above everything under
your feet. Sin no longer dominates you because your present
location is higher than sin. God raises every believer in Christ
so that what dominates others comes under your foot.

As a believer, your sitting posture with Christ is part of your
inheritance. Also, the seat signifies rest. God assures you that
you will rest in Him. Whatever battle of life is facing you right
now, there is an assurance in God that he will fight for you. All
you have to do is watch for the rest. Stop trying to do what God
has already done for you. Whatever God does is forever. If he
had promised you rest, then it would be forever.

Your position in Christ is already an accomplished one. You
do not need to do anything to earn it. It became yours when
you came into God's kingdom. Remember, a king could speak
from His throne without moving around, and whatever He says
becomes a command. God has made you a Priest and King on
earth. Therefore, rule and reign.

REFLECTIVE QUESTION
How does being raised and seated with Christ shape
your perspective and daily life?

New Wine

> Nor do they put new wine into old wineskins,
> or else the wineskins break, the wine is spilt, and the
> wineskins are ruined. But they put new wine into
> new wineskins, and both are preserved.
> MATTHEW 9:17

FOR ANYTHING TO CHANGE in your life, you need first to change something in your mind. An old thinking pattern cannot produce a new life. This is why repentance is a change in heart and not necessarily a confession in words. Change your thoughts; you will change your life. How, then, can you achieve this?

It would be best if you stopped holding on to the hurt from the past. Forgive to be free. Your true liberation is when you no longer feel the sting of pain when you remember the person or situation that once made you cry.

To have a changed life, always anticipate a new and glorious future ahead of you. The mind is programmed to have what you anticipate receiving from life. Your anticipation empowers your hands to work for what you want and allows your mind to produce energies that attract what you believe for yourself.

Subsequently, engage more in personal development. Personal development is desiring a better life and working to have it. Be deliberate about the type of life you want and get resources, books, and materials that change you into that person.

Always Hold on to what adds value to your life and let go of the rest, no matter how appealing it looks. As you do these things, I see a new spring of freshwater flowing out of the well of your heart.

REFLECTIVE QUESTION
In what areas of your life do you need to embrace new wineskins to receive and contain the newness Christ offers?

Cast Your Cares on Him

**Casting all your care upon Him,
for He cares for you.**
1 PETER 5:7

WHAT HAS BEEN THE burden on your heart recently? What has been the situation that makes you constantly soak your pillow in tears? Has a failed project, heartbreak, or family problem become a great concern for you lately? Do you feel helpless in your situation? There is always help available. Our God is our present help in times of need. Take the burdens off your heart and put them in the hands of the greatest burden-bearer. He cares for you.

In the past, I used to be worried about many things. Anxiety and fear of the unknown almost made me lose all that I had. Sometimes, after I have prayed about the things that bother my mind, I still squeeze myself into the corner of my room to shed tears. However, I realised that many of those things that caused fear and anxiety were not actually how they were. I realised that I magnified those situations in my heart.

Rather than allowing the devil to complicate issues for you, why not just take the matter to God in prayers and place them at His feet? Do not try to change the situations you do not have the wisdom to handle. Seek the God of all knowledge to know what to do, and He will direct your ways. God will only teach you what He knows you need to do. Sometimes, He will do what He knows you cannot do. Just trust Him for your life and situations.

REFLECTIVE QUESTION
How can you practically cast your cares on God today?

Trusting God's Perfect Plan

**Your kingdom come, your will be done
on earth as it is in Heaven.**
MATTHEW 6:10

A KINGDOM IS SIMPLY a king's domain. So, when the scripture says, "Your kingdom come," it means that God's domain should come on earth. That was an excerpt from the Lord's Prayer, and it is very significant in our lives today. God's kingdom involves His culture, government, and ways of life. Jesus instructs his disciples (which include you and me) to pray for God's kingdom to come. Peace, joy, orderliness, and righteousness prevail where God's kingdom is.

The coming of God's kingdom should be the undying burden of God's people. Those who love the King eagerly yearn for his kingdom to come. You are responsible for spreading God's influence on the earth. If you begin with where you live or work, many people within those environments will be influenced and would like to be a part of this kingdom.

When you pray and say, "Your kingdom come, O God," there is a real sense of yearning and loyalty. If you love the King, you will yearn eagerly for his kingdom. You cannot say "Thy kingdom come" while you promote your kingdom. Sin is an expression of disloyalty to God. It lifts you and your lifestyle over the will of Christ.

Therefore, pray today that the Lord should be merciful and cancel whatever you have done to hinder His Kingdom on earth.

REFLECTIVE QUESTION
How can you align your will with God's will today?

A Strong Refuge in Times of Trouble

God is our refuge and strength,
a very present help in trouble.

PSALMS 46:1

I DIDN'T CONSIDER GOD my greatest ally when I was much younger. Instead, I used to see him as an angry father standing over me, waiting to pounce on every failure. I'm so grateful I no longer see him this way, as I've discovered he's more kind, compassionate, and gracious than I could ever imagine.

God is nothing like we sometimes wrongly portray or perceive him. As my views have changed dramatically and continue to change, many now see God the way He is. God is your refuge! You can come to Him just as you are, tell Him the deep things of your heart, and share your pain so that He may soothe it and your wounds so that He may heal them.

God is your deliverer. He gives you victory over your oppressors, who hold you back and prevent you from living to your full potential. God is delivering you! I believe that He will cause you to triumph in this situation today. Fix your eyes on Him and the miracle that's on its way!

You can find a place of hiding in Him when storms arise, and life tries to throw its fiery darts at you.

REFLECTIVE QUESTION
How has God been your refuge and strength in the past? How can you rely on Him to help you in your current situation?

The Purpose of Life

Let us hear the conclusion of the whole matter:
Fear God and keep His commandments,
For this is man's all.
ECCLESIASTES 12:13

GOD IS FEARFUL. THIS kind of fear does not mean God wants to be dreaded. The fear of God is awe for Him. It is an act of honour, reference, respect, and submission to God and His word. It is wisdom to fear God because it saves you from actions and detrimental life choices. Your fear of God guides you about how to live your life to please God.

Abraham obediently went with Isaac to the place of sacrifice because he feared the Lord. He has obeyed all the instructions that God gave him. You cannot claim to fear and be disobedient to His word. Your worship and reference to God have much to do with your obedience to His instructions. God honours those who fear Him by revealing His secrets to them (Psalm 25:14).

God is not wicked, and He will never cause you danger. However, there are natural consequences for human actions. Do not take the consequences of your actions as God's punishment for your wrongdoings. God does not do evil; neither does He tempt anyone with evil (James 1:13). He requests that you honour Him and follow His commandments. It will save you a lot of stress. Keep your life safe with God by obeying His command.

REFLECTIVE QUESTION
How can you cultivate a deeper reverence for God in your daily life? What steps can you take to align your actions with His commandments?

Wise People Take Advice

The way of a fool is right in his own eyes.
But he who HEEDS COUNSEL is WISE.
PROVERBS 12:15

THERE WAS A TIME when I had a very good business idea and wanted to execute it. I decided not to mention it to my friends or business people because I felt they would steal my idea and use it for themselves. So, I began all by myself. However, I got to a point where I needed someone with expertise in a particular field. Although I had consultants and business moguls as friends, my ego did not allow me to meet them for advice. Again, I did it all by myself, so the business crumbled before it was built.

Please do not be like Him. There is safety in a multitude of counsellors. It is wise to seek counsel from people you know who have the spirit of counsel or perhaps from people who have done what you wish to start.

Now, you need to understand that even if you might not be a smart person, having competent and intelligent friends will save you from many disasters, especially when you want to make vital life decisions. Who are you, friends? Where do you get counsel whenever you need it? Can you trust your friend's opinion about any matter concerning you? Think about this.

REFLECTIVE QUESTION
How can you cultivate a humble attitude and actively seek wise counsel?

For Your Sake, He Became Poor

For you know the grace of our Lord Jesus Christ, that though He was rich, yet for your sakes He became poor, that you through His poverty might be rich.

2 CORINTHIANS 8:9

JESUS WAS GOD IN human form when he came to earth. He left all he had—the glory, power, and majesty—and came in the likeness of a man just for your sake. Jesus became many things for us to enjoy peace and affluence. Yes! He was poor so that you could be rich.

Imagine how Jesus left all in Heaven and came to earth so that you and I could enjoy riches, glory, and affluence. In God's plan, you are not supposed to be poor because Jesus Christ carried your poverty and nailed it to the cross forever. His divine power had provided for you everything pertaining to life and godliness (1 Peter 1:3).

Anytime you need something, tap into the numerous resources God has made available for you through His word. Speak God's word about any lack you are facing right now, and you will be surprised at the surplus that will come your way. What do you still lack today? Jesus already made provision for your wealth. He gave His riches in exchange for your poverty. Acknowledge all that He has done for you.

REFLECTIVE QUESTION

In what ways can you sacrificially give to others, reflecting the love of Christ?

Sharing Your Faith

That the sharing of your faith may become effective
by the acknowledgement of every good thing
which is in you in Christ Jesus.

PHILEMON 1:6

DEARLY BELOVED, MEN SHOULD always see the faith and life in you. Your words should prove that you are a Christian and a lover of God. The Christian life is a faith-filled life. Therefore, to win men's hearts into the same faith-life, you should share your faith effectively through love. Your love for your neighbour is seeing God in everyone around you. It keeps you from discrimination and ridicule against a fellow human.

The faith life's efficacy is expressed by how you treat other people. Learn to relate to people out of love. God forgave your sin and sent His only begotten son to die for you while you were still a sinner.

Now, you have no choice but to reciprocate that same dimension of love with other people. Forgive quickly and hold no offence against anyone. Your faith is not in your profession alone but in your deeds. The Bible says, "For as the body without the spirit is dead, so faith without works is dead also" (James 2:26). People must see the evidence of your faith.

Proclaim the testimony of Christ's work to others. Show them the Christ kind of love, and let compassion be the motivation for attending to the needy.

REFLECTIVE QUESTION
In what ways can you deepen your understanding of the good things you share for the sake of Christ?

Your Daily Guide

This book of the law shall not depart out of your mouth,
but you shall meditate in it day and night, that you may
observe to do according to all that is written in it.
For then you will make your way prosperous,
and then you will have good success.

JOSHUA 1:8

EVERY MACHINE HAS A manual of instructions. Refusal to follow the manual will lead to a fault and various malfunctions in the machine. It is quite similar for humans, too. As a child of God, you have a daily manual to follow to live a fulfilled life. That manual is God's word, written in the Bible.

When God asked Joshua to lead the Israelites, He gave him His word. After God spoke with Joshua verbally, He left Joshua with a permanent assurance of His presence. Even when Joshua could not see God, He followed God's word amazingly, which brought Joshua tremendous success as an individual and leader.

God's word must be your daily guide. The Bible's instruction, wisdom, and inspiration are sufficient to transform your life. Read, study, and meditate on this word daily. Give time and attention to God's word, and never let it depart from your lips.

REFLECTIVE QUESTION

How can you incorporate regular meditation on God's Word into your daily life? In what ways can you apply the principles found in Scripture to live a prosperous and successful life?

The Dominion Mandate

Then God blessed them, and God said to them,
be fruitful and multiply; fill the earth and subdue it;
have dominion over the fish of the sea,
over the birds of the air, and over every living
thing that moves on the earth.

GENESIS 1:28

WHAT WAS GOD'S INTENT when He made man in His likeness
and put him in a beautiful garden? Why did God say that man
should multiply? Why did God create humanity in the first
instance? You see, God wants the extension of heaven on earth.
So, God had to make a being in His nature, but with a fleshy
body, to take charge in the earthly realm. As God is in heaven,
He has also made you who are on earth.

You are God's representative on earth. Hence, he had given you
the dominion mandate on earth. God's blessing is on your life,
and its purpose is to increase, multiply, and dominate on earth.
Nature is at your command. They all wait to obey you about
anything you declare.

Do not allow the devil to cheat you of what God has given you.
Rule and reign on earth. You have been empowered to dominate.
I pray that your understanding opens to this truth and that you
begin to walk in it.

REFLECTIVE QUESTION

How can you be a faithful steward of God's creation in your daily life? In what ways can you contribute to the well-being and preservation of the environment and its creatures?

Those Who Know Their God

…but the people who know their God shall be strong,
and carry out greater exploits.

DANIEL 11:32

IN THE BIBLE, THE seven sons of Sceva went out in Jesus' name. They knew nothing about the name except that Paul spoke about it. These men tried to cast out an evil spirit from a person's life "in the name of Jesus whom they had Paul preached (Acts 19:13-16)". Alas! The evil spirit dealt with them and sent them away. It was an unfortunate event for the sons of Sceva because the demon in the person recognised the names they mentioned but did not recognise their authority.

To exploit God's kingdom is not based on mere information. Beyond what you have heard about Jesus, you must have a personal relationship with Him. Seek God to know Him. The knowledge of God is beyond mental assent. The word "to know" in the Hebrew rendition is the same root word describing intercourse between a husband and His wife.

So, to know God means to have intimacy with Him. Your knowledge of God comes from spending time with Him every day of your life. You learn how God speaks, His will, ideology, and plans for your life the more you spend time with Him. God unveils deep secrets only to those with a cordial relationship. Do you have a relationship with God? If not, start today.

REFLECTIVE QUESTION
How can you strengthen your knowledge of God and deepen your relationship with Him so that you can stand firm in your faith? In what ways can you resist the deceptions and temptations of the world?

Serve One Another

For you, brethren, have been called to liberty; only do
not use liberty as an opportunity for the flesh,
but through love serve one another.
GALATIANS 5:13

ASIDE FROM YOUR SERVICE to God, why do you need to serve
one another? It would interest you to know that many out there
need your help in many ways you can never think of. People smile
and keep up happy faces, but many fight several issues deep in
their hearts. People battle with unspeakable issues that they
cannot talk to anyone about. Some of these issues will require
you to discern by the Spirit what people go through and make
them see God has them in mind.

As a believer, you must know that God has placed you where
you are as a light to the world. You will realise that you will never
feel fulfilled trying to fix your life to its best until you have helped
someone. Your service to others is a responsibility you owe to
the world around you. Render help as much as you can and be
willing to show people the extent of God's love for them.

Many people are battling with suicidal thoughts and could
be on the edge of giving up. However, God had positioned you
around such people to bring peace, love, and comfort to them
with the Holy Spirit's help. Know that you can only give what
you have. If you have not learned to spend time with the Holy
Spirit as a believer, there is no way He would reveal to you the
problems of others. Learn to spend quality time with the Holy
Spirit as He reveals to you what you need to do to become a
blessing to others.

REFLECTIVE QUESTION
How can you use your freedom in Christ to serve
others in love? In what ways can you cultivate a humble
heart and actively seek opportunities to serve those
around you?

Holiness is Not Optional

**Pursue peace with all people, and holiness,
without which no one will see the Lord:**
HEBREWS 12:14

MANY PEOPLE ARE QUICK to say that righteousness is the rightness of deeds. But let me ask you: what was the right deed that guaranteed us the grace we received from God? Of course, Grace could not have been right. You and I were saved by grace through faith. Even before you were born, Jesus had chosen to die for your sins. Through His death, you were declared righteous and justified before God. Righteousness is God's gift to every human who receives the work of grace through faith in Jesus.

On the other hand, holiness is walking in the consciousness of who you are in Christ Jesus. It is a life you live, not an action you take. As a believer, you do not try to be holy. It is God's nature to regenerate man. The works of Grace make you Holy. You are Holy because God's Spirit dwells in you. God cannot abide by anything unclean. However, you must maintain who you are through the lifestyle you live.

The Holy Spirit teaches you the habit of maintaining the Holy life. This means that you cannot choose to live the way you like. A new Spirit now controls your actions and habits. Dear beloved, you cannot afford to live casually. Your life is in God, and God is in you. Give it all to Him.

REFLECTIVE QUESTION
**How can you actively strive for peace in your
relationships and nurture holiness in your daily life?**

Prayer of Agreement

Again I say to you that if two of you agree on
earth concerning anything that they ask, it will be
done for them by My Father in heaven.

MATTHEW 18:19

TOGETHER, EVERYBODY ACHIEVES MORE. This saying is true.
Whether at work, in school, or during project work, you will
surely get a better outcome when you work as a team with others
of like mind. There is power in togetherness. You do much more
in agreement than you would have done alone.

The scripture makes us understand that if one chases a thousand,
two will send ten thousand to flight (Deuteronomy 32:30). Can
you see the geometric progression when you agree? The same
principle applies to prayers.

The Spirit of God manifests Himself wherever He sees prayers
made in agreement. The devil understands the potency of an
agreement prayer, so he chose to sow a seed of discord in homes.
A family that prays together commands more power and results
than praying individually. Never forsake prayers done in agreement.

Always find time to pray together with your family. Also, never
forsake the gathering of the brethren. These are essential because
the Spirit of the Lord manifests wherever he sees unity, love, and
the bond of one spirit.

REFLECTIVE QUESTION

**How can you actively seek opportunities to engage
in prayer with others and experience the power of
agreement in your own life?**

Walking in the Spirit

If we live in the Spirit,
let us also walk in the Spirit.
GALATIANS 5:25

ONE OF TWO DRIVING forces determines your day: your flesh or your spirit. What is your default way of responding to the natural events around you? Do you leave it to circumstances or try to find reasons for such events? Dear friend, I want you to know that even though we live in a physical world, the spirit realm controls this realm.

There are forces of the Spirit that dictate the order of events in this world. Never be caught unaware. Do not let your flesh take the upper hand in your life. There is a Spirit in you. It is the Spirit of God. This Spirit knows all things and can do many things. But your ignorance of God's Spirit in you can limit your capability in the Spirit.

To walk in the Spirit, you must shun any dictates from your flesh. The flesh will always want things against the Spirit. Both the flesh and the spirit have a voice. The choice is yours to choose which voice to follow. While the flesh always craves pleasure, sensuality, and lust, the Spirit desires God. You can always walk in the spirit and be guided by the Holy Spirit.

REFLECTIVE QUESTION

How can you develop a greater sensitivity to the leading of the Holy Spirit and live in step with Him each day?

Run Against the Tide

> Blessed is the man who walks not in the counsel
> of the ungodly, nor stands in the path of sinners,
> nor sits in the seat of the scornful.
>
> PSALMS 1:1

WHEN A SHIP MOVES on the sea during a storm, moving in the wind's direction becomes difficult. The storm takes control of the ship's movement, and it becomes difficult for the captain to sail successfully unless He has learned well from experience to control the tide. This situation is quite similar to the affairs of the present world. It always seems difficult and sometimes impossible to live against a trend.

The world system is filled with many popular trends that people follow but are not morally acceptable. For instance, people do a lot of dubious acts in their workplace, and it looks as if there is nothing wrong with it. However, the Scripture clearly shows us today that you are blessed when you dare to stand up against any form of immorality happening around you.

The trending immoral lifestyle in fashion, entertainment, and every other aspect of life could look enticing, but you can choose a different route. The Christian life is truly a walk. Most times, this walk does not look appealing.

I encourage you to pursue your walk with God, even if it means living against the tide of this world and how society is structured to operate. It requires sacrifice, but it's worth it!

REFLECTIVE QUESTION

How can you actively guard your heart and make choices that align with God's truth, even in the midst of worldly influences?

Enjoying Harvest in Famine

Then Isaac sowed in that land,
and reaped in the same year reaped a hundredfold,
and the Lord blessed him.
GENESIS 26:12

THE ABOVE SCRIPTURE TALKS about a time when there was a great famine in the land. There had been a drought in Israel for many years, and the people struggled to survive. God told Isaac not to go to Egypt but to sow in the same land with famine and drought. Listen to this: God's blessing is not limited by economic situation or location. If God could bring out water in a desert, there is nothing He cannot do.

You have to follow God's simple instructions, and you are sure to enjoy the benefits later. Isaac was a symbol of blessing through obedience. Isaac never complained or doubted God. All he did was follow simple instructions. Someone is reading this devotional right now; all you need for your financial breakthrough is a simple instruction from God. Please listen to Him and do as He told you to do.

Isaac sowed a radical seed. What happened? He reaped an extreme harvest in return! The economy does not have to be booming for you to be blessed. All the odds can be against you, but when God asks you to do something, and you don't argue or make an excuse, that's when miracles happen. You'll be promoted even though you're not the most qualified. Today, I pray that you will begin to enjoy a great harvest wherever there has been famine, in Jesus' name. Amen.

REFLECTIVE QUESTION
Are there areas in your life where you need to step out in faith and trust God's provision, even when circumstances seem unfavourable?

Empowered by the Spirit

But you shall receive power when the Holy Spirit has
come upon you; and you shall be witnesses to me
in Jerusalem, and in all Judea and Samaria,
and to the end of the earth.

ACTS 1:8

SOUL-WINNING IS YOUR PRIMARY responsibility as God's
child. When Jesus was about to leave the earth, the last words
he communicated to His disciples were to go and make disciples
of all nations (Matthew 28:19-20). You and I must fulfil the
same responsibility today. However, without a strong backup,
we could not go far with that command. Therefore, God sent
the Holy Spirit to empower, guide, and direct us to fulfil this
divine mandate.

The Holy Spirit is God in the life of every believer. He is the
Spirit of God that gives boldness to the unlearned, courage to
the fearful, and power to the weak. The Holy Spirit can make
"nobody become somebody." He is the power that works in every
believer to live above sin and fulfil God's will.

Today, do not harden your heart against the Holy Spirit. Let
Him empower you to witness the good news to people, heal the
sick, and go great exploit on earth. Present yourself to the Holy
Spirit as a useful vessel, and He will do wonders in your life.
Surrender to the Holy Spirit and obey Him as He leads you.

REFLECTIVE QUESTION
How can you embrace your role as a witness for
Christ and actively share the good news with those
around you?

Love Your Enemies

But if you love those who love you,
what credit is that to you? For even sinners
love those who love them.

LUKE 6:32

LOVE IS THE FULFILMENT of all of God's commands. If you can love, then you are victorious over sin. Love is an antidote for sin. Isn't it so amazing that God loves the world that He had to give all He has for the sake of you and me (John 3:16)? God loved us even when we were still sinners. God had shown it by example: to love the unlovable and forgive the unforgivable.

It is easy to fall in love when the other person loves you back. But how about loving those who see us as enemies? How about loving those who hurt us? How can you love just as Christ loved? The Lord commanded us to love all men, including our enemies, and to do good to those who hate us. This shows us that loving bad people is possible.

To love your enemy, you must allow God to work on your heart. There are certain things the Spirit of God in you will want you to do, which sometimes might not be convenient for you, but you will have to do them. Prompt obedience to the Holy Spirit is knowing God teaches your heart to walk in love.

Beloved! Shine the light of love on the world, and this must not be limited to a sect, race, clan, or faction. Love as Christ loved.

REFLECTIVE QUESTION
How can you cultivate a love that extends beyond your comfort zone and embraces those whom society might deem unlovable?

Building on the Rock

He is like a man building a house, who dug deep
and laid the foundation on the rock.
And when the flood arose, the stream beat
vehemently against that house, and could not shake it,
for it was founded on the rock.

LUKE 6:48

THE FOUNDATION OF ANY building determines its strength when a storm comes. Likewise, the foundation upon which you build your walk with God significantly impacts your life when challenges come. You cannot develop your walk with God on dos and don'ts and expect to remain strong when facing challenges. It is impossible.

Your Christian walk is not about morality, rules, and laws. Your walk with God is a lifestyle that must be founded on Christ. Jesus came from heaven to become the foundation for building a beautiful relationship with God. He is the sure foundation who showed God and His ways. Through Jesus, you can approach God as a father and not a scary being who does as it pleases Him.

Beloved! It is essential first to be grounded in Christ before you set out to build. You can also build your business, family, and career on the sure foundation of our Lord Jesus Christ when you put Him first. Today, let Jesus take priority in your life.

REFLECTIVE QUESTION

How can you ensure that your life is built on a solid foundation in Christ so that you can withstand the storms of life?

Integrity Preserves

**For the upright will dwell in the land,
and the blameless will remain in it.**
PROVERBS 2:21

INTEGRITY IS THE QUALITY of standing for the right thing no matter what happens or who approves it. You will know a person of integrity when what they say and do is valid. Integrity is the degree of oneness you possess about any issue of life. You mean what you say, and you say what you mean.

When people say how much you uphold rightness, they will trust you with things of great value. Integrity is a virtue of righteousness. You cannot claim to be of God and lack integrity because our God upholds integrity through His words and name. We live like God on earth. Hence, integrity must be part of our core.

Dear believer, maintain your integrity in your speech and actions. Do not make promises you cannot fulfil so that you will not trap yourself. The preservation integrity offers is that it keeps you from deceit, hypocrisy, and pretence. No one would like to do business with a man of low or questionable integrity. Therefore, you must keep your integrity intact.

REFLECTIVE QUESTION
How can you actively cultivate a life of righteousness and integrity, trusting in God's faithfulness for your security?

The Foolish Millionaire

But God said to him, 'Fool! This night your soul will be required of you; then whose will those things be which you have provided?

LUKE 12:20

IN A WORLD WHERE money has become a yardstick to measure success, it is wise to understand money's concept rather than prioritising what should have been the last thing on your list. Money is a good thing to have. The Bible says money is a defence (Ecclesiastes 7:12). Biblically, money is a recognised entity. You must understand that money is neither good nor bad. It is what you use the money for that defines it.

It would be foolishness to acquire so much money and consume it on frivolities, pleasure, and indecent acts. It is common to see how people use their money for flamboyancy. Jesus called such a person a fool. No matter your money, when you die, it is all gone. What matters most is what you use the money to do.

Do not be a millionaire fool who thinks money will forever flow, so it should be merriment alone. It is wise to invest in people with your money. Whatever you do to others is unto God. Help people experiencing poverty. Bless the needy and use your money to promote God's kingdom.

REFLECTIVE QUESTION
How often do we prioritise material possessions over the things that truly matter?

Speak Life

**Death and life are in the power of the tongue,
And those who love it will eat its fruit.**
PROVERBS 18:21

THE TONGUE IS THE smallest organ in the body, yet it is the most sensitive. The tongue can dictate the pace of your life. You will either be justified by it or condemned by it (Matthew 12:37). The tongue is the outlet with which you release the intent of your heart. God has so much empowered your tongue to bring to pass whatever you say.

Now, you must be careful about your heart's thoughts because the tongue says it and stamps it forever out of the abundance of what is in your heart. Why do you think people who fear accidents become causal or say negative things about themselves eventually become victims? It is simple. Your tongue sends energy to your environment to attract it to your life, whatever you say.

Rather than speaking negatively about yourself, why not declare positivity, possibility, and optimism about your life? Speak of hope instead of fear. Speak of life instead of death. You shall have what you say. Therefore, cultivate the habit of speaking life, and you shall experience life in Jesus' name.

REFLECTIVE QUESTION
Are you aware of the impact your words have on yourself and those around you?

Co-Workers With God

**For we are God's fellow workers;
you are God's field, you are God's building.**
1 CORINTHIANS 3:9

IN GOD'S VINEYARD, YOU are not an employee. You are a co-worker with Him. It is partnership work. God loves to partner with us to bring His will to earth. You will be so surprised to know that He would never do anything on earth without you and me, despite the greatness of God. We are the people God wants to use for the Glory of His name. Therefore, God would have to draw you closer to Himself so that you can work with Him.

Whether you are a believer or a steward in a church, you must understand that the work you do for God is to bring Him glory and not for selfish interest. In return, God would honour you with His presence and reward your service. This is why I say working with God is a partnership relationship.

The Lord calls you a partner. He partners with you to fulfil his will on earth. You are not an employee who demands a salary from a boss. You and God work together to ensure God's glory covers the earth. He gave you his spirit, the Holy Ghost, to dwell in your heart and enable you to do your assignment efficiently.

REFLECTIVE QUESTION
How are you actively co-working with God in fulfilling His purposes?

Love Your Neighbours

**And he said, "He who showed mercy on him."
Then Jesus said to him, "Go and do likewise.**
LUKE 10:37

WHO DO YOU CONSIDER as a neighbour? Why should you love your neighbour despite their unfriendly attitude? What does love do? Your neighbours are more than people within the same compound, apartment, or environment. Your neighbour is anyone you have contact with at the office, home, on the street, or anywhere you find people.

In today's Bible text, Jesus gives a parable of a man who fell among robbers on his way, probably to a business meeting. The supposed man was beaten and wounded heavily. He was disposed of his valuables, and he was left half dead on the road. Everyone walked past the lifeless body on the ground, except a Samaritan who showed mercy to the wounded man.

You see, the act of love is not a religious deed. It reflects God's nature through the way we treat others. God does not see anyone less, and you must not either. Show love to people when you have the opportunity. Be willing to help and always do your best to lift people. The great men who feared God were not necessarily priests, pastors, or bishops. A great man is any man who sees God in other men. Love is God's way of showing others how important they are to God and you. Show love to the unlovable today.

REFLECTIVE QUESTION
Are you willing to inconvenience yourself for the sake of others?

Fight the Good Fight

I have fought the good fight,
I have finished the race,
I have kept the faith.

2 TIMOTHY 4:7

DAILY, THERE IS CONTENTION between you and the kingdom of darkness. It is a fight between gratifying your flesh and pleasing God. The Bible called this a fight of faith. There is contention for your faith, but you must be resilient and never allow the devil to win this war. God has empowered you with all the graces and strength to be victorious; it is now up to you. You can either let down your guard or take up the whole armour of war.

The good fight of faith is against the world's principalities and powers. The implication is that the fight is not physical. It is a war in the unseen realm. You cannot be in between when it comes to this fight. You are either in or out.

People who do not take their faith walk seriously are easily knocked out in this fight. You must never allow the enticement of this present world to make you drift away from God. Guide your heart with jealousy because this is always the point of attack.

Your mind is the battleground for this fight, and you must cherish it. Watch out for what you allow into your mind through your ears and eyes. These are the channels to the mind.

REFLECTIVE QUESTION

Are you staying true to your calling and holding fast to your faith in the midst of adversity?

The Father's Love

And he arose and came to his father.
But when he was still a great way off, his father
saw him and had compassion, and ran and fell
on his neck and kissed him.

LUKE 15:20

IN TODAY'S BIBLE TEXT, the story is a parable Jesus told about a son who left home in a strange land after he had demanded a share of His father's inheritance. It is a well-known story for every Bible student. Most people call it the parable of the prodigal son, but I call it the parable of a loving father. It showed the extent of the father's love towards for wasteful son.

The parable described God's eternal love for humankind. Nothing we did made us deserve His love, and there will be nothing we will ever do that would make God love us less. The Father's love is not a function of our deeds but a reflection of His nature. God is love. You cannot understand love without God. To love your spouse, children, or an unlovable person, you must learn how God loves without minding our ignorance.

Although God loves us all without condition, he hates any sinful act. So, avoiding what God hates and letting our lifestyle bring Him joy will be proper. God finds pleasure in you when you fulfil His divine purpose on earth. Dear friend, stay within the confines of God's love, and you will see that our God is love.

REFLECTIVE QUESTION
How do you respond to God's unconditional love for you?

Service Maintains Life

And strip Aaron of his garments, and put them
upon Eleazar, his son: and Aaron shall be gathered
unto his people, and shall die there.

NUMBERS 20:26

WHAT SUSTAINS THE LIFESPAN of any believer is your service to
God. As long as you are still in active service to God's work and
within your purpose, you are not permitted to die, according to
God's word. The Bible says about David that after he had served
God's purpose in his generation, he died (Acts 13:36). Until your
service on earth is over, no death is permitted to take you away.

This is the mystery of longevity that many fathers of faith
understood that kept them till old age. You are saved for a purpose:
to serve the Lord and bring others to God through your service.
You are alive because of the assignment the Lord has committed
to your hands.

In today's Bible text, when Aaron completed his assignment as
Moses's assistant, there was no more reason for him to remain on
the scene. Sometimes, God could call you a support or a helper to
another man's vision; never neglect it. When you feel too big for
God's divine assignment, He raises a replacement immediately.
The implication is that he will have to call you home.

Now that you still have the time and energy, why not strive to
be in the service of the kingdom of God? When we serve God,
he makes sure we are safe in His will. The day you quit service,
you start dying. Service sustains life, which should be a wake-up
call this morning. Let your service please the Lord!

REFLECTIVE QUESTION
**Are you willing to accept the consequences of
your actions?**

The Extra Oil

**But the wise took oil in their vessels
with their lamps.**
MATTHEW 25:4

TODAY, WE SHALL BE looking into the parable of the ten virgins. The scriptures called five of them foolish and the other five wise. You must note that they were all virgins, which means they were pure, chaste, and sanctified. The extra oil the smart brought while waiting for the groom makes some wise and others foolish.

Extra oil carries such a great message for believers at this time. Undoubtedly, Jesus is coming soon. But many of us have become weary of waiting for His coming. Therefore, we have chosen to enjoy pleasure for a while, and in the process, our oil burns out. The oil is the anointing of God upon your life. Dear friend, it would help if you did everything possible to preserve this anointing.

Prepare extra oil through consistent fellowship with the brethren. Sometimes, we need one another to become strong when we feel weak. You must not forsake the privilege of praying together, studying the word together, and sharpening one another in the spirit. The extra oil is in people who share the same mindset as you. Always keep them close to yourself.

REFLECTIVE QUESTION
Are you investing time in prayer, studying His Word, and seeking His guidance in your life?

Jesus, the Mighty Healer

When evening had come, they brought to Him many
who were demon-possessed. And He cast out the spirits
with a word, and healed all who were sick.

MATTHEW 8:16

ONE OF JESUS' PURPOSES on earth was to heal the sick, and he did
not come less. Everywhere Jesus went during His earthly ministry,
it was evident that the messiah was in town. God anointed Jesus
with the Holy Ghost and power for the sole purpose of healing
the sick, delivering the oppressed, and setting the captive free
(Acts 10:38).

Interestingly, there was never a time when Jesus struggled to heal.
He only has to speak, and it is done. Jesus' word carries power and
authority. Therefore, no power of sickness can stand it. Sickness
is of the devil because there is nothing ever good about the devil.
He comes to steal, kill, and destroy (John 10:10). But Jesus came
to restore all that the devil had destroyed, including our health.

All the healing Jesus did in His time was part of the more
significant works you will do, which he talked about when he left
the earth. When Jesus died and went to heaven, He distributed
the same Spirit in Him to everyone who believed. The same
power that heals the sick is at work in you today. Therefore,
exercise your authority over sickness, diseases, and demons by
the Spirit of Christ resident in your spirit.

A good thing to note is that spending time in God's presence
equips you more, just like Jesus would spend time praying to His
Father in secret. Refrain from allowing any activity to take away
the quality time of prayers from you. The goal is to be like Jesus
and do more wondrous works than He did.

REFLECTIVE QUESTION
**How do you approach Jesus with your own physical
and spiritual needs?**

Forgiveness

**But if you do not forgive men their trespasses,
neither will your Father forgive your trespasses.**
MATTHEW 6:15

OUR PASSAGE FOR TODAY is an excerpt from the Lord's Prayer. Our Lord Jesus Christ gave us a portrait of the exact type of prayer that produces results here on earth. He showed us how, when, and how vital the ingredient that prayers contain is. One of the essential requirements for an effective prayer is forgiveness.

Forgiveness is a fruit of the spirit and a sign that you have experienced God's love through Jesus Christ. God forgave you even before you knew you had sinned. Then what would anyone do to you that would make you hold grudges against the person? Forgiveness is not knowing who is right and wrong. It is only a reflection of a soul that has touched God.

If you know God, forgiveness will not be a hard thing for you to do. Many do not understand that forgiveness helps your heart heal from a hurtful and toxic relationship. When you forgive people, you look past their mistakes, making you like Christ.

Consequently, if you desire a practical prayer life this year, you need to master the art of forgiveness. Men will always make mistakes. Know these when relating to people and create room for their shortcomings; this is called tolerance. If you are tolerant, forgiveness will be easy to practice.

REFLECTIVE QUESTION
Take a moment to examine your heart. Are there any grudges or unforgiving attitudes that you are holding onto?

Perseverance

I say to you, though he will not rise and give to him
because he is his friend, yet because of his persistence,
he will rise and give him as many as he needs.

LUKE 11:8

HAVE YOU TRIED GETTING out of bed for an early morning jog in the winter? It would look as though you should never try it again. This is due to the extreme coldness you would experience outside. However, if you have a goal to keep fit, following a routine will help you, and not a cold morning will keep you from doing what you ought to do.

Likewise, there are certain things you might want to do that seem complicated, but you have to do them for the sake of becoming a better person. For instance, studying the Bible day and night is not often convenient. The devil uses a lot of distraction to fight it so that you do not read God's word. Yet, you broke through all those distractions and still did it. Consistent with such activity, even when inconvenient, is known as perseverance.

Perseverance means not giving up. It takes tenacity and resilience to break through obstacles to achieve your goal. If you can persist in wanting what you want, no matter how hard, you will get it. Today's message is simple. It tells us sometimes that what we want might not fall cheaply on our lap. We have to go for it and only stop once we get it. Keep praying until you see your answers.

REFLECTIVE QUESTION

How can you find strength in perseverance and continue to trust in God's timing and plan?

Testimony

Come and hear, all you who fear God,
And I will declare what He has done for my soul.
PSALMS 66:16

TESTIMONY IS TO SPEAK about what someone has done for you. Our testimony as believers is evident to the world, not only through our words but also by our lifestyle. Your testimony is an opportunity to show people what God can do for one and what He can do for all. Do not withhold testimonies because, most times, they are what some people need to hear for a shift in their lives.

Your testimony praises God, shames the devil, and becomes a point of contact for others. Testimony declares your victory before the fight or makes it permanent after the battle. Do not be afraid to testify of God's goodness at any time. Gratitude is the sea for more. When you testify, you show gratitude to the Lord for what he has done for you, which moves him to do more for you.

Your testimony strengthens your faith and that of others around you. Therefore, do not hesitate to testify of God's goodness wherever you find yourself. Has the Lord been good to you? Do well to testify and bring more glory to his name. Tell someone about God's goodness.

REFLECTIVE QUESTION
In what ways can you share this testimony to encourage others in their own journey of faith?

Say No to Laziness

The hand of the diligent will rule,
but the lazy man will be put to forced labour.

PROVERBS 12:24

THERE IS A LAW in physics called Newton's first law of motion. It states that "everybody continues in its state of rest or uniform motion in a straight line unless acted upon by an unbalanced force." Amazingly, this law also applies to our everyday lives. While some naturally tend to be active and hardworking, others need an external drive to push them to work.

Laziness does not necessarily mean not doing anything. It is to know what to do and defer it for later. Anyone who procrastinates tends to laziness. In such a case, you will have to drive such people to work through whatever means you think is the best way to push the individual to work.

Sometimes, you may let a lazy man see the danger of not working on what he needs to do. Other times, you might have to introduce a reward mechanism for every milestone of work covered. If you want to change your life, you must quit laziness. Anytime you feel the urge to postpone a task you could do within the time, it becomes the best time to take action. Or else, you might never end up doing anything.

REFLECTIVE QUESTION

How might your attitude and actions change if you approach it with diligence and commitment?

Sacrifice

Most assuredly, I say to you, unless a grain of wheat
falls into the ground and dies, it remains alone,
but if it dies, it produces much grain.

JOHN 12:24

THE WORLD SYSTEM SHOWS us that to increase your wealth, you need to save. They make it look like conserving resources causes an increase. But this is not true. Only God brings an increase, and he has shown us how an increase comes through His word. The principle is that your seed, money in this dispensation, can only increase when you learn how to sow.

When the seed you have cannot feed you and your family, the wisdom is to sow it. Sowing requires sacrificing what you have for what you hope to receive in multiple ways. God honours sacrifices and would never turn His eyes away. If you desire financial increase, an effortless way is to sow into God's work.

The act of tithing, first fruit, offering, and every other form of giving are God's way to bless His people. Do not follow the bandwagon to believe the lie from the devil. Nobody ever gives who does not receive in return multiple folds of what was offered. Do you want to live in plenty? Are you satisfied with your current living standard, or do you want more? If these answers are yes, then invest in your future by sowing the seeds in your hands.

REFLECTIVE QUESTION
How might your life be transformed if you choose to let go and trust in God's plan?

Hezekiah's Prayer

Remember now, O LORD, I pray, how I have
walked before You in truth and with a loyal heart
and have done what was good in Your sight."
And Hezekiah wept bitterly.
2 KINGS 20:3

THE PRAYER OF HEZEKIAH has excellent significance today because of his words and the posture he assumed when he prayed. God knew King Hezekiah and had to send a prophet to the King to announce his death date. However, this announcement could have met Hezekiah better. So, he had to tell God about it and remind Him of their partnership and relationship.

Amazing! Who dares talk to the Almighty God in such a manner if the person has not developed a stature in the place of fellowship? If I ask you, does God even know your name so that he could send His servant to deliver a word to you? How much do you know about God that could make you negotiate terms and conditions with Him? Your walk with God gives you power with men and the licence to deal with the situation with Him.

King Hezekiah walked before the Lord with uprightness and with a perfect heart. He did what was good in the sight of the Lord. These things gave the King the right to speak back to God confidently. If you have not practised God's presence, there will never be a way you will hear Him when He says. Learn God's presence through prayers and see Him giving you excellent restoration just as He did for King Hezekiah.

REFLECTIVE QUESTION

How can you deepen your trust in God's faithfulness and mercy as you bring your concerns to Him?

Divine Supplies

The Lord is my shepherd;
I shall not want.

PSALMS 23:1

A SHEPHERD TAKES CARE of the needs of his sheep, guiding them to green pastures and still waters. Similarly, God lovingly tends to our needs, providing us with everything we require. When we acknowledge God as our shepherd, we find security, contentment, and peace, knowing that He will take care of us.

The economy of heaven cannot be compared to that of the world system at all. There is no loss, lack, or limitation in heaven. Whatever you desire becomes a reality. Surprisingly, God wants you to live by the economy of heaven, even as you are on earth. You are God's ambassador on earth. Hence, you are heaven's citizen, representing God's earthly kingdom. Therefore, your supply is divine.

Your salary cannot meet all your needs, no matter how much. However, I know what can satisfy your needs for generations after you. It is the divine supply from heaven. When heaven meets your needs, many years of struggle, hardship, and lack will suddenly turn around for your best.

Our God can provide for you just as He had promised, and He has promised He is your shepherd, and you will not lack anything (Psalms 23). If you can commit your business, job, and needs to God, He is more committed to giving you all you need. Look to God today for your divine supplies.

REFLECTIVE QUESTION

In what ways can you trust in His provision and guidance, even in the midst of challenges?

Do Good to All Men

Therefore, as we have opportunity,
let us do good to all, especially to those who
are of the household of faith.
GALATIANS 6:10

GOD INSTRUCTS YOU NEVER to cease to do good to people. God meets the needs of others through your act of benevolence. If you do not show kindness to others, how do you expect them to see God through you? God will not step down from heaven to reach out to people. It will be against God's word for Him to come as God to earth and make something happen.

When God needed to visit the earth, He had to come as a human—Christ Jesus. So, God will always commit to the hands of man whatever act of goodness He wants to show to humanity. Therefore, you must not be hard-hearted when God wants to visit an individual or group of people with His kindness through you.

Every answered prayer from God comes in human form. God uses yielded men and women to solve the world's problems. People constantly need a solution to their problems—they want answers. Please do not try to be part of their problem. Show kindness to everyone, especially people of the same faith. Whenever you have the opportunity, do good to all men. You do not have to solve all their problems. But whatever you can do to assist them, please do.

REFLECTIVE QUESTION
What specific acts of kindness or acts of service can you engage in to make a positive difference in their lives?

Empowered to Prosper

Then God blessed them, and God said to them,
"Be fruitful and multiply; fill the earth and subdue it;
have dominion over the fish of the sea,
over the birds of the air, and over every living thing
that moves on the earth.

GENESIS 1:28

GOD'S FIRST COMMAND TO humanity was to be fruitful. There was something more to fruitfulness than procreation that God was talking about here. If procreation were what he meant by fruitfulness, God would not have said, "Be fruitful and multiply. Of course, multiplication is a duplication of ourselves and an increase. However, being fruitful implies productivity.

You are commanded to be productive. Nothing dies in your hands. God has empowered you with the grace to prosper. So, any business, venture, goal, or career you do must grow because prosperity has been infused into your makeup. But the question is, why are many still trying to fulfil this mandate? Fear and Ignorance!

Whatever you fear doing will become impossible to do. God does not create authoritarian fear; it is from the devil. When the devil throws the dart of fear into your mind, it hinders you from doing anything. You have dominion over the devil and his works. Therefore, you must never give room for his deceit in your life.

There is power at work in you. It is empowerment for prosperity. Therefore, I urge you to rise from fear and ignorance and take action that brings you prosperity.

REFLECTIVE QUESTION
How can you show gratitude towards God for the gift of creation through your stewardship?

A New Beginning For You

Now the Lord spoke to Moses and Aaron
in the land of Egypt, saying, "This month shall be
your beginning of months; it shall be the first
month of the year to you.

Exodus 12:1-2

THE ISRAELITES HAD BEEN in bondage for about four hundred and thirty years. It was time for them to be delivered from slavery. Still, Pharaoh made it look like a complex and impossible feat for them. The Israelites had to go through so much suffering and hardship at the hands of this wicked Pharaoh.

Finally, the Lord delivers them with a mighty and strong arm and leads them through the wilderness. So, the people needed a fresh start, and God had to declare that this day marked the beginning of the month. I do not know what you have been through in the past, but just as the Lord made a fresh start for the Israelites, today marks the beginning of a new thing in your life.

You may have wasted much of your life in struggles, pain, and embarrassment. Nevertheless, the Lord is giving you a new beginning today. This season shall be for a blessing, increase, promotion, and liberty for you.

REFLECTIVE QUESTION

How can you embrace a new beginning in your own life and leave behind the struggles or failures of the past?

Call on His Name

**And it shall come to pass That whoever
calls on the name of the Lord Shall be saved.**

ACTS 2:21

THE NAME OF JESUS is full of power and glory. It is not just an ordinary name but an authority to make the impossible possible, change people's lives, and transform the situation. Nothing else can promise salvation and deliverance like the name of Jesus. Jesus's name saves you, regardless of race, tribe, ethnicity, or nationality.

However, Jesus's name cannot save you if you do not believe it. The heart and your tongue work together to activate the power in Jesus' name. First, you need to think and be convinced that the name of Jesus saves, delivers, and is powerful. You must believe your situation is not impossible in the name of Jesus. Once you acknowledge and confess, it becomes a reality.

In the name of Jesus, your confession is to agree with the power in the name and what it can do for you. It is more than just speaking; it is a seal of agreement about the energy in the name of Jesus. No matter the challenges you are going through, call upon the name of the Lord right now, and salvation is yours in Jesus' name, amen.

REFLECTIVE QUESTION

How can you cultivate a deeper reliance on the powerful name of Jesus in your daily life?

Promotion Comes From the Lord

For exaltation comes neither from
the east nor from the west nor the south.
But God is the Judge: He puts down one,
and exalts another.

PSALMS 75:6-7

BELOVED! HERE IS AN answer to a life-long question in the hearts of many. People wonder how others rise to stardom. They ask how someone in a low cadre at the office suddenly rises to a managerial position. Why are some people blessed and lifted while others are not? Many people spend several hours and days running from pillar to post, trying to make ends meet. Yet, their labour had only added little or nothing to their lives. What is responsible for this?

Firstly, know that your skills, hard work, and talent are insufficient to lift you from where you are to the top you desire to be. These things are required to sustain you when you rise. They are not a factor in promotion. Only God lifts men.

Promotion does not come from your boss at work. If you rise by accident or manipulation, you will fall back by the same means, and the end of such a person will be worse than the beginning.

There is a powerful force that lifts men, and this is called the grace of God. Once you have it, everything else comes with ease and comfort. Therefore, stay within reach of God's grace, and He will lift you in due season.

REFLECTIVE QUESTION
How can you cultivate a humble heart and surrender to God's judgment in your own life?

Do Not Limit God

Yes, they spoke against God: They said,
"Can God prepare a table in the wilderness?
Behold, He struck the rock,
So that the waters gushed out...
PSALMS 78:19-20

IMAGINE YOU WALKED INTO a shopping mall and found the governor of your state shopping. You reached out to him and greeted him. Then he told you all your expenses for what you wish to buy at the mall are on him. I assume you would select every item you ever needed from the supermarket that day. Of course, you will never doubt his ability to pay for you once you know he can and more.

If you could trust a man so much to do what he promised for you, why do you limit God in your heart about what He promised to do for you? God's integrity will be at stake if He does not do for you what He has promised you. Sometimes, we do not know how to approach God to receive from Him.

When God promises you, He does not want you to start wishing again for what He has promised. A wish in the presence of promises is a lack of faith. When He promises, you receive it by faith and rejoice, even when you have not seen it. Search the scriptures to find out God's promises for you, and begin to bask in the euphoria of these promises.

REFLECTIVE QUESTION
How can you cultivate a heart of gratitude and trust in God's provision, even in difficult times?

You are gods

I said, "You are gods, and all of you
are children of the Most High."
PSALMS 82:6

As HUMAN BEINGS, WE often forget the immense worth and potential we possess. We underestimate the impact we can make in the world when we align ourselves with the purposes of the Most High. This verse reminds us that we are called to reflect the character of our Heavenly Father and carry out His will on earth.

You need to know your identity to blend into an association you do not belong to. Many of us had allowed the limitations of our environment, situations, and backgrounds to dictate our identity. Your true nature is not what the environment makes of you but what you carry inside you.

Beloved! You are not a mere man. You were created in the class of God, and you are meant for the top. Until you look inward, you might never find your true self. Being in the God class, you must learn to rob minds with Him daily to know about your nature better and begin to live in that godly realm on earth.

REFLECTIVE QUESTION
How can you intentionally embrace and live out your identity as a child of God?

God's Word

**Your word is a lamp to my feet
and a light to my path.**
PSALMS 119:105

WHENEVER GOD SPEAKS, POSSIBILITIES fall into place. God's word carries transformative power to change and make things happen. His word delivers, heals, saves, and restores orderliness. Once God spoke and the earth became void, it became a beautiful garden. You must never underestimate the power of God's word.

Among the many powerful things God's word can do is provide guidance and direction in life. You need God's word to order your steps into His will and to work in His ways. Keeping God's word in your heart shields you from the corruption of this world. A believer can only go as far with God as He can go deep in His word.

Every step of the way, no matter the decisions you have to make, the word of God is a perfect guide in life. If you are confused or faced with a hard choice of options, the word of God can guide you through the decision-making process. It says it is a light on your path; this speaks of direction. You are not only under divine guidance but also divine direction.

REFLECTIVE QUESTION
How can you deepen your reliance on God's Word as a guiding light in your daily life?

Divine Instruction

When He had stopped speaking,
He said to Simon, "Launch out into the deep
and let down your nets for a catch.

LUKE 5:4

DIVINE INSTRUCTION PUTS AN end to any form of struggle in life. If you can hear from God, your journey to destiny becomes easy and fast. Many people still struggle with their finances, marriage, and business because they have learned to do things on their strengths. Human strength is unreliable, no matter how strong, intelligent, and vast you are.

Simon Peter was a professional fisherman. The implication was that he understood the best fishing time, the sea's movement, and how to trap the fish. Yet he worked tirelessly without getting one fish until Jesus gave him a word. Your degree and qualifications are insufficient to provide you with a job that would settle you financially forever. It would help if you had divine instruction.

A word from God can settle you forever. Your ability to hear God's direction about a strategy could be your way to a breakthrough. Never underestimate the power of words. God can use one word to make a miracle out of your life. Be open to His instruction, and you will see wonders.

REFLECTIVE QUESTION
How can you step out in faith and "launch into deep waters" in your own life?

What is Your Harvest?

**Do not be deceived, God is not mocked;
for whatever a man sows, that he will also reap.**
GALATIANS 6:7

DO NOT PERMIT ANY man to deceive you; try not to fool yourself. The principle of life is that you will get out of it what you put into it. It will be an aberration to sleep all day and expect riches to come finding you on your bed. Anyone who assures you of a beautiful future without being intentional about your life is deceiving you.

Whatever you want from life, you have to get it. Every good thing in life comes with a price, and until you are ready to pay the price, you will only keep wishing and assuming. God cannot be mocked. The laws and principles he has set in motion cannot be reversed.

When you plant a seed in agricultural science, it grows and becomes a mature plant with several seeds ready for harvest. One striking thing about sowing and reaping is that the fruit is always more significant than the seed you sow.

If you plant a maise seed, the harvest will be an ear of corn with approximately hundreds of seeds. The act of sowing is the work you need to do for what you hope to get. Therefore, sow wisely. Invest more in your life. Use every opportunity to sow good seeds in your destiny for a bumper harvest of goodness, fulfilment, and peace later in life.

REFLECTIVE QUESTION
What kind of seeds are you sowing in your life, relationships, and actions?

The Name of the Lord

The name of the Lord is a strong tower,
the righteous run into it and they are saved.

PROVERBS 18:10

BELOVED, OUR PASSAGE THIS morning gives us an insight into the protective dimension of the name of the Lord. It describes the Lord's name as a strong tower that guarantees safety for anyone who runs to it for help. There is an attitude that ensures safety. It is to "run." You run in the direction where you feel more safe and secure.

You do not go to God as an option in case what you have does not work. No! You approach God as your only option. Your existence and survival depend on God, as does your safety. You must understand that whatever or whoever wants to attack you must first attack Jesus Christ. You are in Him, and He is in God.

As long as you are in Christ, you are saved and secured from the insecurities, evil, and corruption ravaging the world. Dear friends, nothing should ever separate you from God. Seek Him daily, and only take a step with His approval. Remain in Him, and your destiny will be secured forever.

REFLECTIVE QUESTION
How can you find refuge in God's strong tower amidst life's challenges?

Call Forth Your Miracle

Now when He had said these things,
He cried with a loud voice,
"Lazarus, come forth!
JOHN 11: 43

WHAT DO YOU DO when everything else has failed? You have fasted, prayed, and believed, yet nothing seems to change. Sometimes, the answer to what you desire might not have to come through fasting or prayers but by a declaration of faith. Sometimes, all you need for that miracle is to call forth.

The scripture tells us that God had to speak when the earth was without form and void and everywhere was dark and confused (Genesis 1:1-2). God did not start running around in confusion about what to do. He called forth light, and there was light.

Consequently, when Jesus got to the tomb where Lazarus was for four days, He did many things, but nothing changed until He said, "Lazarus, come forth..." Jesus' weeping did not bring his friend back. The rolling away of the stone did not change anything until Jesus declared it by the Spirit. You have to call forth your miracle in faith and watch God bring it to pass. Call on that miracle today and see God bring it to you in Jesus' name. Halleluiah!

REFLECTIVE QUESTION
In what areas of your life do you need the resurrection power of Jesus?

Honey from the Rock

He would have fed them also
with the finest of wheat; And with honey
from the rock I would have satisfied you.

PSALM 81:16

HALLELUIAH! I AM EXCITED to bring you the word of the Lord today. Our God can satisfy your hunger with honey from the rock. This is more than an assurance of hope; it is a declaration of God's capability in your life. Through the scriptures, we see God turning around impossible situations to give hope and joy to many who trust him. Today, you are not an exception if only you can trust God for your desires.

Are you on the verge of giving up on yourself because of your present situation? Do you need more clarification on how these things can be? What is the correlation between honey and rock? I want to tell you today that our God is very able. You can count on him to do it if he has said it. God brought water from the rock for the Israelites in the wilderness (Numbers 20:3-13). He is the same God today, and he can feed you with honey from the rock.

Speaking of Jacob in Deuteronomy 32:13, the Bible says that Jacob was made to suck honey from the rock. No wonder the man did so many exploits in his days. The rock is a dry place. Nothing sweet should come out of it. But the Lord says He will give you honey from the rock. Expect a miracle today. God will favour you from where you least expect it. You will enjoy breakthroughs even in the face of an economic downturn. This is God's word for you today!

REFLECTIVE QUESTION

How can we ensure we're positioning ourselves to receive God's abundant provision?

Why Fasting?

However, this kind does not go out
except by prayer and fasting.

MATTHEW 17:21

To GAIN STABILITY IN your walk with God, you must develop and sustain the ability to fast and pray. Fasting involves starving your flesh so that your spirit can gain more energy. Therefore, it is a "must-do" for every believer who is serious about their walk with the Lord.

Our Lord Jesus clearly showed that some things will only shift if you engage in fasting and prayer. Specific challenges of life you must overcome require more from you than just morning prayers. You need to engage in fasting to make your spirit align with divine instructions. No wonder Jesus had to fast for forty days and nights before he began his ministry here on earth.

Whenever you starve the flesh of all pleasures, your spirit becomes sensitive to what the Lord wants to do. Beloved! I encourage you this morning to resolve to engage in fasting and prayer. You will be amazed at how life's challenges and difficulties leave on their own accord. Work on your schedule and include a period of fasting and prayer. Remember, God still answers prayers, and he will answer you today!

REFLECTIVE QUESTION

How can you incorporate prayer and fasting into your daily life to strengthen your faith and overcome challenges?

Arise and Eat

And the angel of the Lord came again the second time,
and touched him and said, Arise and eat;
because the journey is too great for thee.

1 KINGS 19:7

THERE WAS A TIME in Prophet Elijah's life when he was discouraged and afraid despite being a great prophet of the Lord. He thought he had come to the end of the road and that his life was going to end. He even lamented that he was not better than his ancestors, all because a witch threatened him.

Similarly, you might be discouraged right now about the issues in your life. It could be challenges at your workplace or threats from every side of your life. Whatever the challenge is, there is good news for you today. God is sending divine help to you.

While Elijah was sleeping and probably waiting to die soon, the Lord had other plans for him. There was still an assignment for him. So, an angel from the Lord brought food to him for the new assignment ahead. See, challenges come because you are about to enter a higher phase of your life journey.

Therefore, when the problem hits hard, God is not ignorant of it. He is always on standby to lift you up and above. The place the Lord is bringing you into requires energy, and you must eat now of God to have the strength to advance powerfully.

REFLECTIVE QUESTION
When you feel overwhelmed and exhausted, how can you trust in God's provision to renew your strength?

Trust in the Lord

**Trust in the Lord with all your heart,
and lean not on your own understanding.**
PROVERBS 3:5

TODAY'S BIBLE TEXT IS wise counsel for anyone passionate about success. It admonishes you to put your entire trust in the Lord and never to rely on human logic. I know you have a way you wish it could be done. Sometimes, you must have planned it all out by yourself. However, let God lead you. Remember, it is not in man to order his way. There is a defined wisdom that silences any nonsense, and this wisdom could only come from God.

God knows the end of a matter from the beginning and knows what is best for you. All you have to do is trust him with all your heart. This means that your trust in God should be absolute. You do not trust him with your health, and you lean on understanding your finances. It must be final. Trust Him wholeheartedly.

As you do your business, I encourage you to put your whole trust in the Lord. Trust his wisdom and counsel. Let him direct your choices, and let his word guide you. God bless you.

REFLECTIVE QUESTION
In what areas of your life do you struggle to fully trust God? How can you surrender control and lean on His wisdom and guidance?

More Than Conquerors

Yet in all these things, we are more than conquerors through Him who loved us.
ROMANS 8:37

A CONQUEROR HAS FOUGHT battles and has never been defeated in any. This implies that victory is synonymous with being a conqueror. Such a person is seen as powerful, invisible, and unbeatable. Interestingly, this ought to be the life of every believer. Nothing is permitted to pull you down because you have the host of heaven at your side. The mighty man in battle is the one in charge of your war. So, victory is guaranteed.

The Bible does not call you conquerors because you fought the battle. God has done it for you through Jesus Christ. God's love for you is so great that He stands in your defence anytime and any day. You do not have to fight a single battle. All you need to do is ensure compliance with whatever He wants you to do.

Dear beloved, you are not disadvantaged. The creator of the ends of the universe is on your side. Call on Him, and He will fight till the end for you. You are more than a conqueror through the love of God in Christ Jesus. Stop calling yourself what God has not called you. Arise and enforce compliance in the place of prayer. You are more than Conquerors!

REFLECTIVE QUESTION
How can you live out your identity as a conqueror through Christ in your daily life?

The Battle is the Lord's

And he said, "Listen, all you of Judah and you
inhabitants of Jerusalem, and you, King Jehoshaphat!
Thus says the Lord to you: 'Do not be afraid nor
dismayed because of this great multitude,
for the battle is not yours, but God's.

2 CHRONICLES 20:15

YOU WILL NOTICE THAT the Lord fights and defends them from
their enemies each time the Israelites face a battle-like situation.
In the Bible text above, Jehoshaphat was afraid because many
enemies were fighting against him. It was the time of his life when
he did not know what else to do. These other enemy nations were
more potent than his army, and as a man, he was afraid.

However, everything changed when the people began to praise
the Lord's name. The Lord comforted them and assured them it
was their battle. Beloved, whatever the struggle of your life is, I
want you to trust the Lord in it. The fierceness of the situation
does not mean the end of your life.

No battle is too fierce for God or a mountain too high for Him.
Whatever God says He will do, He is more than able. Once He
says the battle belongs to Him, you have nothing to fear. Rest in
His unfailing word and see how God will bring the challenging
situation to your feet.

REFLECTIVE QUESTION
How can you release your fears and surrender your
battles to God, trusting in His plan and provision?

You are God's Heir

And if children, then heirs—
heirs of God and joint heirs with Christ,
if indeed we suffer with Him,
that we may also be glorified together.

ROMANS 8:17

IMAGINE IF YOU WERE an heir to the wealthiest man on earth! Amazing right? Of course, it is. You get to inherit all his assets, property, and names. The sweetest part is that you only need to work for some benefits. The assets automatically become yours because you are his heir.

Likewise, the Bible declares that you are an heir to the creator of the universe. All that your father has given to you so that you will lack nothing. Remember what the 24th chapter of Psalms says? "The earth is the Lord's and the fullness thereof, the world, and they dwell therein."

The whole universe belongs to God, your father. Think about it. Beloved, you are not hopeless! The whole earth is yours. You are an heir of God, and everything He owns belongs to you. Rise today in the power of this revelation and begin to command things around you for your good.

You are God's heir!

REFLECTIVE QUESTION

How does understanding our identity as heirs with Christ impact how we live our daily lives?

By Faith

Now the Just shall live by faith...
HEBREWS 10:38

YOUR FAITH IS THE purchasing power in the economy of the spirit. The book of Ephesians tells us that we have been blessed with all spiritual blessings in heavenly places. However, we live bodily in the physical realm, and blessings exist in the Spirit realm. Therefore, you need faith to access what is available in the spirit.

Faith is your ability to trust God's word concerning you despite the odds. You must accept God's word as the final say in all your affairs. The dynamics of faith are that you must first know what God says about a situation. Articulate the word into you through meditation, and release it in your time of need. So, if the word of God has not become part of you, it becomes difficult to exercise your faith.

You will exchange your faith for the victory you have not seen yet. One way you will see evidence of faith is that you have joy in whatever you pray about. Joy is an indication of an answered prayer. When you pray, stop once you get to that point where streams of joy begin to flow. Lastly, faith is potent when you do things out of love. Let love lead you to pray and declare out of a heart of love.

REFLECTIVE QUESTION
In what areas of your life do you need to exercise greater faith and perseverance?

Not of Works

**Not of works,
lest any man should boast.**
EPHESIANS 2:9

IT IS EXCITING AND refreshing to know that your salvation and all the following blessings were given free of charge. You did not have to either pay for it or work for it. Grace is a provision from God without human effort. However, grace does not allow laziness. God gives you by grace what you can never have on your own, which is the salvation of your soul.

How much would be enough if you had to pay for God's grace? If you had to work for your salvation, how long would you be able to redeem yourself? Beloved! The mercy and grace of God in your life are a gift. Nobody works to earn God's eternal gift. He chose to show us mercy even while we were still in the bondage of sin; his only son came to die for our redemption – it is all a gift.

Remember today's bible verse the next time you feel intimidated because you think you are not doing enough of what God requires from you. Nevertheless, do not take God's grace for granted. Grace is no licence for sin. Instead, it should keep you from sinning.

REFLECTIVE QUESTION
How does understanding that salvation is a gift of grace impact your relationship with God and your daily life?

Help From Above

I will lift up my eyes to the hills—
From whence comes my help?
My help comes from the Lord,
Who made heaven and earth.

PSALMS 121:1-2

THE PSALMIST UNDERSTOOD THE importance of acknowledging God's help. It is absolute when God helps a man because God is Omni Potent. All power belongs to God alone, who can use it as He wishes. God raised a man from the dungeon hill and made Him rule over nations. He enthrones one and dethrones another.

If God blesses you, no man on earth can undo the blessing. This is why your total reliance must always be on God and fellow men. I can tell you for free that men's help is limited. A man can only raise you to the level of his arm. But when God lifts you, the sky becomes your starting point.

However, learn to recognise God's help. God could use the person expected to lift you beyond your most expansive height in life. Never despise people. When you are within God's will, no relationship you have with people is by accident. Respect men, appreciate relationships, but trust God.

REFLECTIVE QUESTION
Where do you tend to seek help in times of need?

Victory With God

When you pass through the waters,
I will be with you, And through the rivers,
they shall not overflow you. When you walk
through the fire, you shall not be burned;
Nor shall the flame scorch you.

ISAIAH 43:2

THE LORD GIVES YOU this assurance today. Beloved! You are not alone, irrespective of the hard times, challenges and failures you experience. God is with you to see you through it all. He makes you pass through the storm to build strength in you. He made you experience those rejections to have a better offer He had prepared for you.

Anything you lost was never yours. God has a better offer for you, but He needs you always to recognise He is here and near. Therefore, do not be discouraged. You are not alone. When it seems like you are drowning or getting burned, remember that you are not alone.

No matter what you are going through, be cheerful and let the Lord lead you through it all. The challenges are meant to teach you genuine trust and obedience to the Lord. Do not despair; you will come out victorious.

REFLECTIVE QUESTION
How does knowing that God is with you in the midst of difficulties give you comfort and strength?

Prayer That Works

If my people, which are called by my name,
shall humble themselves, and pray, and seek my face
and turn from their wicked ways; then will I hear
from heaven, and will forgive their sin,
and will heal their land.

2 CHRONICLES 7:14

THE ABOVE BIBLE TEXT starts with a posture when you pray. It is not how you kneel, stand, sit, or walk while praying. It is a posture of the spirit called humility. It takes humility to go to God in prayer. Pride makes you try everything yourself. This will lead to a vicious life cycle or cause you to struggle. Humility is the state of seeing God in all you do.

The prayer of a humble man is a sweet-smelling savour to God. He can never resist it. God declares to Himself that He detests pride but gives grace to the humble. Sometimes, you wonder while you have not received answers to your prayers. The challenge is that you have yet to learn humility. Stop focusing on yourself in prayer. Let your focus only be on God. This is the humility of the heart.

Whenever you pray in humility, the Lord hears and answers your prayer. He gives grace to the humble but resists the proud. Henceforth, as you pray to the Lord, approach him with a broken spirit and a contrite heart. Let your humility speak out to the Lord, and He will hear and answer you.

REFLECTIVE QUESTION
How can you apply the principles of humility, prayer, seeking God's face, and repentance in your own life to experience restoration and healing?

Living Above Sicknesses and Diseases

Who Himself bore our sins in His own body
on the tree, that we, having died to sins,
might live for righteousness—
by whose stripes you were healed.

1 PETER 2:24

IS IT POSSIBLE TO live without being? This is a question you should ask me right now. With the wave of sicknesses, diseases, and pandemics that have recently plagued our generation, one might be tempted to think it is impossible to live a sickness-free life.

This morning, I want to announce that you can live above sickness and disease. Sickness was never God's original plan for humanity. Sin brought sickness and death to the world. Sickness is a direct consequence of sin. Now, living above sickness and disease is to stay away from sin.

A life in Christ is secured from any form of sickness or disease. Your salvation is your gate pass to divine immunity. However, it would help if you were careful about your lifestyle and environment. Over 50% of illnesses result from poor hygiene and dirty environments. Right now, I decree healing upon anyone sick in the name of Jesus.

REFLECTIVE QUESTION

How does understanding the depth of Christ's sacrifice and the healing power of His wounds impact your daily walk with Him?

This is Your Season

He has made everything beautiful in its time.
Also, He has put eternity in their hearts,
except that no one can find out the work that
God does from beginning to end.

ECCLESIASTES 3:11

BELOVED! GOD'S GOODNESS IS not seasonal. He is good at all times. Sometimes, we measure God's goodness by the level of our good deeds. We quickly assume that God will do likewise if we can do one good deed. Let me tell you, God's goodness has nothing to do with your deeds.

Was it your deed that gave you grace? Could it have been your work that gave you wealth? Is your anointing from you? Let me tell you for free that everything you are and have is from God. There is something called alignment when you want to receive from God. Alignment is being sensitive in your spirit to capture what God does per season. Every day is God's day, but the day you decide for Him is yours.

God is doing something now. People who know it have aligned themselves for the season. Never be caught unaware when God is in your neighbourhood. Make this your season for change and transformation. Align yourself in prayer and be watchful.

REFLECTIVE QUESTION

How does the recognition of the eternal perspective impact the way you approach the seasons and circumstances of your life?

God is For You

What then shall we say to these things?
If God is for us, who can be against us?
ROMANS 8:31

THIS IS GOOD NEWS! God is for you. He is beside you to walk you through life's journey. God is in you to direct your steps in life. He is for you at every crossroads of your life. It would help to have a strong force to win battles and succeed in life. Know this assuredly: God is not the most potent force you need in life. He is the only force your life depends on.

Our God is all-powerful. When he takes a stand for you, he goes all out to see you victorious. When God is for you, you are sure of an embarrassment-free life. No one can stand against Him who survives the light of day.

Now, He said He was for you. This is enough to keep you at rest. Let his words in Psalms 105:15 be in your ears throughout the day: "Saying, Touch not mine anointed, and do my prophets no harm." You are God's anointed, and no evil is permitted in your direction.

REFLECTIVE QUESTION
How does the truth that God is for you give you confidence and courage to face any challenges or opposition in your life?

Give God the Permission

So I sought a man among them
who would make a wall, and stand in the gap
before Me on behalf of the land,
that I should not destroy it, but I found no one.

EZEKIEL 22:30

BELOVED! IT CAN BE shocking to reveal that until you give God access, He will never intervene. God is a Spirit, but he does not force himself on others as demons do. If you do not give God access, there is little or nothing He can do. Friends, sometimes we assume for God. We think He should do a sure thing for us, even when we refuse to call on Him for it.

In Genesis 18:26, Lot and his family were spared from Sodom and Gomorrah's destruction because Abraham asked for God's permission for His relative. The most exciting part of this story is that God would have spared more people if Abraham had asked further. This means that God will never turn down the request of His people as long as it is within His will.

Do not be silent about whatever you are going through now and need God's intervention. Cry to God in prayer. Express your heart to Him and remind yourself of His words to you. Allow God, and you will see the transformation in that situation.

REFLECTIVE QUESTION

How can you be an intercessor, standing in the gap for others and seeking God's intervention in the brokenness of the world?

Righteousness Exalts

**Righteousness exalts a nation,
but sin is a reproach to any people.**
PROVERBS 14:34

PRAISE GOD! TODAY'S TOPIC inspires me because it highlights a simple divine lifting strategy and promotion. I have never met a man who has not loved success, promotion, and growth in his entire life. The very essence of our creation is hinged on dominion and increase.

In God's kingdom, several principles work for promotion. One of them is righteousness. Righteousness is God's gift of salvation to everyone who receives the life of Christ. It allows us to deal rightly with God and man. Righteousness helps you not just to do good and shun bad but to stay away from evil.

Promotion comes from God only when He sees that the work of righteousness is complete in you. If you manipulate yourself to the top, you will need your strength to keep you at the top, which can be very frustrating. But if God lifts you, nothing can bring you down. Today, let the work of righteousness find root in your life by living rightly before God and man.

REFLECTIVE QUESTION
How can we actively pursue righteousness in our personal lives to contribute to the strength and prosperity of our society?

You are Royalty

But ye are a chosen generation, a royal priesthood,
an holy nation, a peculiar people; that you should
show forth the praises of him who called you out
of darkness into his marvellous light.

1 Peter 2:9

Do you think you are worthless? Are you going through some challenges and doubt God is concerned about you? I have good news for you today. God made you in His image and gave you the royal mandate to rule and reign. You are from a royal tribe (1 Peter 2:9).

God had chosen you before the earth's foundation so you could take charge like Him. Never underestimate your potential. There is more to you than you think. Learn to see yourself through the mirror of God's word and not through your circumstances or environment. I encourage you today to walk with confidence in who you are.

Royalty doesn't wallow in dirtiness. Regardless of what has happened in your past, I want you to see yourself in a new light today. Princes don't beg to rule, nor do princesses succumb to oppression. Stand tall and speak God's word against anything that does not reflect royalty in your life.

REFLECTIVE QUESTION
How does understanding our identity as chosen and called by God empower us to live a purposeful and impactful life?

Overcoming the Spirit of Fear

For you did not receive the spirit of bondage again
to fear, but you received the Spirit of adoption
by whom we cry out, "Abba, Father.
ROMANS 8:15

FEAR IS THE PRIMARY enemy that obstructs miracles. It attacks your belief in God's power. The spirit of fear makes you think that what you dread most will indeed happen to you. Fear manifests in the form of unbelief and doubt. But the truth about fear is that it is never real. It is from the devil. Nothing from the devil is original.

The spirit of fear was never part of your makeup at creation. God made you by His Spirit, and fear was never part of God's makeup. Never invite the spirit of fear into your life. The spirit of fear finds expression when it sees self-doubt, negative thoughts, and words. Let faith find expression in you.

Faith is believing only in God's word and acting accordingly. Fear and faith can never coexist. Interestingly, both fear and faith come from what you hear. If you hear wrongly, you will allow fear to dominate your life, but when you hear the word of truth, the life of faith becomes your reality.

Dear believer, embrace faith today. Choose to hear and listen to God's word alone, irrespective of the voices around you. Rebuke the spirit of fear now and walk in the victory of being called a son of God.

REFLECTIVE QUESTION

How can understanding and embracing our adoption into God's family free us from fear and empower us to live in the fullness of His love?

You are Special

For thus says the Lord of hosts: "He sent Me after glory,
to the nations which plunder you; for he who touches
you touches the apple of His eye.

ZECHARIAH 2:8

WHAT A LOVING GOD we have! You will agree that the Bible promises God's defence and special treatment for all his children. God is intentionally concerned about you and everything that is yours. There is nothing God cannot do for you because of the depth of love He has for you.

You are the apple of his eye. This means no evil can touch me as far as you are in God. You carry God's nature in you; your body is His temple of worship. As long as God cares for you, He does not want you to be careless about your life. Avoid whatever does not give glory to God.

Live your life in the reality of a son who always seeks to make His father happy. He had a special interest in you right before you came out of your mother's womb. Therefore, the gifts, talents, and abilities He had deposited in you are to be used to the glory of His name. You are unique in God's sight, and let this be your daily declaration.

REFLECTIVE QUESTION
How does understanding that we are the "apple of God's eye" impact the way we view ourselves and our relationship with Him?

The Lord is Your Helper

Unless the Lord builds the house,
they labour in vain who build it; unless the Lord
guards the city, the watchman stays awake in vain.

PSALMS 127:1

ARE YOU ON THE verge of giving up on yourself? Do you feel helpless and hopeless? Does it feel like nothing seems to work in your life? Today, I bring you good news from the throne of God. Your dreams are valid, and your life can still be filled with goodness, regardless of what has transpired in the past.

God is your helper. When God helps a man, other men begin to favour him because God would have put his thoughts in their hearts. Help from God can eradicate every nonsense you have battled with for years. How can you then access this help? There is no better way to get help from God than by helping others.

Jesus said, If you can do this to the least of your brethren, you have done it to me (Matthew 25:40). Amazing! Your help to others is a great help to God, and He will surely reciprocate. Also, prayers allow you to access help from the Lord. Learn to help others and pray alongside them. I see the Lord sending help to you from Zion in Jesus' name.

REFLECTIVE QUESTION

How can we cultivate a mindset of acknowledging our dependence on God and trust in His provision in every area of our lives?

The Antidote to Sin

Your word I have hidden in my heart
that I might not sin against you.
PSALMS 119:11

LET ME SHARE WITH you an uncommon truth. Many people say it is impossible to live without sinning. This is untrue. Jesus, our perfect example, walked on earth, and all through His year, no iniquity was found in Him.

Remember, he was also human on earth. The truth is living above sin is very possible and realistic. If it were not, God would not have said that, for we do not have a High Priest who cannot sympathise with our weaknesses but is, in all points, tempted as we are yet without sin (Hebrews 4:15). How was Jesus able to achieve this remarkable feat?

Sin thrives in secrecy. Once the devil allows you to sin and cover it, then he makes you do more and more and then finally draws you away from God. Exposing your mind to God's word is an effective antidote to sin. Meditation on God's word searches your heart to reveal what does not look like God in you. Every time the temptation to sin comes to you, it should meet God's word in your heart, which fires it back.

Also, fellowshipping with God enables you to live above sin. Spend quality time with God at all times, and the grip of sin will weaken in you. As you step out today, please cultivate the habit of meditating on the word. Hide it in your heart, and let sin be far from you.

REFLECTIVE QUESTION
How can we prioritise and incorporate God's Word into our daily lives, allowing it to shape our hearts and guide our paths?

Follow the Process

For the earth yields crops by itself:
first the blade, then the head,
after that the full grain in the head.

MARK 4:28

IMPATIENCE HAS BECOME THE norm in this generation. Everybody desires a quick way to achieve their goals and objectives. Today, you see a lot of get-rich-quick schemes to deceive many people and lure them with unrealistic promises.

Whatever you get without a process will never stand the test of time. Fast food, get-rich-quick schemes, and a lot of success and pressure in this generation had sent many to untimely grace.

Whatever is good has a process. The finished goods you see all over the market did not become what they are by mere accident. All products are first raw materials before they pass through a manufacturing process. Dear friends, there is a process for everything you want in life. Do not try to jump the gun.

In your attempt to get things done quickly, do not forget to follow the process. There is a time to sow and a time to reap. You do not expect a harvest if you have planted nothing. As a matter of truth, the fruits you will reap in your life in the next five years are the seeds you are sowing presently, either knowingly or unknowingly.

Today's word is an admonition to you that there is a process to everything in life. Do not jump protocol, or you will keep moving in a vicious cycle of an unending journey. Follow the process for the results you desire in life. The man who follows the process understands the progress and can teach others after him. Ask the Lord for the grace to follow the process.

REFLECTIVE QUESTION
How can we cultivate patience and trust in God's timing as we faithfully sow seeds of faith and allow Him to bring growth and fruition in His own perfect way?

Grow in God

As newborn babes,
desire the pure milk of the word,
that you may grow thereby.

1 PETER 2:2

ONE OUTSTANDING CHARACTERISTIC OF living things is their growth. Every living thing must grow. The moment you were born again, the life-giving Spirit of God dwelled in you; thus, you became an alive Spirit. It is against the laws of nature for you to remain stunted.

Our bible passage for today exposes us to the exact formula for spiritual growth. It compares our spiritual growth to how a baby grows by taking milk. Our spiritual milk is God's word. The more of the word you have in you, the more you grow in God. You do not want to be spiritually malnourished. Therefore, you have to eat the right proportion of the word. The dosage is daily. Everyday intake of the word guarantees speedy growth in God.

Decide to grow today and back it up with corresponding actions involving a regular word intake. Grow until you come into the measure of the stature of the fullness of Christ. Never stop growing until you become like Christ in spirit, character, and life.

REFLECTIVE QUESTION
How can we cultivate a hunger for God's Word and allow it to deeply nourish and transform our spiritual lives?

Give Thanks Always

In everything, give thanks:
this is God's will in Christ Jesus concerning you.
1 THESSALONIANS 5:18

THANKSGIVING IS YOUR OBLIGATION to God. You must make it a habit always to develop a heart of gratitude for everything. A grateful heart will receive more from God. Let me tell you for free: this is not God's best for you yet. No matter where you are, it is not your final destination. God has more for you in store. But how will you receive more if you had not thanked Him for the previous ones He did?

Thanksgiving is a spiritual exercise that activates greater opportunities in life. In good and bad times, the Lord deserves your thanksgiving. Nothing about you is alien to God. He always has your best interests at heart.

So, whatever happens in your life, know it is for your God. There is always a provision for thanksgiving wherever you see God's act. Therefore, do not be ignorant and do not know what you ought to thank God for. As you cultivate the habit of thanksgiving today, the Lord will ride on the wings of your praises and deliver miracles, signs, and wonders to you.

REFLECTIVE QUESTION
How might adopting an attitude of gratitude change your perspective?

Sight and Size

For all the land which you see,
I give to you and your descendants forever.
GENESIS 13:14-15

THE FUTURE YOU STEP into is the one you have envisioned. Your ability to see and imagine what God has promised plays a crucial role in realising His plans for you. The scope of your vision in God's kingdom—how you see yourself in light of God's promises— determines your spiritual stature.

Ask yourself: Do you see the greatness God has declared over your life, or do your current circumstances constrain you? Sometimes, your environment can cloud your vision, making you underestimate what God has in store for you. It's important to distance yourself from any influence that limits your ability to see God's best for you.

What is your self-perception? Do you see yourself as a victim or a victor, a success or a failure? Your attainments in life are often as vast as your vision allows. Today's scripture encourages you to envision your future even before it unfolds. Cultivate your mind's eyes to see beyond the immediate and dream bigger.

REFLECTIVE QUESTION
How does God's promise in Genesis 13:14-15 inspire you to trust in His faithfulness?

God Blesses Faithful Stewardship

His Lord said to him, 'Well done, good
and faithful servant; you have been faithful over
a few things, I will make you ruler over many things.
Enter into the joy of your Lord.

MATTHEW 25:23

GOD'S BLESSINGS ARE RESERVED for those who steward their
gifts and responsibilities with faithfulness. The rewards from
God aren't just for casual followers but especially those who
serve diligently and faithfully. Serving God isn't just an activity;
it's an expression of our devotion, done in a manner that reflects
our commitment to Him.

God's word today reminds us that every act of faithfulness, no
matter how small, is seen and valued by Him. When you serve
with a heart full of love for God, your actions resonate far beyond
what you can see. Even when your efforts feel unrecognised or
unrewarded, God is preparing a greater reward for your faithfulness.

If you've been investing your time and energy into your local
church, community projects, or helping others, know that these
acts of service are planting seeds of blessing. The divine principle
is clear: your work for God, done in love and faithfulness, will
reap a harvest of blessings.

REFLECTIVE QUESTION
**How can you faithfully steward the gifts and
opportunities God has given you?**

Seeing Yourself Through God's Eyes

But the Lord said to Samuel, 'Do not look at
his appearance or at his physical stature,
because I have refused him. For the Lord does not
see as man sees; for man looks at the outward
appearance, but the Lord looks at the heart.

1 SAMUEL 16:7

THIS PASSAGE REMINDS US of the importance of seeing others
through God's eyes rather than judging based on external
appearances.

Much like Gideon, who saw himself as less than what God
had destined him to be, we often underestimate our potential
due to our circumstances or self-perception. God's view of us
vastly differs from how we might see ourselves or how the world
defines us. He sees beyond our fears, limitations, and the external
factors that confine us.

Your true worth and success lie in recognising who you are in
God and living out that reality. Don't let your environment or
background dictate your identity or potential. Your life is rooted
in God's plan, and what He has planted in you is sufficient to
make a significant impact. Open your mind to see as God sees,
and embrace the fullness of your identity in Him.

REFLECTIVE QUESTION

**How can you cultivate a heart that sees others
through God's perspective?**

Claiming Victory With God

Yet in all these things, we are more than
conquerors through Him who loved us.

ROMANS 8:37

THIS POWERFUL STATEMENT REMINDS us that through Christ's
love and power, we can triumph over any challenge or trial that
comes our way.

Reflect on the past year as a testament to God's unwavering
presence and support in your life. The challenges you faced were
obstacles and opportunities for God to demonstrate His love and
strength in your life. Each victory, each moment of triumph, is
a celebration of your partnership with God.

As you look forward to what lies ahead, remember that the
God who has been your constant companion will continue to be
by your side. He is the author of your story, and with Him, you
are equipped for whatever comes your way. Your past victories
are not just memories; they are foundations for the greater things
God has planned for you. Step into the future with confidence,
knowing that, with God, you are prepared for a journey of
continued victory and blessing.

REFLECTIVE QUESTION

**How does the truth of being "more than conquerors"
impact your perspective on challenges and trials
in your life?**

Winning With God

> I will lift up my eyes to the hills—From whence
> comes my help? My help comes from the Lord,
> Who made heaven and earth.
>
> PSALM 121:1-2

PAUSE FOR A MOMENT and reflect on the year that has passed. It's been a rollercoaster, with highs and lows, but the most important thing is this: you made it through. Your resilience is commendable, but remember, it's not just your strength that carried you; God was with you every step of the way.

Think about the challenges you faced this year. Those long, sleepless nights, the overwhelming worries, the moments you felt utterly alone—it wasn't solely your courage that saw you through these trials. God was there, bolstering your spirit and lifting you when you were down.

When life's uncertainties shook your world, He stood firm as your rock. His promises were your anchor, steadying you amidst life's tumultuous waves. Each new day was a gift from Him, a reminder that He's always by your side, cheering you on.

Celebrate the victories of this year. They're not just fleeting moments of joy but tangible evidence of God's enduring love for you. Each triumph is a chapter in your life's story, co-authored by you and God, a testament to the incredible team you make.

So, step forward into the future, not just with your plans but hand in hand with God. He empowers you beyond measure. The victories of the past are seeds of hope and promise, growing into a future filled with even more of God's blessings and breakthroughs. Remember, with God, you are always ready for the amazing journey ahead.

REFLECTIVE QUESTION

How does recognizing God's role in your victories and challenges impact your mindset for facing uncertainties in the upcoming year?

Dear cherished reader,

AS ANOTHER YEAR COME TO AN END,
remember that your journey of faith is a continuous,
unfolding story. Each day is an opportunity to
embrace new beginnings, deeper connections, and
the limitless grace that surrounds you.

As you step into the next year, may you carry the
lessons learned and the wisdom gained on this
transformative path. Your faith is a beacon, guiding
you through challenges and illuminating the beauty
in each moment. Embrace the coming days with
hope, courage, and a heart full of gratitude.

May the pages of your life be filled with joy, love, and
purpose. Walk confidently into the future, knowing
that you are not alone—divine love accompanies you
every step of the way. The best is yet to come.

Blessings for a joyous and fulfilling year ahead.

With faith and encouragement,
DOUGLAS ASANTE

www.ingramcontent.com/pod-product-compliance
Lightning Source LLC
Chambersburg PA
CBHW020905100426
42737CB00043B/145